Uranus the Awakener

Electrifying the Intellect

By

Alan Richards-Wheatcroft

Copyright Alan Richards-Wheatcroft, 2025
All Rights Reserved
Without limiting the rights reserved above under copyright, no part of this publication may be reproduced, stored in, or introduced into a retrieval system, or transmitted in any form or by any means (electronic, mechanical, photocopying, scanning, recording or otherwise), without written permission from both the author and the publisher, except in the case of brief quotations embodied in reviews and articles.

The scanning, uploading and distribution of this book via the Internet, or via any other means, without the written permission of the publisher is illegal and punishable by law. Please do not encourage electronic piracy of copyrighted materials.

ISBN: 978-0-86690-697-5
Cover design by Celeste Nash
Adobe Stock image_415753793
Sutterstock image_162791

Requests and inquiries may be mailed to the publisher:
American Federation of Astrologers, Inc.
6553 S. Rural Road
Tempe, AZ 85283
www.astrologers.com

Acknowledgements:

Thank you,

To Kathryn Silverton, for providing the perfect 'Uranian' conclusion to what I consider to be my ultimate life achievement — commemorating the triple conjunction of the Sun, North Node and Mercury, which is square Uranus in my natal chart. May the *force* continue to be with you.

To Samantha Kane-Kennedy, for *electrifying* my senses with your quintessential candour, and enlightening sincerity. Your brilliance and foresightedness have been the mathematical icing on this Uranian cake, so to speak.

To Celeste Nash, for your Uranian healing, guidance and insight; and for your ultimate contributions. You have utilized and electrified your Uranian transits very well my dear friend. A tribute to you!

Electrification is a form of elevation. When the brain is electrified-elevated, via the Uranus archetype, anything is possible. Thus, when the brain is electrified-elevated via Uranus, a direct channel is opened into the universal mind of God.

On the whole, astrology is a universal/Uranus discipline. Therefore, only when a sufficient amount of the brain's intellect has been electrified-elevated, will astrology be fully understood.

Alan Richards-Wheatcroft

Table of Contents:

Acknowledgements	iii
Foreword by Kathryn Silverton	vi
Prologues:	vii
Introduction	viii
Chiron: The Psychological/Intellectual Healer	1
When Uranus is Intercepted	5
Outer Planets in Elevation	17
Part One: The Profundity of Uranian (Cerebral) Karma	19
Part Two: Uranian Illness and Disease	73
Part Three: Electrifying the Brain's Intellect	123
Epilogue: Conclusion: The Future is Uranus	173
About the Author	183
Afterword	184
Index Other Titles Published by the American Federation of Astrologers	185

Foreword

By Kathryn Silverton

In a most Uranian fashion…Alan and I stumbled upon one another when he was attempting to locate the esteemed author and astrologer, Bill Tierney. As luck would have it, I was able to help him make his desired connection, and Alan subsequently asked me to pen his foreword. As a professional astrologer with over 40 years of study under my belt, I was honored and thrilled to oblige, and my thirst for the unusual was quenched when I read the manuscript.

What would a book on the subject of Uranus have to be in order to complement the nature of the planet? By definition, it has to be unusual, an alternate take on the subject, innovative and out of the box. Alan checks all these boxes in this treatise on what some astrologers deem the planet that rules their craft. Expect to come away with numerous 'aha' moments as you feast on this brilliant take on a most fascinating subject.

Alan's expertise as an astrologer is evident in prior works on astrology and healing, as well as his work on the planet Neptune. In this literary delight, he offers up numerous examples of how Uranus's role has played out in the lives of well-known figures. His focus on the electrical nature of Uranus and its karmic implications are spot on! The reader will be amazed to learn such goodies as to why people are drawn to certain geographical locations, and how gifted individuals have implemented their natal Uranian placements to accomplish their goals.

My hope is that once you have devoured this masterpiece, you will be motivated to consume his other works, if you have yet to do so! Happy reading, and may your brain feel electrified by the lovely morsels contained within.

Sincerely,
Kathryn Silverton

Kathryn is a certified professional astrologer, and author of Lunarcasts 2012. She also serves on the board of directors at the American Federation of Astrologers (AFA). Kathryn is the President of the Metropolitan Atlanta Astrological Society.

Prologues

"Even matter called inorganic, believed to be dead, responds to irritants and gives unmistakable evidence of a living principle within. Everything that exists, organic or inorganic, animated or inert, is susceptible to stimulus from the outside."[1]

Uranus Glyph

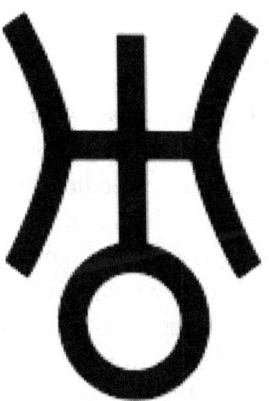

The glyph of Uranus symbolizes a person's head, with a protruding antenna. In practice then, Uranian innovative, and ingenious ideas can be relayed like electrical discharges directly to the brain.

Introduction

"Uranus is both a much-loved and a much-feared archetype in astrology. It is the hallmark of all that is new and wildly different during a given period. Its reputation as the 'Cosmic Trickster,' the Awakener, the accelerator of thoughts and events, is unchallenged in astrology, as is its association with intellectual brilliance, cultural innovation, and technological invention."
Marilena Marino

This book has been *synchronized* with the wholly new cerebral patterns of the Aquarian Age. Therefore, it has been drawn up to offer entirely new ways of examining planet Uranus; hence the modern-day ruler of Aquarius. Uranus is a forward-thinking and forward-looking planet. Therefore, it presses us into continuously riding the 'shock wave,' that is often associated with sudden and progressive changes. Uranus allows us to meet the future with our eyes wide open, and our brains restructured. Moreover, Uranus liberates us from the influences and heaviness of extremism.

Neurological Summary

Uranus is considered to be the *oddity* of the cosmos. Furthermore, there are many who still fear its erratic, impulsive and unpredictable nature. Notwithstanding, Uranus embodies the sagacious and erudite expressions such as, inspiration, liberation, brilliance, intellectual artistry, and abstract vision. These are the vital components or integrants that support the brain in its psychological pursuit for intellectual absolution. Hence, it is these Uranian integrants, which *unbind* the brain from its electrically-charged neuro karma (for more information, see Part One).

Saturn transmutes physical karma into spiritual realization, whereas Uranus extricates the brain from its karmic shackles; thereby releasing more of the brain's intellect. Neuro karma is applied to the brain, courtesy of Uranus, because the brain didn't succeed in consolidating more of its intellect throughout its previous incarnations.

The unique qualities associated with Uranus are unsurpassed, meaning that its power is *unparalleled* to any other sphere in the cosmos. What's more, Uranus is the planet that stimulates the senses, particularly in an electromagnetic capacity. This means that highly creative and innovative ideas are released in the brain, and principally after the individual has endured a *wake up* call in some way, or an extreme warning of some description. This planet is, after all, known as the cosmic alarm clock, or, to be more precise, the intellectual *awakener*.

Often, this type of neuro trauma, hence the wake up call, manifests as a sudden shock, or a convulsion, which are considered to be contrasting neuro impulses. Thus, this is how the singular energy of Uranus works — through the lightening impulses in the brain. Neuro impulses of this magnitude are adjudged *fittingly* as neuro karma, for which the conclusion is neuro liberation; hence to be *freed* from those apprehensive and unpleasant thoughts, and repetitive ideas, which tend to stick to us like neuro sealant.

Innovative and inventive ideas are also released in the brain during and after the onset of sudden neurological trauma, such as epilepsy. Epileptic seizures, which are examined in detail throughout Part Two, are a typical example of Uranus's penchant for higher creativity and inventiveness, which are indiscriminately expressed via the brain. These are the neuro/medical components for brilliance (genius). Albert Einstein was a classic example of acquiring brilliance via a neuro-brain disorder (for more information see, when Uranus is Intercepted).

Uranus and Neuropeptides

Of course, it is not always necessary to undergo a debilitating disease, such as epilepsy, in order to attain a higher level of creativity and innovative expressiveness. Most comprehensively, the energy of Uranus *regenerates* the neuropeptides located in the brain — turning up the intellectual volume — fabricating the cerebral blueprints that outline inventive ideas and creative suggestions (see diagram). [2] It is simply a case of being able to 'tune in' to the brainwave patterns in our brains.

The neuro vision of Uranus is *unlimited*; meaning that its dimensional capacity for knowledge is *limitless*. This makes Uranus the perfect acronym for intellectual superiority. This, intellectual superiority is essentially a 'master stroke of conceptual genius,' which is naturally developed once the brain begins to release more of its cerebral capacity, hence its underlying intellectual potential (for more information about the function of neuropeptides, see section, When Uranus is Intercepted).

The next diagram designates the social and creative portions of the brain (frontal lobes), which are saturated with neuropeptides — Uranian dimensions that are widely associated with Uranian subversions

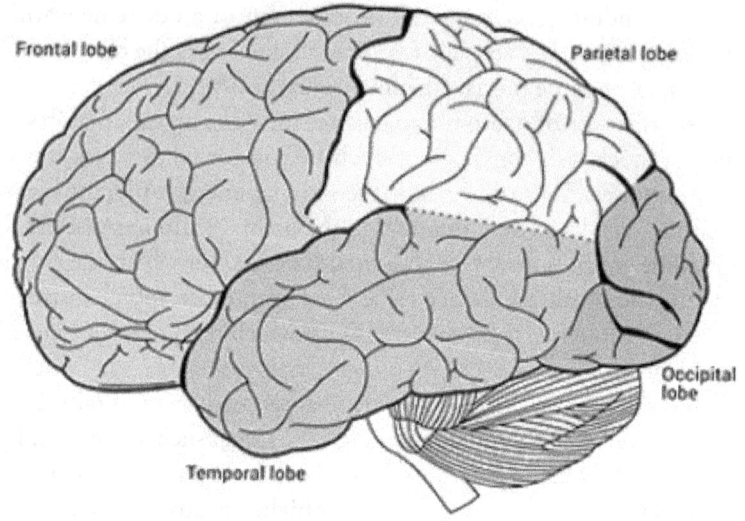

and innovations. Neuropeptides *expand* the potential of these innovatory regions. Subsequently, this neuro undertaking of Uranian activity helps the brain to release more of its ingenious intellect.

It is often said that a human being only uses up to ten percent of the brain's cerebral capacity, especially while in a state of consciousness. This incredulous notion was depicted in the movie, *Lucy*, starring Scarlet Johansson. However, a more detailed and realistic explanation of this cerebral theory on the brain's capacity for intellectual superiority is detailed throughout Part Three.

Meantime, I refer to the 'conscious state' in this way, simply because whilst in the unconsciousness state of sleep, the brain naturally *consolidates* more of its cerebral capacity, especially in a magnitude that is both emotional, and reasoning. This innate function is necessary, because it assists with the replenishment of the cell structures during the body's sleep cycles. Moreover, this is often why our dreams depict an involvement within events and circumstances, which are beyond the normal frame of reference; and which would be deemed as *impossible* in the logical state of consciousness, such as events depicted in the movie, *Lucy*.

Advancements in Uranian Technologies

Consider, what we have accomplished with our so-called active intellect so far? Over the course of the past fifty years, there have been colossal and monumental advances in technology. However, what we refuse to consider, or even understand, is exactly where the initial ideas for such brilliance emanate from in the first place. Intellectual ideas, especially those concerning advanced technology have been *conveyed* from those Uranian higher minds — intellects that were once sentient. Now they are a part of the evolved collective inhabitants of the spirit world, such as the intellect of Albert Einstein.

Yet, this current technological revolution of innovative thoughts and ideas far outweighs our present intellectual progression. The ingress of Uranus in Aquarius in 1995, through to 2003, marked a significant *shift* in ideas for technological advancements. The problem is, we have deployed a large percentage of these technological advancements to manipulate, rather than to liberate, the intellectual shackles that unnecessarily *bind* humankind. This is a further reason why a great many individuals are not progressing intellectually.

Simply, we do not fully understand the fundamental purpose of technology, mostly because of our current state of non-progression. For example, why do so many abuse cell phone technologies? Thus, cell phones are highly-developed communication devices, and were not intended as a 'focus for technological obsession.' Cell (mobile) phones were initially developed and deployed to be used solely in emergency situations. For example, if the car breaks down in the middle of nowhere. Or, at the scene of an accident. In these scenarios, cell phones are 'life savers.'

There are however many more technological advancements, which are ready to be passed on to humankind, from the spirit world. However, they will continue to remain 'pending' because of our overall lack of progression, and our understanding of brain functioning. According to the *Akashic Records*, it is hoped in spirit that these advancements can be eventually dispensed at Uranus's ingress into Virgo — beginning in 2045. If, by then, the Earth has not reached the cataclysmic point of 'no return,' there should be enough spiritually enlightened and responsible souls to take full advantage of these entirely new Uranian technologies.

Meanwhile, at this crucial staging post in our physical and psychological evolution, hence the twenty-first century, human beings should have *consolidated* around thirty percent of the brain's overall intellect.

According to the *Akashic Records*, a high percentage of the population should have consolidated one hundred percent of the brain's intellect in the initial stages of the Aquarian Age — around 2040 — the point in which we should all be telepathically linked.

The technological advancements, which mankind currently applies to his way of life, are only compliant with our overall and current state/lack of cerebral progression.

Uranus and Cetaceans

Curiously, the dolphin is the only mammal that *consolidates* all of its brain's intellect. Thus, this marine life form is completely responsive while in the state of intellectual consciousness. [3] The dolphin's sleep patterns are however very different from that of a human being. According to the science author Kevin Kurtz, dolphins let their right side of their brain go to sleep, while the left side remains active, and conversely. Ordinarily, this bodily function regulates their breathing, but it may also prove that the dolphin's intellectual capacity *exceeds* that of a human being.

The dolphin is essentially a mammal, which exhibits ethereal and innovative distinctions — from the Uranus and Neptune dimensional dominions of consciousness. In addition, the dolphin doesn't display the capacity for manipulation. Instead, the dolphin displays an image of being permanently liberated from its psychological net of neuro karma. This is why the dolphin gives the impression of being contented, and *free*, by which it has *colonized* its own brain. Unfortunately, it is human beings that manipulate, and eliminate these magnificent and highly-intelligent creatures.

Initially, the dolphin has emanated from a higher and a much more distinctive realm of consciousness; and this is the reason why the dolphin has managed to develop a unique Uranian sonar system — more advanced than anything mankind has invented. In order to develop this marine technology, the dolphin has successfully *harnessed* a large percentage of its multifunctional receptor cells — around thirty percent. Multifunctional receptor cells are essentially the cornerstones of the dolphin's unique Uranian energy. For more information about receptor cells, see Part Two.

The dolphin is a highly intelligent mammal, which mankind should not, under any circumstances, be destroying, especially for monitory profit. By committing these barbaric acts, he is unknowingly *disman-*

tling the innovative image of his own technological future. Alternatively, we should learn by example, and *consolidate* our own unique brilliance — drawn from these distinctive Uranian advancements — reproduced via the excessive intellectual aptitude of the dolphin. In other words, rather than destroying it, we should all learn to communicate (telepathically) with the dolphin. Thus, we have much to learn, and to gain from this magnificent mammal.

Those who are needlessly and knowingly killing these animals for incentive and gain will incur colossal amounts of cerebral karma, which will come to pass in spirit.

Chiron

According to the *Akashic Records*, Chiron was once a Moon of Uranus. A cosmic cataclysm, which occurred eons ago, propelled Chiron across millions of miles of space. Today, Chiron is caught in the distant orbit of Saturn. Chiron's Uranian influence upon Saturn is why the ancients designated the ringed planet as the traditional ruler of Aquarius. Chiron also provided healing to the Saturn archetype, which ultimately provoked a resolve to a disorganized cosmos — in the aftermath of such a prolific event. Therefore, the ancient mythological narrative of 'Chiron the Wounded Healer,' was essentially depicting Saturn karma, which I shall explain in greater detail throughout the Chiron prologue.

The cataclysm, which propelled Chiron into Saturn space, also had shocking consequences upon Uranus. As a result, Uranus orbits the Sun, literally tipped over, and on its side. Thus, the circumference of Uranus is dramatically out of all proportion with the rest of the cosmos. This is another reason why Uranus is referred to as the 'oddity.' The significance and the consequences of this are also explained in the Chiron prologue. In truth, Uranus is rebelling, because one of his cosmic children (Chiron) has been swept away, and in effect, *exiled*. Some ancient minds believed that Uranus *ostracized* Chiron, similar to his mother in Greek mythology.

This notion does however, correspond somewhat to the narrative of Chiron in ancient mythology; hence the myth in which Chiron withdrew from the world because of his immortal wound — inflicted by an arrow — a wound in which he could not die from (see next section).

Part One: The Profundity of Uranian (Cerebral) Karma

It is important to point out that the natal chart remains the main influential force in the life of the individual, up to the point of the second Saturn return (approximately between 58 and 60 years of age). After the second Saturn return, the natal chart becomes a contrasting influence — alongside the solar return chart. This is because each of us experience transformations throughout life. Throughout all of my publications, the majority of my case studies concern the specific influences of the natal chart — before the onset of the second Saturn return.

Throuhout this book for the purpose of a more defined interpretation, I always allow ten degrees orb between the major planetary ascpects.

Part One, is perhaps, the most significant and pronounced section of the book. Therefore, I have outlined many distinct Uranian notions and cultures — pointing to why so many souls have been *impaled* upon the Uranian cross of cerebral karma. In our current global situation of non-progression, this is perhaps the main reason why mental illness is proliferating. Mental illness can also be a *repercussion* of a psychological impasse — from the karmic recesses of a previous incarnation. Or, it can simply be the result of a profound and recent shock. Either way, mental illness is occurring at an alarming rate, because souls are not *evolving* in the way they have agreed to do before they incarnated.

Cerebral (Uranian) karma is a sub-branch to a much greater impression. Most, if not all forms of conventional karma, affects the soul only — by which the effects are exhibited throughout the physical body. However, Uranian karma is unique because it impacts the brain's intellect. The brain is essentially representative to the central network, hence the main computer, that oversees the primary functions of the physical body. [4] This is essentially all a part of the 'oddity syndrome' that encompasses the Uranus archetype, because Uranian minds are often considered to be 'technology geeks.'

Interestingly, those who exist solely within the Uranian domain of consciousness shouldn't ignore, or disregard their soul's intellect. Unfortunately, many in this field of consciousness do just that. Part of their incarnation concerns the *consolidation* of their soul's intellect, via the Neptune archetype. In some cases, those who have a powerful Uranus in the chart, suffer from soul unawareness and depletion, because Neptune's influence is often *weak*.

Specifically, Uranian karma depicts universal destiny; and it is universal destiny that lies at the core of the Uranus archetype. Universal destiny still applies if, for example, an individual's life is terminated, or compromised via methods that are considered to be atypical, and unusual, and which are considered to be Uranian. So, for example, being struck by lightning, or assassinated fits this Uranian frame of reference. Or alternately, the assimilation of an individual's intellectual objectives or identity are notably uncommon systems of procedure, that all operate within the Uranian archetype; and which all lead to Uranian karma.

The assimilation of other people's ideas is currently on the increase. One such example is through the expanding notion of copyright theft. These are all multiplex classifications of intellectual karma; and which symbolize the element of shock — each representing a specific guise within the nucleus of the Uranus archetype. Homosexual and lesbians, have the ability to shock the stauncher conventionalists. Gay people, as they are referred to today, invariably possess an extreme Uranus influence in their natal charts, as we shall discover in Part One.

Generally, the influence of Uranian karma is more *electrified* and *stimulating* than conventional karma; meaning that its overall intent is via the element of surprise. Thus, the element of surprise is certainly the theme for assassination. The anticipation and the application of Uranian karma is something we really foresee — arriving like a bolt from the blue yonder. Unlike other forms of planetary karma, Uranian karma is delivered within specific time frames and parameters. These are the domains where tumultuous turbulences or disruptions of energy, which are directed towards the collective, are predominantly active. For example, Uranian karma is implemented via natural electrical disturbances, such as electrically-charged storms, and earthquakes. Those who are personally affected by these devastating interruptions are receiving their Uranian karma, in the upmost sense of the word, and for whatever the reasons involved.

Living under the strict conditions imposed by martial law is another example of functioning Urania karma. This is because; at the head of the authoritarian establishment is a despot, or a dictator. Despots are typically Uranian be design. Living under such unyielding rules is what leads to uprisings and revolutions, which are once again all Uranian by design, to which the end game is often *liberation*.

Alternatively, Uranian karma manifests in the form of a *revelation*, which ultimately causes shock to the cognitive system. [5] Just how the karma is exemplified is dependent on the position, and the condition of Uranus in the natal chart. However, the lightening effects of Uranian karma has the potential to release more of the brain's intellect. In this case, profound shock, for example, is often its ultimate weapon that elicits more of the brain's intellect. So, for example, if a person is killed by electricity, more of the brain's potential will be released once the soul tenants the afterlife. How it is utilized however, or even recognized, is solely dependent on the level of intellectual evolution, the soul has attained in physicality.

Karma, in its many guises, doesn't just affect the soul. It affects every physical organ throughout the human body. The brain is indeed a unique and individual organ, meaning that it can operate *solely* without the influence of any of the other primary organs, which the brain oversees in some way. Uranus is often referred to as the *awakener*. This is because the brain is the only organ that doesn't require rest. When we sleep the organs regenerate. The brain's way of regenerating however, is to *expunge* those unwanted cerebral files, which contain outdated ideas.

Moreover, the brain has developed this natural course of development, in order to *balance* intellectual karma. On occasion, there are some files left *intact*. During reincarnation, these files are *reactivated*; and therefore, they manifest as Uranian intellectual karma. Under these circumstances, this is what would happen if an individual intently *assimilates* another individual's intellectual objectives. The karma, which would be applied because of this deliberate underlying measure, would most likely manifest as a Uranian type illness or disease. If then, the individual *refuses*; and thus, *fails* to expand his or her cerebral capacity; the brain will be the focus of intellectual karma during the next incarnation — or in spirit. Interestingly, spirit is the domain by which the soul prefers to remain in.

Additionally, I examine the position of Uranus in the natal chart to exactly determine the strength of intellectual karma; and how it will eventually transpire. Thus, to take in the shape of the life with the individual concerned. These intellectual revelations have been highlighted by examining the appropriate celebrity case studies — whose life has been shockingly obstructed, or even terminated by the unfortunate and shockingly negative impact of Uranus in the chart. In effect, this meant that Uranus wasn't *elevated* to a high enough level of reasoning.

Part Two: Uranian Illness and Disease

Throughout Part Two, I have investigated, in depth, as to why so many souls have succumbed to Uranus-orientated illness and disease, such as seizure disorders. Seizure disorders, and in particular, epilepsy, which is on the increase, particularly in the US, is caused, in part, by the damaging effects of electricity on the physical body — most likely occurring in a previous life. We incarnate into a specific country, so that our karma can be appropriately *balanced*. Whatever type of karma we are confronted with in physicality, the country of our origin provides the ideal environmental conditions, which we need to *sustain*, and thus *maintain* our intellectual karma.

In the USA, where intellectual karma is extensively high, there are over three million of its citizens who suffer from epilepsy. This is in

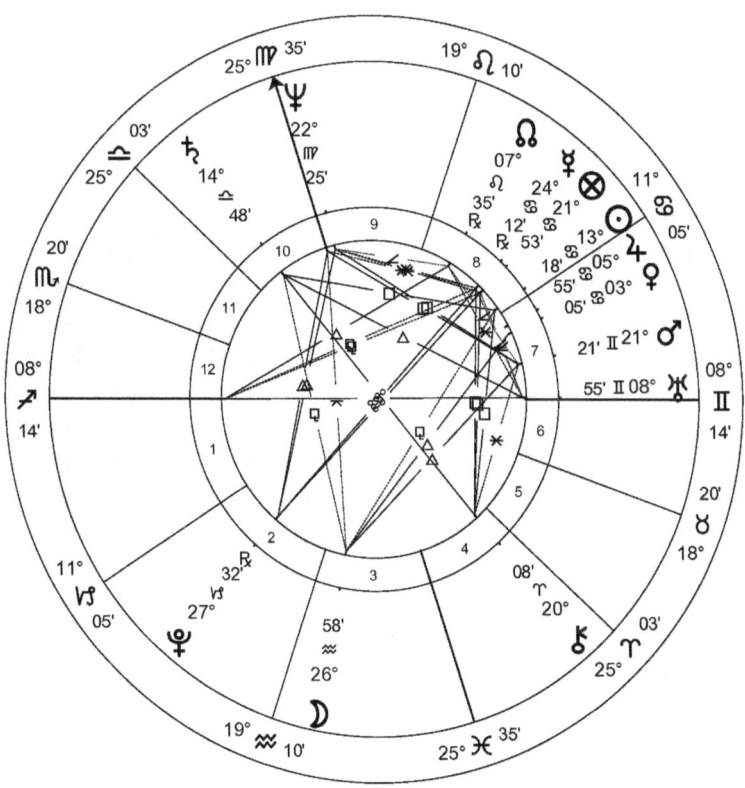

Sibly Chart for USA, 7/4/1776, 16:50, Philadelphia, Pennsylvania

accordance with government statistics. These shocking figures are unmistakably *pronounced* by the position of Uranus in the US Sibley chart — exactly opposing the Ascendant — from the sixth house of health.

In this position, Uranus determines that the US is a country that will always carry the immense burden of intellectual karma — sustaining individuals with mental health problems — partly because of its 'karmic attraction' to electricity. These are also characteristics that are symbolized by Uranus opposing the Ascendant, and its wide trine to Saturn.

The origins of the US's cerebral karma are simply *unfathomable* and *arcane*. Nevertheless, it is a fact that simply exists. The US's intellectual karma is further exhibited by the opposition between Mercury and Pluto; combined with Mercury's half-square to Uranus. Interestingly, the US is ranked second behind Brazil for the most lightning strikes on a particular country. These statistics would also act in accordance with the position of Uranus in the US chart. [6] Moreover, the US is the only country that still enforces the death penalty by the electric chair, in approximately five of its primary states. This shocking tally is also in accordance with the countries increasing levels of intellectual karma.

Psychosomatically speaking, epilepsy is caused by a fear of embracing the *reality* of life. In essence, the brain ultimately rejects new ideas and suggestions, which would lead to psychological stagnation and disintegration, which is often the psychological cause of epilepsy. However, these are only mirror images of a past life; because in a physical capacity, the brain has been compromised or damaged previously — leading to intellectual *inactivity* in the current life. Such shocking events of misfortune would *compromise* the nervous system, especially during the soul's next physical incarnation. In all practicality, the individual would most likely incarnate with Mercury or Uranus retrograde. This would further indicate the likelihood of incurring intellectual karma.

Seizure disorders are also the result of death caused by brain abnormalities, which occurred in a previous incarnation. These are common complexities of Uranus-orientated dis-eases, which are examined in detail, along with other Uranian infirmities, such as heart attacks, diseases of the arteries, and sudden fatal accidents throughout Part 2.

Sudden fatal accidents however, give the appearance of being in the wrong place at the wrong time — when in actual fact the brain is attempting to *balance* its Uranian (intellectual) karma. You may be familiar with the narrative that chronicles an individual, or a group who miss their flight, for whatever reasons, and then subsequently they discover that the plane they had intended to board had actually crashed. In the natal chart, this lucky event would be representative of a strong and positively aspected Jupiter — coupled with *earned* Saturn karma from previous incarnations.

Lightning strikes are also a major cause of storm-related death; and lightning strikes traditionally symbolize the concept of being in the wrong place at the wrong time. This is a Uranian concept, and one that it shares with illusion-orientated Neptune. According to the NWS storm data, over the last thirty years, there are on average 45 *reported* lightening fatalities a year, which seems marginal. [7] However, the true figures denoting this type of fatality frequently go *unreported*.

By and large, death from lightening, and other more common forms of electricity discharge, such as being killed by electric shocks, causes other problems, and abnormalities in the body. Examples of this include, muscle spasms, necrosis, thrombosis, and motor and sensory function abnormalities, which are all connected to Uranus's conceptual programming of intellectual karma.

Most intriguingly though, thrombosis has its karmic roots buried in the fatal aftermath caused by severe electrical discharges. The American actor James Stewart developed a DVT (Deep Vein Thrombosis) in his leg, which became a pulmonary embolism, which was the cause of his death (for more information, see Part Two).

Part Three: Consolidating the Brain's Intellect

Throughout Part Three, I have outlined some remarkable and extraordinary methods that are designed to increase the overall intellect; and which will help to further *consolidate* more of the brain's capacity. This is all by way of the amazing Uranian potential — highlighted within the natal chart. In this respect, the natal chart is the 'pivotal catalyst' to *consolidating* the brain's intellect — courtesy of Uranus. Aspects to Uranus in the natal chart determine just how much intellectual artistry can be measured overall within the brain. Its celestial sign and house position however, determine just how this brilliance can be *sharpened* even more, and executed in its own unique way — for the distinct purposes of intellectual innovation.

Moreover, a classic example of this Uranian brilliance is *covertly* housed in the natal chart of the amateur astronomer and TV presenter Patrick Moore. I use the term *covertly* because, what is not widely known however, is that Patrick Moore secretly *advocated* the use of astrology. This revelation was revealed shortly after his death in 2012, by the husband and wife astrology duo, Derek and Julia Parker, who knew him 'personally.' [8]

Both Derek and Julia Parker have Uranus square Pluto in the natal chart. So, they were the right people as it were, to reveal the truth (Pluto), about Patrick Moore's adoration of astrology (Uranus). Therefore, we will examine the details of how he managed to keep his interest in astrology an undisclosed secret, especially from his peers.

To a greater extent, this cosmic confidentiality concerns secretive Neptune, which is close to the IC, in Moore's chart. Initially, Neptune's wide conjunction to the IC means that this point in space is transcended into a 'subterranean place' in his natal chart. Furthermore, the fourth house has essentially become a deep ocean of secrets. Which are taken directly to the grave — endorsed by Neptune's responsive tenure. Neptune is also in mutual reception with the elevated Sun; which is closely conjunct

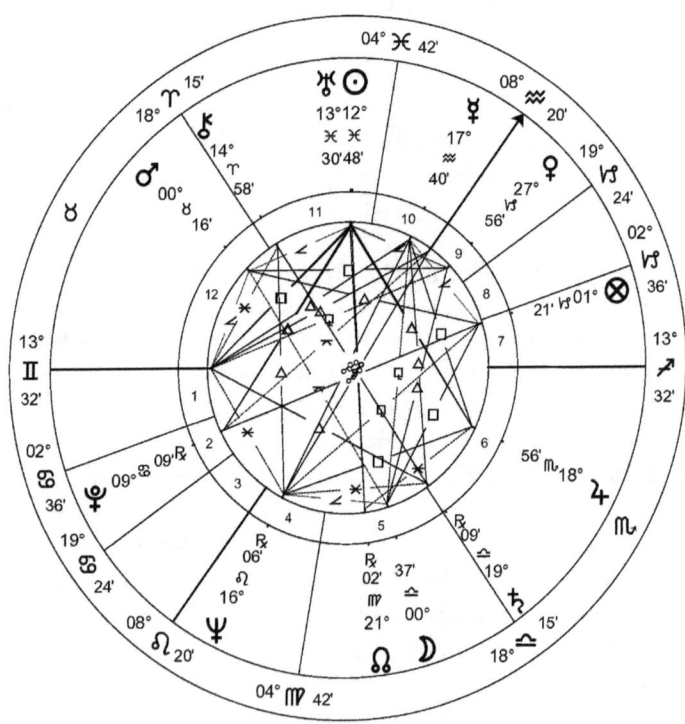

Natal Chart for Patrick Moore, 3/4/1923, 10:00, Pinner, England,

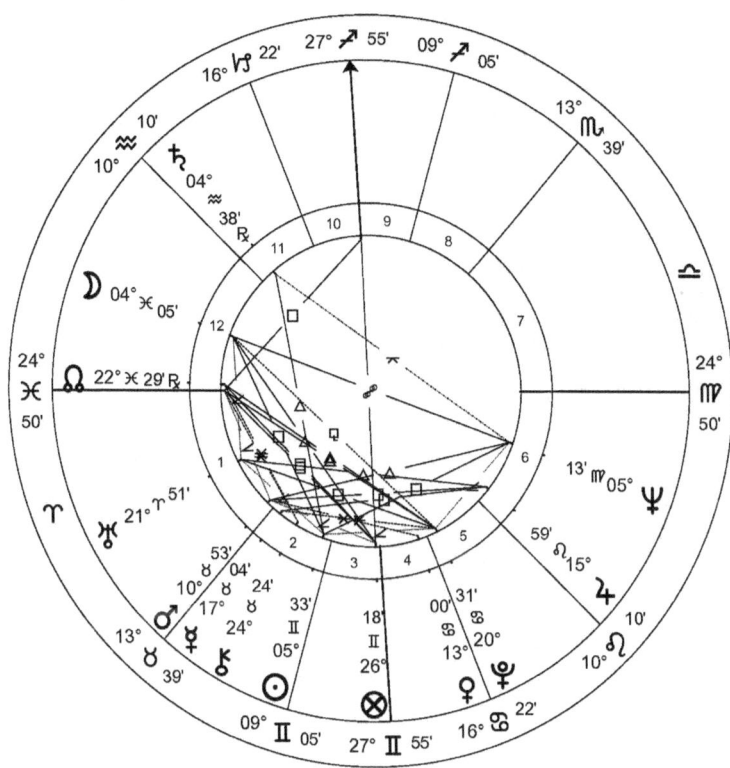

Natal Chart for Derek Parker, 5/27/1932, 02:50, Looe, England,

astrology-orientated Uranus. So, it was no coincidence that Moore was able to guard his ultimate secret of being an enthusiastic supporter of astrology.

Neptune's opposition to the MC and Mercury means that Moore was able to *reluctantly* disguise his interest, by continually sneering and pouring scorn on the very mention of astrology, especially when he was being interviewed. This plan of action was fabricated in order to avoid any suspicion. Neptune's quincunx to Uranus also means that he was able to keep up this pretence, until long after his death, when the shock of such a revelation surfaced. In effect, the adjustment associated with the quincunx, which in this case was concerned with the paradox of non-believer and believer of astrology, emerged *shockingly* after his death.

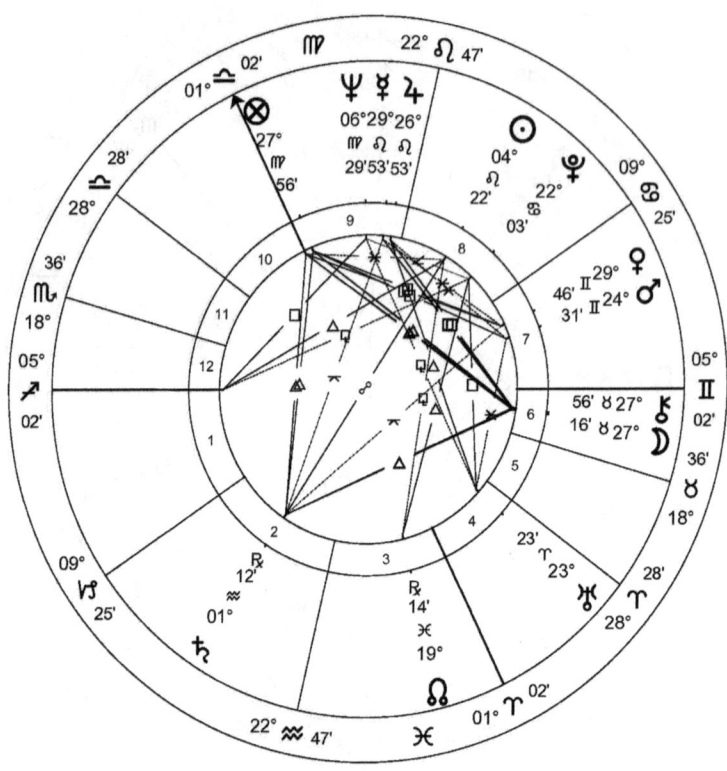

Natal Chart for Julia Parker, 7/27/1932, 17:00, Plymouth, England

Neptune in the fourth house, and in this case, denoting the watery grave, *drowned* this ultimate secret — a secret that could never be allowed to emerge from these watery depths. Otherwise the shame, denoted by Leo and the Sun, would have been too much for him to endure. Especially, throughout the scientific world — a coterie of disillusioned authority figures to where the stereotypical disbeliefs of astrology have become a routinely commonplace conception.

As a final thought, Part Three of this book contains a selection of the familiar, and the more modern-day case studies that have already, and continue to reach the pinnacle of their success, by releasing more of the brain's intellect. Sometimes however, Uranus 'tricks us' into believing that we are much more erudite than we actually are. This is a common conception, especially when Uranus, is in frictional aspect to Neptune, such as the quincunx. Here, the adjustment posed by the quincunx would be to elicit more of the brain's intellect — accomplished by laying down some complicated challenges for the brain to comprehend. All of the case studies in Part Three depict this intellectual quality.

Forethought

On the whole, this book represents an intellectual journey into the higher and ingenious recesses of the planet Uranus; and what can be accomplished, as a result of consolidating more of the brain's intellectual capacity. I hope that you find this book interesting, helpful, and perhaps intriguing.

Thank you for buying this book.
Blessings to you dear reader.
Alan Richards-Wheatcroft.

Chart Data

- Sibly Chart for the US, 4th July 1776, 16:50, Philadelphia, USA, Placidus Houses, Mean Node.
- Natal Chart for Patrick Moore, 4th March 1923, 10:00, Pinner, UK, Placidus Houses, Mean Node.
- Natal Chart for Julia Parker, 27th July 1932, 17:00, Plymouth, UK, Placidus Houses, Mean Node.
- Natal Chart for Derek Parker, 27th May 1932, 02:50, Looe, UK, Placidus Houses, Mean Node.

References

1. A quote from the inventor and futurist Nikola Tesla.
2. Neuropeptides are present within the brain; and are involved mostly in ventilatory and cardiovascular regulation. For more information visit: www.sciencedirect.com.
3. Information courtesy of www.quora.com.
4. Information courtesy of the Akashic Records.
5. Information courtesy of the Akashic Records.
6. Statistics courtesy of www.statista.com.
7. Information courtesy of www.springer.com.
8. Patrick Moore's secret interest in astrology was revealed in 2013. Thus, it came to light in an article published by the Astrological Association of Great Britain (AA).

"Chiron reminds us that only through recognizing and accepting our inner wounds can we find true healing."
Lisa Tenzin-Dolma

Chiron: The Psychological/Intellectual Healer

In Greek mythology, Chiron was considered to be a wise, but unattractive entity. Thus, Chiron was a centaur — part man and part horse. According to mythology, Chiron was accidentally shot and wounded by Hercules, with a poisoned arrow.

Chiron was a powerful physician; however, he was unable to heal from his wound, which, in time, became unbearably painful. Legend implies that Chiron was the son of Cronos (Saturn), and therefore he was immortal. According to mythology, Chiron renounced his immortality to the god Zeus, in order to free his close friend Prometheus, who was being punished for stealing fire from the gods — imparting it on humankind. After Chiron's death, Zeus freed Prometheus, and fixed Chiron in the heavens, as the constellation of Sagittarius.[1]

As with all known aspects of Greek mythology, the myth of Chiron is solely a metaphor. Today, the story is mostly concerned with how we cope with psychological distress, and ineluctable physical defeat, which are all an essential part of the human condition. Often, the injury that refuses to heal is purely a psychological wound, denoting deep set anguish, and doubt.

It can also refer to a hurt, which can orchestrate feelings of being *ostracized* from others. Ostracism is primarily a Uranian characteristic. Chiron is also a collective influence, similar to Uranus. In addition, Chiron symbolizes that which we *freely and unconditionally* give to others — without expecting anything in return.

Furthermore, Chiron's association with anguish and doubt, coupled with his knowledge of medicine, is why this cosmic entity has been linked to the intellectual and impressionistic sign of Virgo.

Healing/Electrifying the Psychological Wound

In the natal chart, Chiron symbolizes the point in which 'psychological healing' should naturally occur. Chiron's healing can only manifest in a psychological capacity, because the physical wound is only a metaphor, similar to the legend. If, however, we were physically injured in a previous life, it can only be reflected as a psychological impairment in the current incarnation.

In addition, Chiron's individual potential for psychological and intellectual healing, should be expanded *exponentially*, and within the ascendancy of the collective. Therefore, by using the phrenic healing potential of Chiron to heal another soul actually assists in the *balancing* of our personalized Saturn karma. Thus, Chironic healing should be *targeted* at the collective, but only when the individual has been *healed* in an intellectual capacity, which automatically triggers a release of the brain's concealed cognitive abilities.

So, how does Chiron healing manifest in the natal chart?

For example, if Chiron tenants the first house in Aquarius, the individual has within them the potential to become an evolved teacher — *spawned* from the suffering of early life struggles. These souls have it within them the potential to continually, but steadily, traverse an intellectual and innovative path of life. Once the cerebral karma has been balanced, the individual can freely impart wisdom and knowledge within an organized communal mainframe. In essence, they have the aptitude for inspiring others into *consolidating* more of the brain's intellect. On a personal level, this individual act of intellectual superiority also helps these souls to *consolidate* more of their own brain's intellect.

If Chiron is situated in the eighth house and in Pisces for example, the individual needs to offset his or her cerebral karma, against the immense range of their emotional compass. Overall, this means that their intellectual capacity is often superseded by their unconstrained emotions. In a previous life, their emotional capacity was mostly the focus of attention. Currently, they must learn to govern their emotions, so that there is more room for cerebral expansion. Once this has been achieved, the individual can then begin to heal other people's wounds, especially through intellectual compassion, and through acts of sheer kindness and reassurance. Ultimately, this will *transform* their souls.

If Chiron tenants the sixth house in Virgo, the individual is often drawn to medical matters. But more importantly, the individual is concerned with how the brain elicits its influence over the physical body, and therefore all illness and disease must surely have psychological connections. In most cases however, this notion is true. But it is often the individual concerned who has become *preoccupied* with their own reserved intellectual misfortunes, and analytical insecurities. Therefore, these souls must learn to balance their systematic viewpoints with their innate psychological imperfections. Then, they will be able to impart Chiron healing to those souls who are just as insecure and self-conscious, as they were beforehand.

Interestingly, Chiron in Virgo souls often impart their healing within charitable organizations. Here, they can provide a psychological refuge for the impoverished, and the unfortunate. Hence, those souls who have, for varied reasons, become psychologically compromised.

Essentially, these are some examples, which distinguish the fruits of a strong Chiron response.

The Separation

Today, Chiron is deemed mostly as a Saturn entity. This is because Chiron's perihelion lies in Saturn's zone of control. Furthermore, this is why in Greek mythology, Chronos (Saturn) was Chiron's father. However, Chiron's aphelion still lies within the distant influence of Uranus. In a way, this can be considered as 'Chiron's comprehensive healing potential' — governed by two separate but distinct spheres of potential.

The consequences for Uranus however, were catastrophic. Uranus has been mortally wounded in the process; and because Uranus is a sphere of pure intellect, the wound has opened up a psychological gorge in this spherical cosmic brain, which essentially *symbolizes* the modern-day Uranus archetype. Principally, Uranus now functions on the rim of psychological impairment. Metaphorically speaking, its brain is now where its cosmic arms should be.

The separation of Chiron from Uranus is both alarming and extreme. During this monumental cosmic cataclysm, which occurred eons ago, and which compromised the entire solar system, Chiron was dragged away from the gravity pull of Uranus. The impact literally *tipped* Uranus onto its side. This is the image we still see today. This is why Chiron is deemed as the wounded healer, because it is continuing to *heal* from this traumatic event in cosmic history. This cosmic portrayal ultimately symbolizes the earthly child, who has endured a difficult birth into the world — a transitional point in which a psychological wound has been karmically created. The separation of Chiron from Uranus is the main reason why human beings are not progressing in the intellectual-spiritual capacity.

Thus, Uranus is only operating at a fraction of its intended potential. This is mostly why the planet is misunderstood. In essence, the purpose of Uranus is to *evoke* more of our brain's intellect — a characteristic that it also needs to do in its current predicament of attempting to heal itself — due to the psychological loss of its twin entity, Chiron.[2]

References

1. Information source, Wikipedia.
2. Information court of the Akashic Records.

"A mind once experienced by a new idea never returns to its original dimension."
Marilena Marino

When Uranus is Intercepted

When Uranus or Aquarius is *intercepted*, timidity is often a concern, particularly throughout the course of adolescence. Often, these people prefer to remain inhibited, rather than express themselves in an intellectual capacity. In all cases however, those who have Uranus intercepted are 'highly intelligent and creative,' but they don't actually realize it, until much later in life.

A very respected and well-liked celebrity figure who is 'on route' to overcoming these noticeable facets, is the American actor Matthew McConaughey (see case study below). Additionally, someone who did acquire the reputation of 'intellectual genius,' but who didn't actually have Uranus intercepted, was the German physicist Albert Einstein. Einstein did however; have an unmistakable opposition involving Uranus and Jupiter; and which also included an intercepted polarity on the midpoint of this Uranus-Jupiter opposition — making the configuration one of extreme significance (see case study further on).

Uranian Intellectual Karma

Dyslexia is a common mental health condition. However, it shouldn't be confused with autism, which is a lifelong developmental disorder. Research does suggest that dyslexia, which is a learning brain disorder, affects a large percentage of those who have Uranus, or Mercury intercepted. Dyslexia is also apparent when Mercury and Uranus are frictionally aspected in the natal chart, particularly when they square Neptune, or when Mercury is square Uranus.

Unfortunately, when the individual is under the influence of this mentally impairing condition, he or she actually believes, and most likely accepts the notion, that they are dim, or just plain stupid. Most likely, it is also the cruel remarks of others that have made them feel that they are intellectually compromised. However, this misconceived concept couldn't be farther from the truth; because those whose brains have become seriously *unbalanced* by dyslexia have the potential to go on and become 'intellectual geniuses.'

Moreover, when Uranus is intercepted, or frictionally aspected with other planets in the natal chart, such as the Sun or Mercury, the brain has the capability to *generate* sizeable amounts of infrared radiation, or infrared light. Thus, infrared radiation is the epitome of electromagnetic energy, which the brain generates naturally, as brainwaves. However, infrared energy resonates at a much higher wavelength. Dyslexia *tangles* and *snares* brainwaves. It also *dampens* and *obstructs* the movement of infrared radiation — until the condition subsides.

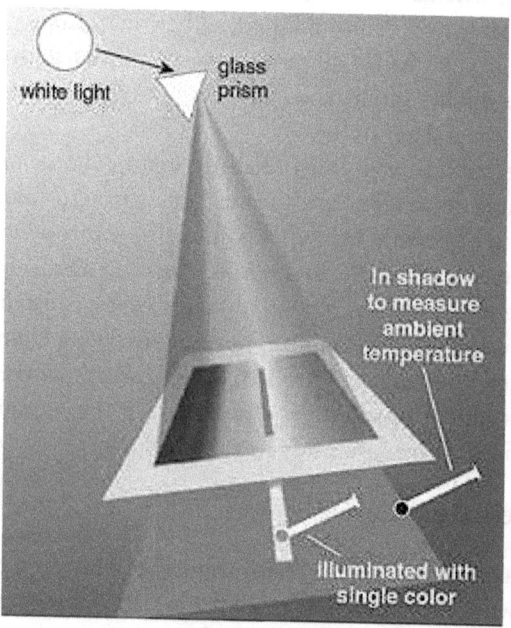

Once the brainwaves are unravelled however, which can be achieved via stillness, and intellectual enlightenment, the Uranus intercepted individual becomes *receptive* to elevated thinking, and intellectual cleverness.

Interestingly, William Herschel, the discoverer of Uranus in 1781, also discovered the existence of infrared radiation (see diagram),[1] in 1800.[2]

The diagram above shows Hershel's notion of infrared light, which is being created in; and thus, filtered through a prism. This is similar to the notion of 'intellectual genius.' Thus, this is where ideas and suggestions are manufactured in the frontal cortex of the brain; and thus, *refined* through the brain cells, particularly the neurons.

Uranian Intellectual Distinctiveness

When Uranus is intercepted in the natal chart, the individual possesses a strong sense of technological/intellectual acuity, which is distinctly recognizable. Moreover, they don't suffer fools, or to coin the phrase, they don't suffer sociopaths. Thus, this is an unmistakable idiosyncrasy that gives the appearance of someone who is *different* — separating them from the rest of society. Hence, it is an intellectual looney kind of thing. But then again, this notion is so far from the actual truth.

Possessing such a higher level of intellect gives them the *appearance* of being different; when in fact, they are, in physical form, just like everyone else. The only real difference is that they possess extraordinary levels of intellectual distinctiveness. It is however, their free-spirited perspectives on life, which separates them from everyone else. For these are the quietly subversive souls, who wish to *liberate* the collective from the shackles of authoritarian domination.

Furthermore, the Uranus intercepted/frictionally aspected soul is often associated with the 'overly-enthusiastic professor' type of personality. But this is purely a myth, because in actual fact, all the Uranus intercepted soul is attempting to do is simply being recognized for who they actually are. Thus, they are kind, considerate, and extremely intelligent, and not the mad, crazy and disassociated person that these infrequent characterizations in the natal chart are generally associated with.

They are the pioneers of humanitarian/technological justice — cut from the philanthropic cloth that, without any form of constraint, *computerizes* the cosmic brain — representative of the Uranus archetype.

Uranian Intellectual Genius

There is a distinct and unmistakable indication, or an intellectual pointer, which points to the intellectual genius; and that is the symbolic halo. The halo is a crown of light rays, circle or disk of light, which surrounds the head in a vertical fashion. Now that Uranus 'sits on its side,' and its rings orbit vertically, the planet *mirrors* a halo around a person's head. This is yet another symbolization of the intellectual genius. Those souls who have Uranus intercepted, or frictionally aspected in the natal chart, are more likely to have a prominent halo around their heads, which is often yellow, blue, or green in color.

Furthermore, and according to the *Akashic Records*, the intellectual genius can often detect the presence of a halo around another individual. Thus, a sure sign of intellectual superiority.

Uranian Intellectual Similarities

When Uranus is intercepted, it acts very similarly to when Uranus is positioned in the twelfth house. Hence, this is often a case of intellect and ideas, which are being *suppressed*. Thus, the suppression of the intellect is the crucial element of an intercepted Uranus, and is particularly prevalent throughout adolescence. Hence, the suppression of the intellect is perhaps the main cause of the individual's innate timidity of expression, and particularly where the release of new ideas is concerned.

Throughout their lives, the Uranus intercepted soul *appears* to carry the heavy upended weight of cerebral karma. However, it has not occurred as a karmic blueprint; but more like the imposition of an impending obstacle. Therefore, this is a karmic provocation that will pose a major challenge to their all-embracing intellectual progression, which is similar to the expression of dyslexia. Dyslexia is also concerned with the twelfth house.

Yet, these souls are evolutionary *evolved* in a cerebral capacity. However, they have chosen to incarnate, in order to expand their knowledge, which is connected to the higher functions of the brain — previously unexplored cerebral zones. This case in point is similar to the natural plight of the impressive and all-evolved dolphin.

It is not until much later in life, hence around the second Saturn return, that the individual is given the innate opportunity to express themselves *fully*. In other words, they become *inundated* with ideas. It is usually at this developed juncture in their lives when the intercepted Uranus soul finally begins to develop their inborn potential — towards intellectual genius, and unsurpassed brilliance. It is then, that the quest to completely master their intellect begins.

A strong case in point, which represents someone who strived towards the complete mastery of the intellect, was the German physicist, Albert Einstein. Although Einstein's Uranus wasn't intercepted, it was however, opposing Jupiter in Aquarius, the sign with which Uranus naturally rules. Uranus is also squared to an intercepted Pluto. This cosmic setting was, in effect, similar to Uranus being *wholly* intercepted.

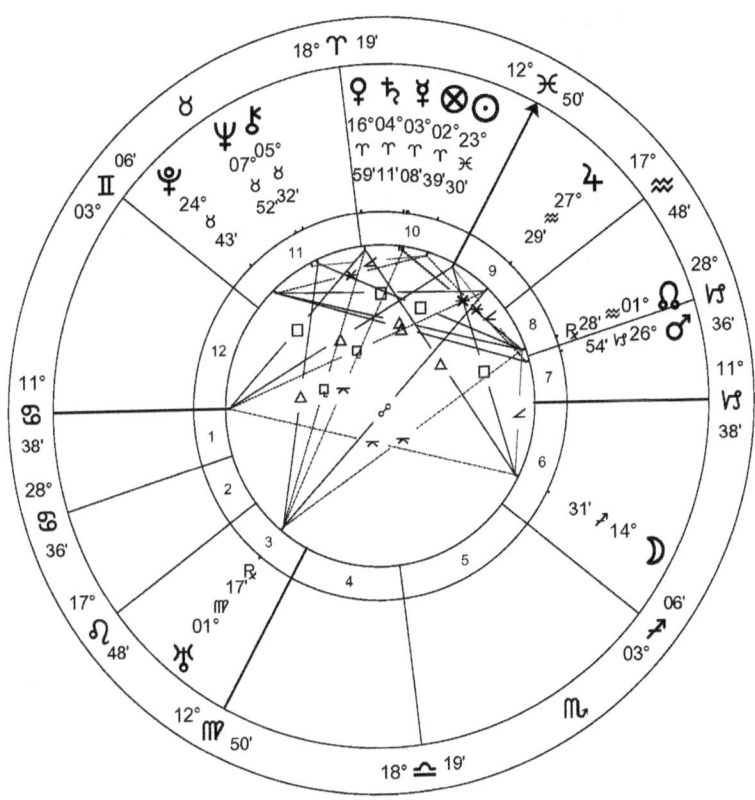

Natal Chart for Einstein, 3/14/1879, 11:30, Ulm, Germany

Uranus's Intellectual Footprint — Albert Einstein

Albert Einstein was considered to be one of the greatest, and perhaps most influential physicists of all time. Initially, he began his career as a patent clerk. Yet, he was appointed as an associate professor in 1909. [3] However, it wasn't until much later in his life, (at 76), that he developed his legendary principles on special relativity. These exceptional philosophies established that the laws of physics are the same for everyone, despite their individual status. For example, light travels at the same speed despite the way in which it is contained. The development of his special relativity was an important milestone in Einstein's life, because it meant that he was able to *graduate* towards his own remarkable notion of intellectual genius.

In the natal chart for Albert Einstein, the centerpiece is most definitely the dissociate Uranus-Jupiter opposition — symbolizing the possible expansion of the cerebral intellect — which will only transpire through measures that are both *incompliant* and *rigid*. In other words, if we are unwilling to make necessary changes to our lives, they will be forced upon us regardless. For Einstein however, this was not the case.

Steadily, he graduated towards the status of intellectual genius, which wouldn't become apparent until much later in his life. This was due, in part, to Saturn's elevation in the chart (see footnote 1). Meanwhile, a dissociate aspect of this magnitude generally means that there will be considerably more obstacles to overcome, than if the aspect was *unequivocal*, hence in the same aspectual relationship (see footnote 2). Thus, overcoming obstacles was certainly the case for Albert Einstein.

Moreover, Uranus squares Pluto; and Pluto's degree is pitted (deficient), according to William Lilly.[4] Thus, Pluto's blemished degree is *intensified* due to Pluto's interception. For Einstein, transformation would be a slow and lengthy process, which is always the traditional nature of Pluto. In effect, Einstein had to literally *grapple* for everything he considered to be of scientific, evolutionary and spiritual value.

Uranus is also quincunx Mercury. Mercury's degree in Aries is dark, according to Lilly. So, Mercury doesn't manage to generate light in the chart — despite the fact that Mercury lies close to the Sun; and would therefore *naturally* reflect the Sun's light energy. Mercury's close conjunction with Saturn is, in effect, a cosmic coup d'état. This is because Saturn *seizures* Mercury; and holds it firmly in its concrete grip. In essence, there was not much room to navigate his ideals — administering them only to those supportive minds.

Einstein was epileptic. Therefore, he endured a lifetime of epileptic seizures, which ironically may have assisted him in his work. I have heard it said that shortly after an epileptic (grand mal) seizure, a person

Footnote 1
Elevated planets literally mean planets that are at the 'pinnacle' of the chart. These are planets that are usually around, or nearest to the MC (refer to next section, Outer Planets in Elevation).

Footnote 2
Dissociate aspects occur when the planets, which are in aspect, are situated close to the end, or the beginning of a sign, and have a relatively large orb. For example, if the Sun lies at one degree of Aries, it would be in dissociate square with a planet at twenty-five degrees of Sagittarius — although the signs themselves are in trine to each other. Only when the Sun reaches one degree of Capricorn, would it be deemed as being in the same aspectual relationship.

can become very inspired by the presence of renewed intellectual ideas, and spiritual knowledge.

But, with all of this Uranus influence in the chart, it is hardly surprising that Einstein was epileptic — considering also that Uranus tenants the cerebral-medical third house — naturally ruled by Mercury — considered to be Uranus's understudy. Nevertheless, the quincunx between Uranus and Mercury means that an adjustment needed to be made within the cerebral confines of his brain. In essence, his brain would need to be *consolidated* — establishing equilibrium between the left and the right side of his brain. Hence, to *harmonize* these separate but distinct cerebral elements.

Once the adjustment denoted by the quincunx has been inaugurated, the burden of epilepsy would have been relinquished. It is not certain however, whether Einstein actually overcame this debilitating and harsh condition. However, and despite this debilitation, Einstein became one of the greatest and accomplished minds of the nineteenth/twentieth century.

To quote one of his profound expressions, "we cannot solve our problems with the same thinking we used when we created them." Very Uranian!

An Intellectual Impression of Technological Magnificence

The elevated Sun (top of the chart) in Albert Einstein's natal chart *did* however provide sufficient light, by which he could successfully manoeuvre his inner mechanical vessel towards the distant beacon of intellectual radiance. In addition, his stoic determination to succeed in his particular field of expertise had been progressively *supported* by the mutual reception between Mars and Saturn. Here, Mars tenants the sign of Saturn's domicile rulership, Capricorn, to which Mars is in its exaltation, and Saturn tenants the sign of Mars's domicile rulership, Aries, to which Saturn is in its fall.

But overall, it was Einstein's oblique and dissociate opposition between extensive Jupiter and conceptual Uranus, which *stamped* and *secured* his intellectual footprint; and which will leave a distinct impression in the erudite minds of others, for generations to come.

Predominantly, Einstein was an ambassador for revolutionary (quantum) science, and advanced mathematics. Thus, his evolutionary mission was to aspire other like-minded intellects into becoming the intellectual geniuses of today — disseminating technological development.

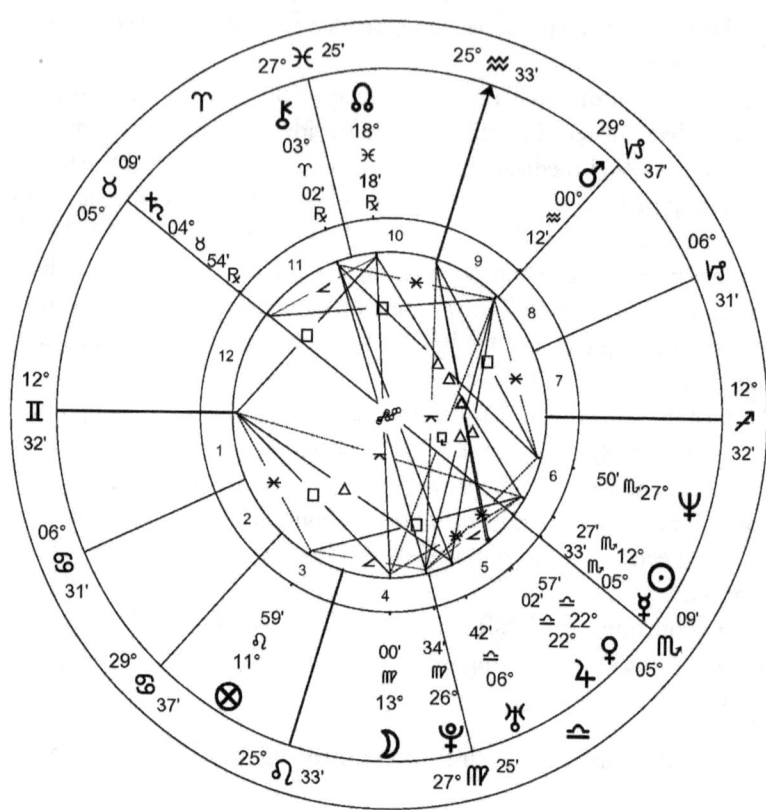

Natal Chart for Matthew McConaughey, 11/4/1969, 19:34, Uvalde, Texas

The Intellectual Humanitarian — Matthew McConaughey

Matthew David McConaughey is an intellectually-accomplished actor. The foundations for such a life privilege were elementally conceived from an earlier life — managing the prospect as being a reserved, and a self-effacing individual.[5]

In the natal chart for Matthew McConaughey, Uranus is intercepted — through which its 'apprehensive undertones' can often be discerned throughout the majority of his acting roles. However, the socially-reticent, but collectively-creative influence of the intercepted Uranus is particularly apparent in the 1997 science fiction movie, *Contact*. Here, McConaughey starred alongside Jodie Foster, who has Uranus elevated, and opposes Jupiter, in her natal chart (see natal chart for Jodie Foster in Part

One). In the first quarter of the movie, McConaughey was somewhat reluctant to voice his socialist opinions and higher-minded beliefs — until much later in the movie — at which point he decides to be more intellectually assertive. Hence, his reluctance to stand up and be counted for created a slight conflict between these two principle characters in the movie.

Interestingly, in a composite chart, there is a semi-sextile between McConaughey's Uranus, and Foster's Uranus. The general consensus determines that Foster possesses the potential to *sustain* the upper hand over McConaughey. It also determines that with careful *nurturing*, Foster has the potential to win over the intellectual sentiments of McConaughey. This was certainly the case, especially when Foster continually *cited* the paradigm of 'technological invention,' which the movie is based entirely upon.

However, when an intellectual synthesis was created between these two Uranian minds, a dual compromise was eventually reached. Towards the climax of the movie, they were both in total agreement, especially where their viewpoints were concerned. The purpose of this 'movie review' is to determine that intercepted houses and planets are normally hidden from view. However, with determination and careful consideration, they can be easily accessed, as McConaughey successfully demonstrated in his role in *Contact*. But this is only relevant in the movie world of fantasy, and not in actual reality. Throughout the acting profession, these two dualistic elements can be easily *synthesized*.

Uranian Disinclination

The notion of fantasy and reality was highlighted in an interview on the *Tonight Show*, hosted by Jimmy Fallon. Here, McConaughey explained his reluctance to realistically campaign to become the governor of Texas. To him, it was just an apprehensible and fantastical notion, which would be typical of Neptune's square to the MC. Initially, his family had put him forward for the role, which is often a distinguishing characteristic of the Moon in the fourth house, and its trine to authority-orientated Saturn. But he later declined the opportunity.

'Disinclination' is a typical response to an intercepted Uranus, which in this case, is accompanied by a quincunx to contracted Saturn. Saturn lies on the cusp of the twelfth house. In addition, Neptune, the natural ruler of the twelfth house, is square the MC — eliciting the fear factor. Furthermore, Venus and Jupiter, which are also intercepted, are exactly conjunct. Essentially, this stellar combination makes McConaughey a 'nice guy,' in a cool and reserved kind of way. But it does very little for his overall confidence, especially when it comes to expanding his external light of creative invention.

Literally, McConaughey has to 'dig deep' into his subconscious in order to acquire that which most people take for granted; such as the predisposed actions that follow initial thoughts. Ideally, these are his convictions that aspire for him to build upon his initial confidence. Originally, it was a distinct lack of confidence, which prevented Matthew McConaughey from becoming the governor of Texas. He also feared that his involvement would create political chaos, which is a further characteristic of an intercepted Uranus. Ironically, his chart suggests that he would have carried out this duty *impeccably*.

Uranus's trine to the Ascendant is however, a testament to McConaughey's overall acting success — tinged with moderate amounts of intellectual doggedness and fortitude. These cosmic traits are particularly evident in his movies, *The Gentlemen*, and *The Lincoln Lawyer*. However, in order for McConaughey to *reach* a 'higher state of mind,' which he spoke passionately about with Jimmy Fallon, he would need to make the impartial adjustment demanded by the quincunx between Saturn and Uranus. This is an adjustment, which represents fairness within the realms of intellectual stability and authority — pressuring McConaughey further into becoming the intellectual nice guy — as set out by his Venus-Jupiter conjunction.

Throughout the course of his lifetime, Matthew McConaughey *has* always had the potential to reach the psychological state of 'intellectual genius.' This is similar in many ways to the plight of Albert Einstein. Perhaps, he has made the first step towards this, with his recent appointment as a professor of practice.

The Professor of Practice

In recognition of his outstanding work as a teacher, and a mentor to the University of Texas students, and with respect to his career as an award-winning actor and producer, Matthew McConaughey has been appointed as a professor of practice at the Moody College of Communication, starting in the fall 2019 term.[6] Thus, the appointment of this truly remarkable accolade is a testament to the fact that McConaughey has managed to *synthesize* the dualistic elements of fantasy and reality, which is supported by intellectual Uranus.

This professor of practice status is perhaps a testament to his intercepted Uranus — trine to the Ascendant. Aspects to intercepted planets tend to vanish in the midst of time; until that is the planet is remembered *psychologically*, in which case they can be easily accessed. Moreover, and in light of this amazing achievement, McConaughey has no doubt made the required adjustment between Uranus and Saturn. This being the case, McConaughey is destined to become an ambassador of intellectual genius. This is the underlying purpose of an intercepted Uranus.

The honor to become an ambassador of intellectual genius was further endorsed recently. In response to the 2022 Texas school massacre, in which nineteen children and two teachers were killed, McConaughey made a passionate plea for the gun laws to be altered in America. He appealed to US lawmakers to pass gun control legislation, where he urged congress to "reach a higher ground."

Metaphorically speaking, McConaughey was also referring to himself here, because he has ultimately *raised* the vibration of Uranus in his chart — reaching the higher ground of his chart, so to speak. In addition, his speech is reminiscent of the trine between Uranus and gun-loving Mars in humanitarian Aquarius, which *ungulates* towards clemency. McConaughey also met with President Joe Biden to discuss the matter further. His speech came in wake of the massacre at an elementary school on May, 24, 2022 in his hometown of Uvalde.[7]

In my opinion, this notable act of mercy would have extended McConaughey's credentials to become a perpetually-accredited professor of practice, which leads me to conclude this section with a perfectly befitting quote from Matthew McConaughey. "Give thanks. Appreciate what you do have…the more we give thanks, the more we receive to be thankful for. Gratitude is the gift that always gives back."

Chart Data

- Natal Chart for Albert Einstein, 14th March 1879, 11:30, Ulm, Germany, Placidus Houses, Mean Node.
- Natal Chart for Matthew McConaughey, 4th November 1969, 19:34, Uvalde, USA, Placidus Houses, Mean Node.

References

1. Diagram courtesy of www.americanscientist.org.
2. Information source Wikipedia.
3. Information source Wikipedia.
4. Christian Astrology (1647), page 116, denotes deficient and fortunate degrees.
5. Information source Wikipedia.
6. Information source www.news.utexas.edu.
7. Referring to the school shooting in May 2022. Information source, the Guardian newspaper.

> *"When you don't follow your nature there is a hole in the universe where you were supposed to be."*
> Dane Rudhyar

Outer Planets in Elevation

Throughout this book, and throughout my previous publications, you will have noticed that I make frequent references to 'elevated planets.' Traditionally, planets in elevation mean that there is an important distinction to be made. On one level, a planet positioned above the horizon in the horoscope represents energies that are more visible to those around you; and therefore, they are comparatively more exposed to public view. However, on another level, and particularly when the outer planets are elevated, these planets become significantly *immersed* in karmic energies, as a result of the measures we take in life — whether positive or negative.

Likewise, when Saturn, Uranus, Neptune or Pluto are elevated in the natal chart, these planets act as *catalysts* for the differing vibrations, which are associated with karma; meaning that these planets are accumulating karma, which is gathering in some form at this current moment in time. The natal chart is, after all, a cosmic lens — projecting the entire life journey. Thus, the life journey comes complete with stumbling blocks and opportunities for growth and expansion — masterminded and kept in motion mostly by transits, and progressive solar arcs. Thus, the outer planets are the *significators* of causality.

Mostly, we refer only to the karma we are balancing now, which has been acquired from previous incarnations. But the truth is, the karma from previous incarnations must have accumulated somehow. The outer planets, especially when in elevation, are the 'cosmic clues' to acquiring karma in our current incarnation — impacting us in spirit, or in a future incarnation. If we chose to reincarnate, the karma that accumulated in the previous incarnation will be applied. The exact nature of the karma is unique to the specific planet (see list below).

The fact that some planets are elevated in the natal chart means that we have to become 'more aware' of the energies of the particular planet/s under consideration. For example, if Uranus is elevated, we must be more aware of how we interact collectively, and how we relay information to the wider audience. When Uranus is elevated it is easy to dominate a person/s with radical views, and extremist observations. As a result, we may end up doing serious harm to another person/s intellect, with information they are not qualified to deal with intellectually, which in time can cause cerebral breakdown.

On the other hand, if, we *confuse* someone in a mental capacity, especially with religious or spiritual viewpoints, via preaching, we will accumulate karma via the Neptune archetype. Thus, if the planet is in elevation, the karma will most likely come to pass in spirit. This is particularly the case with Uranus and Neptune.

Saturn and Pluto on the other hand, are more generalized in their methods. Therefore, these planets press us into balancing our karma in physicality — making certain it is completely balanced before we return to spirit. However, Saturn and Pluto make sure that any outstanding karma is inherently *imprinted* upon the psyche upon our return to physicality. There is no escape, so to speak.

All of this information can be located in the *Akashic Records*, and through some reliable, impressionable spirit intermediaries.

Outer Planetary Karma

Saturn: Physical/Somatic karma.
Uranus: Intellectual/Phrenic karma.
Neptune: Religious/Prescient karma.
Pluto: Psychological/Generative karma.

Outer Planetary Karmic Disciplines

Saturn rules the physical framework (the corporeal center).
Uranus rules the brain (the reasoning center).
Neptune rules the soul (the heart center).
Pluto rules the spirit (the life force center).
The life force functions as a 'transformational bridge' for the body (Saturn), the mind (Uranus), and the soul (Neptune).

PART ONE

Uranus is the God of Perception and Lightning

(Lightning is the Equivalent to the Emergence of 'Sudden New Ideas')

> *"I know the thoughts that surround you, because I can look inside your head."*
> From the 1969 song, Where Do You Go to My Lovely, by Peter Starstedt.

The Profundity of Uranian (Cerebral) Karma

This line is a piece of the outro, which is the final verse of Peter Starstedt's innovative song. Thus, the entire narrative of the song is cerebrally *karmic* in nature; and therefore, it is *very* Uranus. A brief interpretation would imply that the main character in the song is evading her karma; and in this case, her cerebral karma — donning an alternate disguise.

I selected this particular song, because it is typical of the unbridled thoughts (Mercury), and the uncontrolled vision (Uranus), which 'whirl' through the minds of so many souls today; and which ultimately leads to the onset of cerebral karma. Remember, what we see (Mercury/Uranus), and what we think (Mercury/Uranus), are the principles that orchestrate cerebral karma.

Peter Starstedt is perfectly suited to singing this illustrative song. Primarily, this is because he has a close conjunction of Saturn and Uranus in his socially-orientated seventh house; meaning that he is highly self-aware, creative, grounded, and practically-minded of himself, and others. The degree of Uranus is *fortunate*, according to William Lilly. The fortunate degree makes him intellectually-perceptive. Essentially, *where did you go to my lovely*, is an intellectually-perceptive arrangement. Uranus, is also trine to Neptune (music, and intellectually intuitive melodies). This configuration makes him all-knowing.

The Eyes of the Mind

Traditionally, Mercury rules the eyes. However, Mercury's rulership is concerned solely with the overall movement of the eyes, whereas Uranus is concerned with ocular vision, perception and observation. Essentially, these innovative characteristics are governed by the higher mind, which represents an assemblage of elevated truths, to which are housed within certain parts of the brain. Thus, they are subsequently *released* (liberated) via sudden electrical impulse activity; hence cerebral lightning. These electrified/elevated truths are representative of innovative ideas, and cerebral vision quests; hence contemplative thinking, to which Uranus has its rulership over.

When engaging with the brain for the purposes of a vision quest, it is advisable not to ingest conventional drugs, stimulants or hallucinogens, in order to achieve your objective, otherwise the brain will accumulate

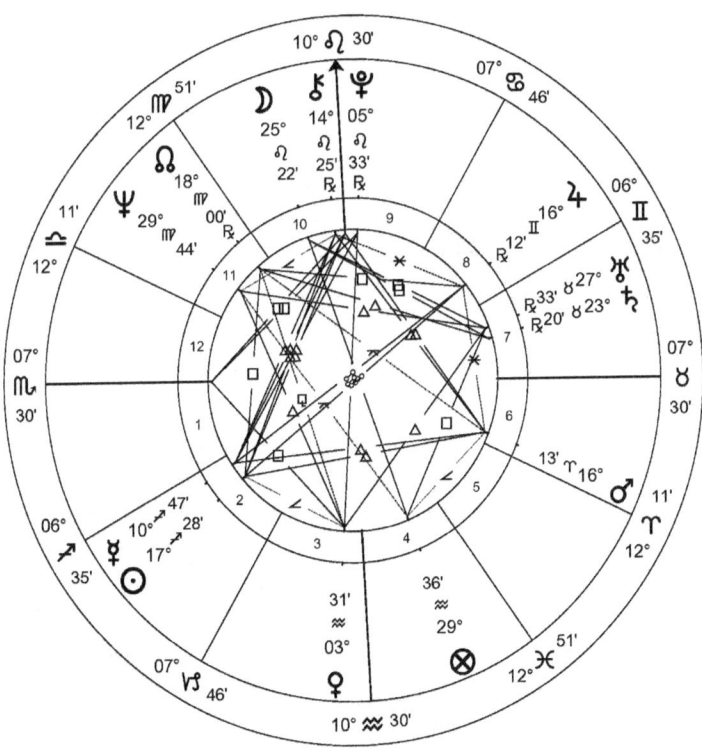

Natal chart for Peter Starstedt, 12/10/1941, 04:00, New Delhi, India

imposing cerebral karma. This is what happened to Marie-Claire, the genuine character in the Peter Starstedt song. The use of the 'elevated imagination,' which is the result of supreme intellectual thoughts, is all that is required. Cerebral vision quests are a particularly good way to receive answers from intellectually imposing questions.

In order to reach this supreme and accomplished cerebral state of being, the brain needs to be purged of doubt, indecision and uncertainty, and recharged with certainty, conviction and absolution, which is the primary mission of Uranus. Thus, to be able to look inside of someone else's head is merely a visual and cerebral perception — distinguishing impressionable observations. If these higher-minded attributes are not attained throughout incarnation, the brain will *amass* elevated levels of imposing cerebral karma. Moreover, when we manipulate others, especially with the power of our thoughts, the consequences of our actions will be severe.

It is important to point out that every organ in the body carries with it a specific form of karma; because the organs are overseen by the chakras, which are colorful reflections of the brain, and the soul. Thus, the brain and the soul are the principle catalysts for every type, and condition of karma.

According to the *Akashic Records*, the brain (Uranus), and the soul (Neptune), are the only two 'fields of vision,' which remain active in the spirit world of transformation (Pluto).

Uranian Vision

Speaking purely in a Uranian capacity, Peter Starstedt's song is about a character attempting to *balance* her Utopian karma, and who is in fact Peter Starstedt's actual wife. However, the outcome of her efforts may not have turned out as she solely intended. Perhaps, she should have looked inside her own head to discover the answers to her questions, which those around her, in the song, could actually recognize. Unfortunately, the song is representative of the overall level of intellect upon the Earth today, which is, in some cases, truncated, and falls very short of the specific requirements attached to the twenty-first century.

Metaphorically speaking, being able to look inside our own head, and into the heads of others, especially when employing the Uranian higher-minded measure of telepathy, should be an extremely relevant factor to this current 'staging post' in our collective evolution.[1] Hence, I refer mostly to the preliminary divisions of the twenty-first century — proficiently referred to as the Aquarian (Uranian) age of enlightenment. Thus, the long-awaited arrival of the Age of Aquarius, which is being heralded by those higher intellectual minds; is representative to the collective path of Uranian evolution. This symbolizes the age of higher reasoning, and ingenious intellectualization.

Unfortunately, many will simply disregard the existence, and the importance of the Age of Aquarius. Discounting this Uranian epoch of intellect is chiefly due to a lack of understanding, and cerebral perception that exists today. Perhaps, to these 'unenlightened souls,' the Age of Aquarius is merely an extension to the current global predicament; hence the age of hopelessness — generating progressive quantities of illness and disease — and which in this case are predominantly cognitive (cerebral) disorders examined in Part Two.

Otherwise, there are a multitude of souls who will attain intellectual superiority, as a result of this periodic phenomenon. Because to them, the Age of Aquarius will be viewed as the age of intellectual enlightenment. Essentially, the Age of Aquarius symbolizes a period of intellectual healing and reasoning. Consistently, our fate lies with the intelligible ideas and free-thinking choices, which we make in life, to which secures our ultimate destiny and purpose.

Unfortunately, in our modern-day world, so many individuals are continuing to *amass* increasing amounts of cerebral karma, primarily because of illogical thinking, and decision making. Far too many succumb to illusion-based temptation — rather than directing their thoughts towards their powers of higher reasoning. A further problem is that many continue to *renovate* outdated ideas and abstract opinions — *rehashing* that which has preceded. Alas, these 'cerebral echoes in time' represent inexorable inducements for the onset of psychological infirmities, particularly dementia and Parkinson's disease.

Theoretically speaking, we cannot successfully recreate an antiquated objective, or an idea, which has reached its pinnacle of virtue — long ago in the past. For example, and in some cases, the criminal mind represents a highly intelligent person, who uses his or her intellect to manipulate, and thus alter a previous situation, for their own personal gratification. If, however, they manage to succeed in their psychological pursuit, they will accumulate vast amounts of cerebral karma.

In some cases, however, they will meet with a Uranian death, such as a sudden fatal accident, a pulmonary incursion, or an electrical occurrence, such as an execution. I refer here to the first case study, Ted Bundy (see further on). A specific type of death is, of course, solely dependent on the strength and the condition of their karma, which is displayed primarily by elevated planets in the natal chart.

Uranian Visual Spectrums

Uranus is the planet that *electrifies* the wavelengths that ultimately belong to the future. It does this by *distorting* the karmic undulations that are connected to the past; hence to balance cerebral karma. However, this bygone trend, which recreates events and circumstances from yesteryear, is continuing to create a 'ripple effect.' This is happening because we are simply not *electrifying/elevating* our brains in the way we should do. Uranus presses us into acquiring new initiatives, and state-of-the-art ideas. Thus, Uranus urges us to embrace the prospect of 'avant-garde' innovation.

Currently, the 'distinct absence' of Uranian innovation, is why so many are considered to be 'brain dead.' In addition, there are many revolutionary groups and autocratic individuals who are attempting to remove the individual's natural desire for liberty and freedom. But, in most cases, this oppressive Uranian revolution, which is sweeping the globe, merely increases the already high levels of despotism in the world. Consequently, this global dictatorship is occurring because so many individuals, particularly in authority, have become *devoid* of new ideas and creativity. That is why so many appear to have no visual cognizance whatsoever. In all cases, these disturbing scenarios represent Uranian catalysts for the onset of cerebral karma, and, of course, illness and disease.

At the same time, it is important to point out that those who become *addicted* to technology are accruing large amounts of Uranian (cerebral) karma, particularly those who suffer from nomophobia, which is a fear of being without a cell (mobile) phone. Technology addiction is also a catalyst for the onset of illness and disease. Metaphorically speaking, this unfortunate compulsion is viewed in spirit as *misusing* and *perverting* the higher-minded ideas of those who have created the technology in the first place. The purpose of innovative technology is to liberate the collective. However, weapons of mass destruction 'do not' *liberate*; they merely destroy the physical and cerebral seeds of the collective. Furthermore, weapons of mass destruction *enhance* the cerebral karma of those who have created it. Thus, weapons of mass destruction is simply a Uranian term for 'misguided vision.'

But perhaps more importantly, those who mishandle technology, for example, using it against the will of the collective, and for the purpose of suppressing and tyrannizing, face their own personalized cerebral persecution. The electrical impulses in their brains will be *hyperactive* — displaying within their visual perception images of the devastation and suffering they are imposing. Uranian punishments are often transmitted through Neptune's dreams.

One such example, which exemplifies this type of Uranian behaviour, is with the Russian dictator, Vladimir Putin, who continues to bring tyranny to the people of Ukraine. Putin accuses the people of the Ukraine as being 'drug addicts,' and 'Nazis.' Perhaps what Putin is actually doing is seeing an immoral reflection in his own head, rather than the heads of those he accuses of being corrupt and iniquitous.

Uranian Karma

According to J.S. Zaveri, 'The brain's commanding presence orders sensation, movement, thought, and a lifetime of memory. The central nervous system, which is a labyrinth, hence a maze of nerve fibres, links all areas of the body to cells in the fabric of the brain.' [2]

What an inspiring proclamation, and one that is perfectly relevant to the acquisition of cerebral karma. Speaking purely in a sole capacity, our brain works in order to close open loops. Thus, an open loop is a task left *unfinished*. Cerebral karma is created specifically on that truth. For example, psychological (mental) illness, is provoked when a life task is simply ignored, or seriously overlooked. Although the time of birth is debateable, the favoured natal chart for Vladimir Putin does suggest a psychological illness, or cancer is imminent, especially if he continues to *violate* and *dishonor* the fundamental purpose of his elevated and afflicted Uranus. Ideally, because Putin has placed himself in an important position of authority, his elevated Uranus is meant to *liberate* the people of Russia from preceding aggressive influences — namely the outdated communist regimes and existing influences.

Most definitely, Putin represents a contemporary figurehead of modern-day Uranian innovation. Visually, he even looks the part. Alternately, Putin is capable of *escalating* this outdated form of psychological belligerence to his own psychological advantage.

If that is the path he chooses, he will ultimately sign his own Uranian death warrant. He may even be assassinated?

Sudden fatal incidents, such as assassinations, occur when assurances, commitments, and the word of honor is deliberately broken, which in turn affects others. This was also the case for President John F. Kennedy (see case example). Although J.F.K. was considered to be a good president, he lacked distinct Uranian innovation. Characteristically, he was an *unexciting* president. During his brief tenure of the White house, for just over two years, J.F.K. demonstrated an *inability* to carry through his thoughts and ideas in the form of legislation. [3] Because of this, many citizens of the US agonized in a multitude of ways. To this day however, his execution was believed to be the result of a major conspiracy, which can be attributed to Uranus and Neptune, in his natal chart. [4]

Electrical shocks are indeed a wake-up call — functioning primarily as sudden and deliberate warnings — indicating that change is required in life. In essence, the onset of an electric shock is *disconcerting*. To receive an electric shock implies that we must try *harder* to achieve our cerebral objectives in life. Hence, to accomplish what we agreed to do; and we mustn't disregard our karmic responsibilities, as a result. This was certainly the case for the American businesswomen Martha Stewart. Stewart revealed in an interview with *Ellen DeGeneres*, that she was struck by lightning on *three* separate occasions. [5] These 'wake up calls' are indeed consistent with the position of Uranus in her natal chart (see case example).

Death by electricity only occurs when the brain is *overloaded* with cerebral karma, as was the case with Ted Bundy. In effect, electricity purges the brain cells — neutralizing the counterproductive karma that pervades the physical and spiritual bodies. Death by electricity is the brain's psychological preferred option, particularly when the brain can no longer *close* the karmic loop holes.

Solely, we manifest cerebral karma simply by transmuting patterns of thought. Thus, when we engage in a specific type of behaviour, whether it is good or bad, that particular measure will undoubtably create a necessary consequence. This is often the case where homosexuals and lesbians are concerned. Their sexual preferences are concerned mostly with Mercury and Uranus — invariably creating cerebral karma. Thus, when Uranus is involved, it is our intended thoughts alone that create the cyclic pattern of cerebral karma — good or bad.

Moreover, in order to avoid obstructive cerebral karma, we must be more conscious of how to *engage* with the minds of others.

Furthermore, we must learn to think *creatively* and *innovatively*, in order to avoid the prospect of amassing negative intellectual karma. Thus, creative thoughts sustain the mind, in its universal quest for intellectual perfection — making it the quintessential acumen for intellect and comprehensive knowledge.

Intellectual Resolutions of Uranian Karma

Physical karma is essentially balanced via sustained soul meditation. However, in order to balance cerebral karma, we need to *electrify/elevate* our brains through creative endeavours, and ingenious ideas. We all have the potential to do this, regardless of our circumstances. The harmonious vibrations that are discharged from our creative undertakings *resonate* in the brain; thus, recreating as a type of mindfulness, or psychological calmness. In truth, the brain is designed for that very purpose — *reconciled* by innovative expressions and developments. Therefore, when the brain is expanded to its current capacity with expressive inspiration, it becomes *immersed* in a concentration of neurons — born in the creative areas of the brain that are rich in neural precursor cells. [6]

Neurons are created in the brain (Uranus), and are essentially information messengers (Mercury). Moreover, they have the potential to increase the brain's capacity further. Uranus is a wide-ranging cerebral planet, and new Uranian inventive ideas *nourish* the brain cells. Thus, these new ideas are transformed into electrical impulses (neurons), which recharge the *brain*; and which *electrify* more of the brain's capacity, therefore balancing cerebral karma.

Currently, so many brains are in a state of *collapse*; hence de-electrification.

Therefore, they are being compromised by increasing levels of cerebral karma — generating insufficient amounts of intellect. This is partly why so many succumb to brain tumors, and other Uranian infirmities, as well as sudden fatal incidents, and of course, electric shocks. Speaking of which, perhaps the famed electric shock, in the extreme form of electrocution, was administered to the 1970s serial killer, Ted Bundy. Bundy did expand his brain to a degree, but for entirely the wrong reasons. Thus, Bundy was an intellectual psychopath, who used his intellect in order to manipulate.

Theodore Robert Bundy was an American serial killer, and rapist. He is considered to be one of the most notorious criminals of the late twentieth-century.

Bundy was extremely intelligent, but also manipulative. Bundy sexually assaulted a multitude of women, between 1974 and 1978 — including underage girls.

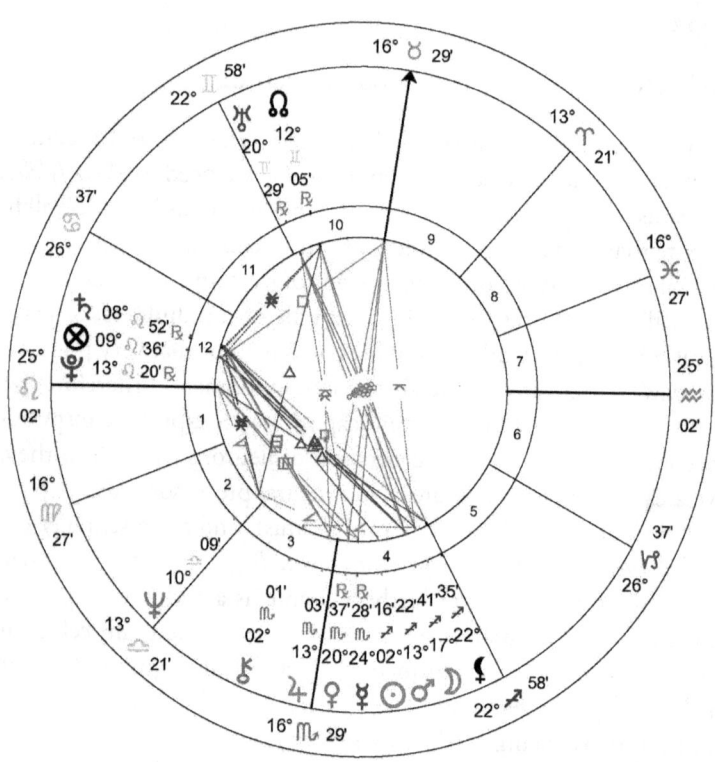

Natal Chart for Ted Bundy, 11/24/1946, 22:35, Burlington, Vermont,

Although he confessed to the murder of 28 women, it was estimated that he was responsible for hundreds of deaths. Bundy was later executed in 1989, by the infamous electric chair. [7]

The Uranus-Ruled Natal Chart

In the natal chart for Ted Bundy, Uranus is very pronounced; thereby exhibiting its superior domination in the chart. So, from its elevated position (top of the chart), Uranus opposes Mars, the South Node, and the Moon, which are all conjunct. The opposition from Uranus to the Moon would most likely mean that Bundy's emotions were *turbulent*, and most likely *unpredictable*. Thus, he was bordering on being 'emotionally unstable.' This would account for the sudden changes to his temperament, which he was notorious for displaying. However, Bundy, it seems, learnt to rationalize his emotions. This meant that he was able to justify his behaviour, especially to the authorities. Therefore, the powers that be were confounded by his violent exertions.

On top of all this, Uranus opposes the Black Moon, which is also conjunct the Moon. This means that his 'emotional unstable behaviour' was a feature of a previous life. This is a karmic feature, which is also confirmed by the South Node's conjunction to Mars; and the South Node's wide opposition to Uranus. Furthermore, the degree of the Black Moon is pitted (deficient), according to Lilly. Traditionally, the Black Moon represents a person's primitive impulses and behaviour in the rawest form. It expresses a dark side of the personality, which is buried deep within the psyche. In effect, Ted Bundy was a person who could turn on the charm, whenever he needed to. Alternatively, he could be excessively aggressive and irresponsible — displaying little or no empathy and remorse. These are characteristics that he honed in a past life, and he had every intention of using them in a future existence (Uranus). Characteristically, Bundy was the quintessential psychopath.

Uranian Projections

Ted Bundy most definitely had *unbalanced* cerebral karma, which was buried deep within the farthest recesses of his brain. This karma had most likely manifested in the form of 'unenlightened convictions.' This, he exhibited as an evolutionary insurrection — revolting against those who he wished to manipulate. In this case, it was his unfortunate victims. These previously mentioned subverted tendencies are now projected via his Black Moon, and its pitted degree in Sagittarius. In addition, they are displayed via the Black Moon's opposition to Uranus, which tenants dichotomous Gemini. Uranus in Gemini is paradoxical, because both of these stellar bodies are *interchangeable*. Hence, they are almost identical — symbolizing the prospect of coherent change — without any rational thought being applied. Essentially, Uranus in Gemini is an airy combination of certifiable components that *swept* through Bundy like a passing tornado. In essence, it seriously compromised his brain.

Essentially, these cosmic patterns manifest as significant cerebral karma, which remain *unbalanced*. Additionally, the natural ruler of Sagittarius, Jupiter, and the natural ruler of Gemini, Mercury, are both pinpointed in Scorpio. Venus, also in Scorpio, is considered as being *almost* besieged; thus, Bundy lacked empathy. In addition, there is little or no brain chemistry that is evident. Moreover, an astrological pattern of this magnitude implies that his brain manufactures thoughts that are *murky*, and which are likely to invoke powerful impulses, which are sexual in nature. These shadowy tendencies are also displayed via Pluto in the twelfth house, and its square to the MC — with Uranus lying on the midpoint of the square. As a result, Bundy's actions sent shock waves around the world.

This, it seems, was the similar pattern of previous incarnations. However, because of the stellium between Jupiter, Venus and Mercury, it was unlikely that very few measures were taken in response to his dark thoughts throughout his previous incarnations. In other words, nothing of a violent nature had occurred. Had it been different however, his soul would not have been allowed to reincarnate. But, because of the elevation of Uranus in the chart, denoting a powerful brain, and its relatively close proximity to the North Node, his perverted thoughts, relating to sexual manipulation, and eroticism, were *metamorphosized*. Such is, this *ignis fatuus*-based *opportunity* to murder his victims was most likely the result of Uranus's opposition to Mars; and Mars's sextile to Neptune — opportunities being the relevant recommendations of the sextile. The Moon's opposition to Uranus however, indicated that many of Bundy's victims were, in fact, young women, or adolescents.

All-in-all, the Uranus elevation, at the head of the chart, and its opposition to the Moon and Mars, meant that Bundy was able to glimpse inside the heads of his victims — imploring and violating their disconcerted thoughts. This in turn, would have augmented his perverted capabilities; and therefore, it would have *aroused* him sexually.

Uranian Adjustments

Another noticeable, and perhaps significant aspect in the chart, is Uranus's exact quincunx to a confined Venus. Venus is in its detriment in Scorpio. This meant that Bundy had severely repressed feelings. However, according to those who knew him, Ted Bundy was deemed as 'intellectually charming;' which is most likely the result of the conjunction between Mercury and Venus. Perhaps in an odd sort of way, the quincunx configuration proved to be his 'ideal companion.' Bundy managed his life in the form of utilizing his intellectual charm, which he could *readjust* at any given time.

This meant that he could become emotionally compromised at the push of his psychopathic button, so to speak.

Inherently, Ted Bundy was a Dr. Jekyll and Mr. Hyde type of character. In essence, the quincunx would have posed as the perfect, opportunistic, and divergent weapon of multiple disguises — exploiting it to his advantage — at any given time. This characteristic would have also been *personified* by the mutual reception between Mars and Jupiter; and Mars's conjunction to the South Node.

Meanwhile, the potential positive implications that were bestowed by the sextile, between Neptune and Pluto, were mostly 'wiped out.' This is because of the 'defective degrees' of the planets concerned. Ten degrees of Libra (Neptune) is *dark*, according to Lilly, and thirteen degrees of Leo (Pluto) is *pitted*. Hence, these cosmic deficiencies, so to speak, would also *superimpose* the effects of the Uranus-Venus quincunx in the chart — inhibiting its maladjusted influence.

The Uranus-Venus quincunx was most likely the 'primary indicator' of Bundy's cerebral karma. Thus, Bundy would have had sufficient opportunity to adjust his personal temperament; whereby he could have *relinquished* his dark and erotic thoughts. Ordinarily, a quincunx between Venus and Uranus acts as the catalyst for perverted lust — from which its prurient influence emanates from a previous life.

The elevated-electrified influence of Uranus; with its sextile to the Ascendant in the chart, meant that Ted Bundy could very well have become one of the greatest inventive minds of our generation. Instead, he corrupted his intellect with twisted thoughts, and abnormal desires. Thus, Ted Bundy became one of the most notorious Uranian serial killers of our generation.

Pluto's square to the MC, coupled by Uranus, and the North Node, both on the midpoint of the Pluto/MC aspect, determines that death (Pluto) will occur in typical Uranian style. In this case, it was via electricity. He spent a total of nine years on death row before his execution. Interestingly, nine is Pluto's number in numerology. During his execution, Ted Bundy's brain would have been electrified. But for the wrongness of all reasons. Thus, Uranus's penchant for electrification can either elevate the brain's intellect, or overthrow the intellect, via subversion.

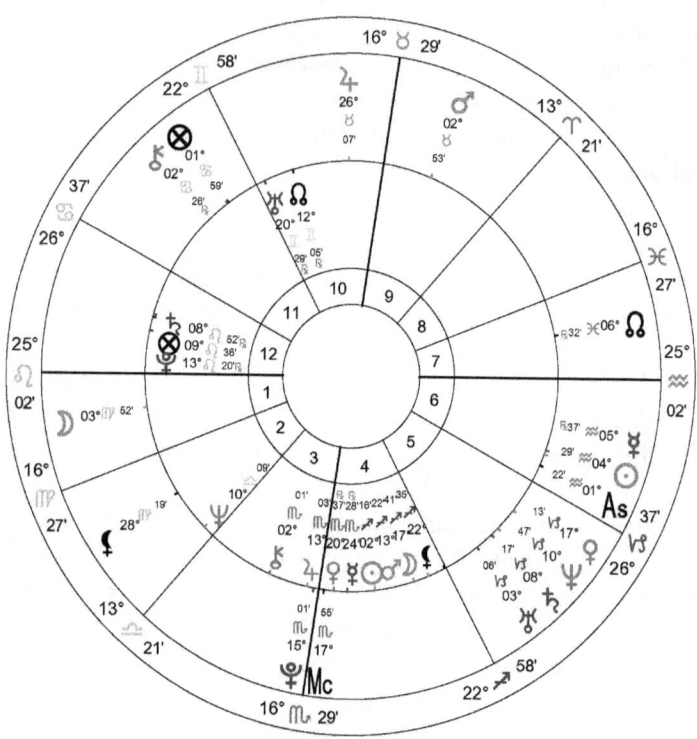

Inner Ring: Natal Chart for Ted Bundy, 11/24/1946, 22:35, Burlington, Vermont
Outer Ring: Death Chart for Ted Bundy, 1/24/1989, 07:16, Gainesville, Florida

Uranian Egalitarianism

On the 24th of January 1989 (a Neptune day), at 7:16 AM, Ted Bundy was executed via the electric chair.

The death chart is, in actual fact, a testament to his fate, and his ultimate demise.

In the death chart, Uranus lies at three degrees of Capricorn. In the natal chart +Uranus is domicile, meaning that it tenants its natural house, hence the eleventh. In addition, Uranus conjuncts Saturn at eight degrees of Capricorn. Saturn is also domicile, in its ruling sign of Capricorn. Saturn tenants the twelfth house in the natal chart. In addition, Neptune lies at ten degrees of Capricorn, and in its fall, and is also in the twelfth house.

Neptune is domicile, as Neptune naturally rules the twelfth house domain. Uranus is at the head of this triple transit conjunction.

Transit Uranus however squares Neptune in Bundy's natal chart. All of these configurations are extremely powerful and revealing — concealing karmic implications. Thus, death, as a result of self-deception, was inevitable. Ted Bundy received *three* death sentences — coinciding with the *three-planet* conjunction in the death chart.

And, with Uranus at the head of the conjunction, death had to be typically Uranian; and in this case, it was administered via electricity.

Ironically, the Descendant in the death chart is Aquarius, which is naturally ruled by Uranus. The Sun also tenants the sign of Aquarius. The Sun is debilitated in Aquarius. Mercury is also retrograde. Essentially, Bundy's past crimes had caught up with him. With Saturn in the twelfth house in the death chart, and also in the natal chart, Bundy would have to *shoulder* the karma of all his victims — overhanging in spirit. In addition, this burdensome Uranian stellium is extending the severity of Bundy's crimes. It is also indicating that Bundy will *not* escape the harsh anticipated justice in spirit (twelfth house, Saturn and Neptune).

In the natal chart however, Uranus was Ted Bundy's potential liberator. However, because he *abused* the elevated position of Uranus, Uranus became Bundy's judge, jury, and executioner in the death chart. Tenanting Saturn's sign of Capricorn means that Uranus will amass evermore cerebral karma — discharging it on the astral brain of Ted Bundy — although his remote return to physicality now lies in the hands of his intellectual spirit guides. But, it will be a long way in the making, if ever at all.

Interestingly, the locality of his death was kept a close secret for many years. [8] I find that to be largely expected, considering the condition, and the strength of the twelfth house (secrets), in both the natal, and death chart.

Uranian Intrigues

After Bundy's execution, his brain was removed in the best interests of science. It was hoped that some abnormalities could be found, which indicated the cause of such violent behaviour. Researchers examined the organ thoroughly. Injuries to the brain have, indeed, been found by some researchers to cause criminality. In Bundy's case however, no such evidence was discovered. [9]

It seems, that after his Uranian style death, the scientists (Uranus) wanted to glimpse inside of his head.

Furthermore, and similarly depicted as the title to Peter Starstedt's song, those who were fondly close to Bundy are perhaps wondering, where have you gone to my lovely?

What a stylish testament however to an individual who gained a reputation as one of the main contributors, who accorded Uranus with the often-unfavourable reputation, it is known for today.

In my opinion, no evidence pertaining to his twisted perversions was ever found, simply because he had cerebral karma, which was *buried* in the deepest recesses of his Uranian brain. All types of karma, which are merely expressions of energy, are invisible to the naked eye. This is mostly the reason why planets that tenant the twelfth house, particularly Uranus, are often invisible and thus forgotten — until that is they are remembered in later life.

In essence, Ted Bundy should have *remembered* his cerebral karma in later life, which is indicated by Pluto's square from the twelfth house, to the MC, and with Uranus on the midpoint. Effectively, this was the karmic, and the cerebral catalyst, which would transform his brain into the intellectual genius, which he had the potential to become. In an aspect of this magnitude, the divide between brilliance and immorality is miniscule. Thus, that diminutive 'fine line' is the difference between creating Einstein, and Jack the Ripper. Together, genius and inequity emanate from the Uranus realm of experience; and they are the ultimate manifestations of perception and reality.

Uranian Karma

Death by the electric chair is essentially a subordinate expression upon the diverse spectrum of Uranian karma. Thus, the electric chair works on the premise that electricity is discharged, and conducted directly to the brain, to which the effects are fatal. There are however, other expressions of Uranian karma, which manifest in an electrical capacity — all of which can prove to be fatal. However, in the long-term an electrical discharge can also prove to be exiting, and beneficial in some way. Thus, they can orchestrate lightning changes to a person's life; especially by raising a person's perception towards the true empirical values of their life.

The most common and natural form of electrical discharge are lightning strikes, which are considered to be extremely rare events. Statistics suggest that there is a fifty-percent chance of surviving a lightning strike. Many say that if you are struck by lightning, you were in the wrong place at the wrong time. I don't believe in coincidences, because everything is preordained, particularly when Saturn and Uranus are involved. If someone is struck by lightning, they were 'subconsciously drawn' to the spot where it initially occurred — orchestrated by the Uranus archetype.

Incidents, such as these, occur in order to raise the overall perception; and in particular, towards the existence of Chiron, and its remarkable powers to heal, especially from lightning strikes. It may be that in previous incarnation; the soul *ignored* the existence, and the potential influence of Chiron. This time around however, the individual is being quite literally *pressed* into what can only be described as an 'awakening towards the reality of psychological healing.'

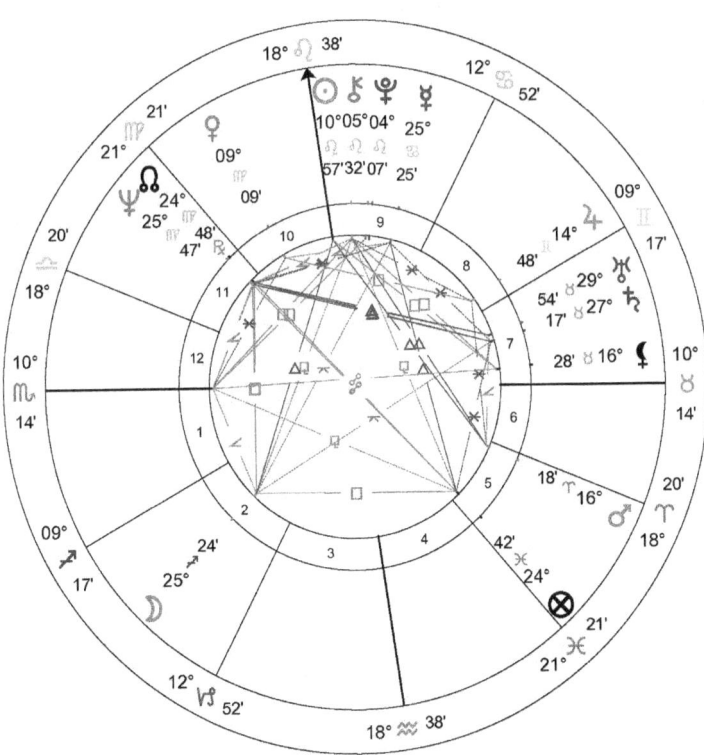

Natal Chart for Martha Stewart, 8/3/1941, 13:33, Jersey City, New Jersey

Someone, who did survive a total of *three* lightning strikes, is the American businesswomen Martha Stewart — exclusively to have her psychological perception raised.

Thus, Martha Stewart was struck by lightning *three* times in her lifetime — orchestrating a lifetime of multiple changes. In actual fact, *three* is a significant number in her life, as we shall see.

Martha Stewart

Martha Helen Stewart is an American retail businesswomen, writer, and television personality. She acquired her success through a variety of business ventures, encompassing publishing, broadcasting, merchandising and e-commerce. She has also written numerous bestselling books. In 2004, Stewart was convicted of felony charges, which related to the *ImClone stock trading case*, and served five months in a federal prison, as a result.

Throughout the course of her life, Stewart has been struck by lightning *three* times. "I just attract electricity; I'm so powerful," she jokingly said on the *Ellen DeGeneres show*. [10] Never a truer word was said it seems. When she muttered those words "I am so powerful," Stewart didn't really understand the true source of her power, or the source in which it emanated from.

Today, it seems she does understand, because Stewart consulted an astrologer. Martha Stewart has a powerful, conjunction between the Sun and Pluto in her chart, which is also combust, meaning that her power was *obstructed*, until around her second Saturn return. Both planets are elevated. Uranus sextiles Pluto, making her an intellectual force to be reckoned with, particularly at this particular point in her life; hence maturity.

Assuredly, it was the sextile between Uranus and Pluto that *saved* her from an electrically-induced death.

The Uranus-Ruled Natal Chart

There is a great deal of karmic (cerebral) connotations attached to Stewart's life. A cosmic collaboration of this magnitude determines that she naturally *possesses* the soul of a revolutionary, who instinctively *liberates* the minds of the collective from all forms of oppression. This means that in her current life, she continues to assist individuals to *purge* their minds of fear and trepidation.

Throughout her life, Stewart has managed to accomplish most of her insurrection-based accomplishments, via her writing. Thus, her books have helped countless souls come to terms with the fear of everyday living. In essence, this is the collective disposition associated with the Uranus-Pluto sextile — with Saturn coming along for the ride as the sextiles dependable chaperone. Still, many today, consider Stewart to be an anarchist. But in reality, she is a passionate advocate — championing all forms of fundamentalist assignments — especially those that are furnished with privilege, loyalty and duty.

In a previous incarnation, it is highly probable that Stewart was responsible for a karmic insurrection, particularly against corrupt leadership and dictators, whose primary objective was to suppress the collective; hence the will of the people. These rebellious characteristics are displayed currently by the besieged Uranus. Stewart was most likely incarcerated for her crimes, in which she languished in a tiny cell — belligerently presented in her current incarnation by Neptune's exact square to the Moon. This 'suppression of her soul' is most likely the catalyst responsible for her claustrophobia, which she is reported to be suffering from.

Exact orb aspects symbolize 'no room for manoeuvre.' Therefore, 'sticking to the job in hand' is the priority. In this case however, there would definitely be little or no room for manoeuvre, as she languished in an inadequate, and cramped cell.

Uranian Humanity

In her current progressive incarnation, *incarceration* unfortunately still 'lies in waiting'— conceivable echoes from the past — relayed by the besieged Uranus — and its close conjunction to pressure-orientated Saturn. But, because of the trine between incarcerating Neptune, and freedom-loving Uranus, Stewart's imprisonment this time around would only be brief, and with the prospect of being potentially *auspicious*. The trine signifies a 'strong point' in the chart, which she has successfully *earned* in a past life. Thus, in that previous life, and when the threads of that current-day trine were being fabricated, in all likelihood she would have been *spared* from whatever punishment awaited her. Thus, this solemn act of humanity is exhibited by the trine between Uranus and Neptune in the natal chart.

Worse luck is that Uranus's position lies at twenty-nine degrees, which is *anaretic*, hence the degree of uncertainty. Saturn's degree is however *fortunate*, according to Lilly. Nevertheless, in this life, Stewart must tread carefully, in order to avoid a *sudden* repeat performance of that horrifically-denounced former incarnation. However, with that fortunately-placed Saturn by her side so to speak, Stewart has, in effect, a viridescent guardian angel watching over her.

The Uranian pattern of karma shown in the natal chart is further elicited by the exact quincunx between the Moon and Mercury. There is no doubt however, that Uranus highlights the extreme cerebral karma, which she must *adjust* her brain from in her current life. Interestingly, there are *three* ways she can adjust her brain patterns from her inherent cerebral karma — displayed via the *three* quincunxes all from the Moon to Mercury, Saturn and Uranus — all of which are connected to the Uranus triple conjunction. Writing at least *three* books will have greatly assisted her in making the necessary adjustment, which has freed her from those echoes of the past (Moon).

Uranian Karma

On the 8th of October 2004, Martha Stewart was sent to *Alderson Federal Prison* to start a five-month sentence for conspiracy, and making false statements. Thus, conspiracy and falsifying information is most likely the result of Neptune's trine to Uranus, and Neptune's square to the Moon. Stewart once remarked that "committing these crimes was easy." This is perhaps a dismissive reflection to the Uranus-Neptune trine.

Neptune also tenants the eleventh house, which is Uranus's natural domain. The Moon's square to Neptune is a further indicator of ever-elusive cerebral karma. The trine between Neptune and Uranus connects them via a semi mutual reception, which is also another important indicator of her cerebral karma. Thus, Neptune tenants the eleventh house (Uranus), whereas Uranus tenants the seventh house (Venus), which is Neptune's lower vibration.

Interestingly, Stewart began her prison sentence in the Venus, and Libra-ruled month of October. Upon her sentence, she took a job, which allowed her to integrate emphatically, and to be an informal liaison between the other inmates, and the prison administration. Very Libran wouldn't you say? In addition, this conforms with the strong Venus influence in her chart — humanitarianly powered by Uranus — employing its liberating resonance from Venus's natural domain. Libra is also on the cusp of her twelfth house (prisons), in her natal chart.

So, is Scorpio, which is ruled by Pluto. Venus is the natural polarity planet of Pluto.

Therefore, it is possible that those she helped in prison, are the very same souls who helped her to navigate the choppy waters of her past life prison incarceration.

There is an additional factor that highlights her admittance to prison. In all likelihood, this configuration has been evoked from a previous life. As a result, Stewart must undertake a radical adjustment. Thus, the position of Uranus in the seventh house means that the core of the adjustment lies at one hundred and fifty degrees, from the seventh, to the twelfth house of prisons. This is representative of the quincunx aspect, and its overall adjustment factor.

Technically speaking, this denotes that she has cerebral karma, which placed her in prison for a *third* time — set in motion by the Uranus triple conjunction, and the *three* quincunxes from the Moon. The triple conjunction includes the Black Moon. Therefore, operating from its Gemini station, the Black Moon *polarizes* the Moon in Sagittarius. Hence, this configuration is a further significator to a past life in prison.

The Black Moon is essentially a cosmic lens, hence a reflection of a past life — projected through the present. The sign of Gemini represents two bodies. Karmically speaking, the Black Moon is the indicator of two previous prison terms. Its current position in Gemini, polarizing the Moon, also indicates that a further prison sentence is highly likely.

Moreover, when we examine Uranus's seventh house tenure (Venus's domicile domain), lying one hundred and fifty degrees from the twelfth house, its position highlights an overall adjustment. Ordinarily, this would most likely underline incarceration as the final time. Furthermore, if we take into consideration the degree of Uranus — shifting it one hundred and fifty degrees, it would place it in the twelfth house at twenty-nine degrees of Libra, which is naturally ruled by Venus. Venus is elevated in the tenth house, and sextile the Ascendant, in the natal chart. This means that slow, progressive, and impartial reconciliation is required in the current lifetime. The sextile from Pluto (Venus's polarity planet), to Uranus corroborates this notion further. It would also indicate that any further incarcerations would be for the purposes of social justice, which is exactly what occurred.

Uranian Lightning Strikes

The fact that Martha Stewart was struck by lightning *three* times, most likely brought about a sudden change to her patterns of intellectual thinking. Perhaps also, those lightning strikes helped to balance her cerebral karma, and therefore liberate her Uranus from its besieged state in the natal chart. Thus, she has nevertheless become one of the most successful, notorious, and outspoken business tycoons of her generation.

Although, the exact dates of the lightning strikes are unknown, it can be confirmed that *three*, the amount of times she was struck, is wholly determined by the *triple* conjunction of Uranus, Saturn, and the Black Moon. In addition, there are *three* major aspects to Uranus; a trine to Neptune, a sextile to Mercury, and a sextile to Pluto.

A further significator to this Uranian kaleidoscope of events lies in the position of the triple conjunction — in the seventh house — naturally ruled by Venus — the *third* astrological body from, and including the Sun. Uranus tenants Venus's natural sign of Taurus, whereas Venus and Saturn are in mutual reception by house position only. The *beneficial* condition of Saturn is perhaps the main reason why Stewart didn't die from the lightning strikes; and because there are no *hard* aspects to Uranus — only soft ones. Thus, the lightning strikes would *never* prove to be fatal.

A final consideration to consider is concerned with the trine between Uranus and Neptune. Thus, Neptune is the natural ruler of the twelfth house of karma. When multiplied, twelve becomes a *three*. This is perhaps additional proof that Stewart's lightning strikes are karmic by design.

As previously determined, Martha Stewart was born with *suppressed* cerebral karma. Primarily, this is indicated by the triple conjunction, where Uranus is besieged, hence its dynamic influence is suppressed. The elevated Sun is domicile in Leo, which is the natural polarity of Uranus and Aquarius. In addition, the Sun conjoins the MC. The Sun and Leo represent fire. There are *three* bodies tenanting the sign of Leo: MC, Sun, and Pluto. This is further cosmic evidence that Stewart was struck by lightning *three* times; and lightning is partially composed of the natural element of fire, to which the Sun is partly responsible. The combustion of Pluto is also a significant factor.

Martha Stewart has always *joked* about this pretty unique occurrence in her life. She frequently refers to being struck by lightning as the "Two

Truths and a Lie game."[11] Ironically, when you multiply two truths, and a lie, it comes to *three*.

Uranian Totalitarians — Kim Jong-Un

Traditionally, Uranus is the planet most associated with despots and dictators. On the whole, this is because the conventional temperament of this planet is, erratic, unexpected, and often violent — negative characteristics that are most associated with oppressive leadership.

Thus, an example of modern-day Uranian dictatorships is applicably illustrated by the North Korean leader Kim Jong-Un. Although Jong-Un's exact time of birth is unknown, it can be confirmed however, that he has Uranus exactly square to his dark and illusionistic Moon — appeasing the close-mouthed semblance of the Black Moon. Thus, Jong-Un is renowned for his secretiveness, and for his volatile, and highly-strung nature, which highlight extreme highs and lows.

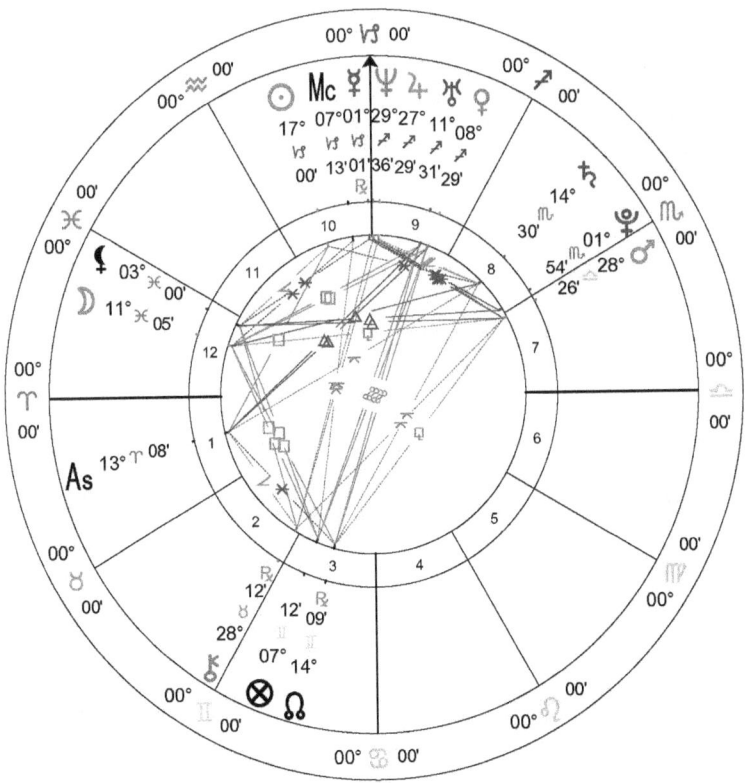

Natural Chart for Kim Jong-Un, 1/8/1984, Pyongyang, North Korea

Hence, he is emotionally *unstable*, which poses as an extensive characteristic within the persona of this suppressive dictator — poignant and emotive characteristics that were set aside in a previous life (Black Moon).

However, because emotionally unstable dictators are *not* normally in control of themselves, they have to somehow compensate for this unbalanced characteristic, by controlling the intellectual thoughts, and the minds of others. Hence, the rudimentary element of volatility, which is attached to the lowest segment on the Uranus archetype, represents the foundational stones for the construction of turbulent environments. North Korea, where Jong-Un resides as its president, is essentially an

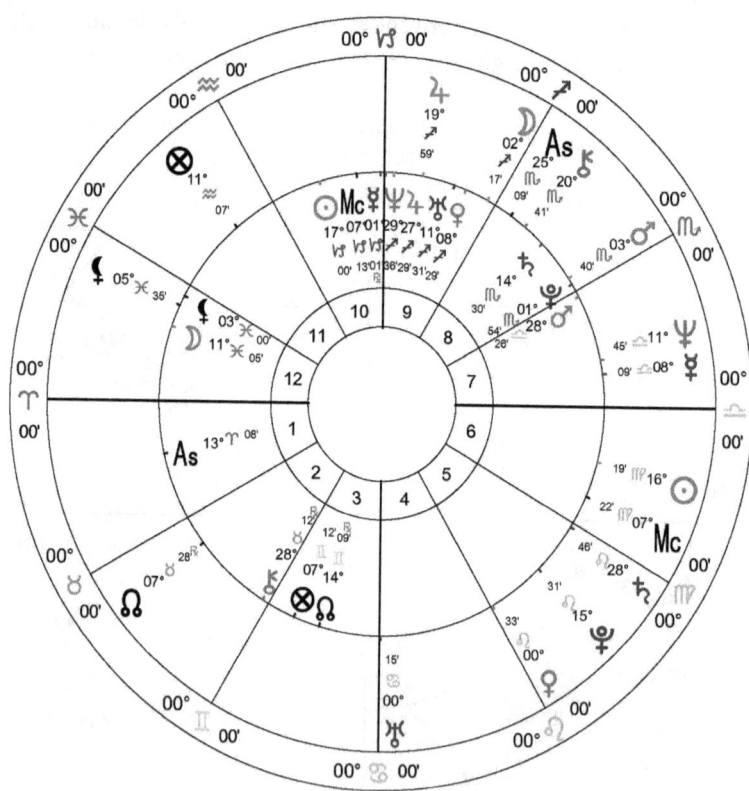

Inner Ring: Natural Chart for Kim Jong-Un, 1/8/1984, Pyongyang, North Korea

Outer Ring: Independence Chart for North Korea, 9/9/1948, 12:01, Pyongyang, North Korea

unsettled and tumultuous country. All of these tempestuous distinctions are fabricated in the North Korea independence chart. The position of Uranus in Cancer in the fourth house, determines that North Korea is a pariah state, where limitlessness and ostracism is prevalent. Thus, where its people attempt to escape from the Cancerian hard shell of oppression, in order to be liberated from their repressive suffering.

The trine from Uranus to Mars symbolizes a determination to succeed in producing weapons of mass destruction, which the authorities keep a close secret (Mars in Scorpio).

When we compare Jong-Un's natural chart with the North Korea independence chart, we can clearly see that his Uranus squares the Sun and MC in the independence chart. A clear sign that Jong-Un must assert his erratic behaviour and cruel perspectives over the collective will of the people — sacrificing their souls for his own brutal requirements. It is fair to assume that the people of North Korea depict their country as an impenetrable tomb — from which there is no psychological escape — exhibited by Uranus's square to Mercury.

Jong-Un is notorious for *not* listening to the advice relayed by his close aids, and his military advisors — unless of course the advice personally *resonates* with his own disillusioned ideals. Thus, these are the classic assemblages of an impressionable dictator, all of which are, unfortunately, and decidedly Uranus. Moreover, these traits oscillate *solely* with a dictator who swings back and forth between emotional and intellectual instability.

Unfortunately, throughout his debateable presidency, Kim Jong-Un is clearly amassing perpetual cerebral karma.

Uranian Duplicity

So, many of the worlds's leading and influential politicians, who have astounded us no less with their insurgent, innovative, but often *duplicit* ideals, possess a tense aspect between Uranus and Neptune in their natal charts.

A classic example of this 'Uranian style duplicity,' was evident in the natal chart of the British Prime Minister, Margaret Thatcher. Thus, Margaret Hilda Thatcher had a quincunx between these two planets. A few members of her cabinet even nicknamed her the 'trickster.' But the quincunx between Uranus and Neptune functioned no less than a catalyst for idealistic innovation — tinged with immovable stubbornness — which ideally needed adjusting. This quality is exemplified further by the quincunx's intersection of the water-based grand trine — with Uranus and Neptune forming a powerful Yod — the finger of God. According to the *Akashic Records*, Yod's determine that God's influence is always with you, and for whatever reasons. It is mostly to learn a particular lesson.

However, because of the potentially *unadjusted* influence of this quincunx, combined with the position of Uranus (fourth house), and Neptune (ninth house), Margaret Thatcher would never 'back down' from her own disillusioned beliefs and ideals. These unpretentious moralities that were also fuelled by Saturn closely conjunct the Scorpio Ascendant in her natal chart. Equally known for her rigid posture and unethical views; she also acquired the hypocorism of, 'Iron Lady.' Traditionally, Mars rules over the element of iron, however in Vedic astrology, Saturn rules over the metal iron. So, this is perhaps no coincidence.

Thus, because of the presence of other overwhelming influences in her chart, such as an afflicted Mars, sitting on the apex of a T-square, Margaret Thatcher would never adjust her overall temperament towards new

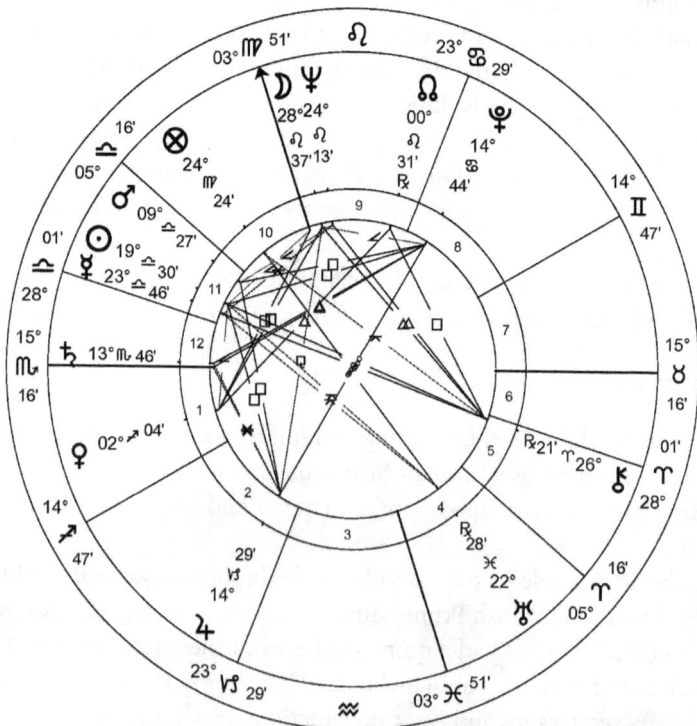

Natal Chart for Margaret Thatcher, 10/13/1925, 09:00, Grantham, England

Uranian visions, and new Neptunian directions. Interestingly, Winston Churchill years of being prime minister came to an end in 1955, and for exactly the same reasons. This was during the presence of a transiting quincunx between Uranus and Neptune — 1952-56. Ironically, Margaret Thatcher quoted Winston Churchill in many of her speeches. Some have said that they were similar personalities. In a composite chart, Churchill's Mars and Jupiter are conjunct Thatcher's Libran stellium.

Churchill also had a square between Mercury and Uranus, whereas Thatcher had a quincunx between these planets. It would seem that the intellectual influence of her nemesis had finally caught up with her, especially with regards to her removal from office, and most likely from her pending death.

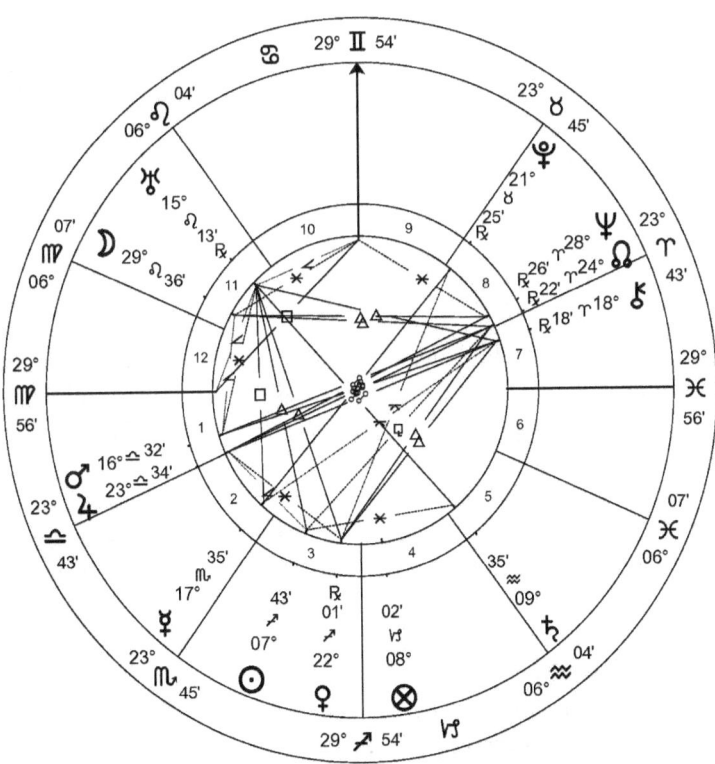

Natal Chart for Winston Churchill, 11/30/1874, 01:30, Woodstock, England

Uranus the Awakener

Uranian Ostracism

Because of her discernible stubbornness, Margaret Thatcher was eventually removed from office — by her own party. Later Thatcher was *ostracized* (Uranus) from the conservative party. However, in order for her to have remained in office, a perpetual adjustment between Uranus and Neptune was needed. Thus, this was an adjustment in which she placed the moral wellbeing of the nation, and its people (Neptune), before her own extreme, projecting, misconceived and impressionable viewpoints (Uranus). Overall, this was an extremely influential quincunx; partly because of its mutual reception. Uranus tenants the sign of Neptune's natural rulership, whereas Neptune tenants the sign of Uranus's detriment.

Regrettably, the radical and indiscriminate perspectives attached to the quincunx were continually demonstrated during her many years in office; and in particular, during the Falkland Island conflict. Also, in her final years of office, in which she demonstrated extreme tendencies. During her many years of being prime minister, coupled by her immovable tenure of number 10 Downing Street, the Uranus-Neptune adjustment, in my opinion, never really transpired. Furthermore, these difficult cerebral characteristics also coincided with the quincunx between Uranus and Mercury. Therefore, she definitely lived up to her title as the Iron Lady!

A Uranian Style Death

It seemed that Thatcher's death was befitting - considering the inferior position of Uranus in the natal chart. Thus, her death was sudden, and occurred in a public place (Ritz Hotel in London). In all likelihood, this type of death is consistent with Uranus in the fourth house of the grave. With Uranus in the fourth house, death is anywhere but home. Furthermore, and similar to her predecessor, Winston Churchill, Margaret died from a Uranian type stroke. A stroke is often consistent with having a difficult aspect between Mercury and Uranus, which they both had.

Margaret Thatcher incarnated to make a difference within the collective seat of consciousness. In other words, she came to Earth to 'raise overall awareness.' Like so many others who have intercepted houses, and planets, their fate is often determined. But the rewards for 'sticking to the job in hand' so to speak, are phenomenal; particularly in spirit. The Uranus-Neptune quincunx was the cornerstone of her natal chart; because Aquarius, which is natural rulership sign of Uranus, is intercepted. Neptune in Leo is also intercepted, along with her Moon and Nodes. Depending on the planets concerned, quincunxes often determine that a positive adjustment also occurs within the collective seat of consciousness, which was the principle feature of Thatcher's quincunx. These are indeed great honors, that were bestowed upon her soul.

Somewhere in her life however, Thatcher strayed from her life path. Instead of raising (Uranus), awareness (Neptune), she manipulated and destroyed the lives of so many. Thus, her quincunx adjusted the lives of the collective, in a negative way. Her true evolutionary vocation was to adjust, and thereby improve the lives of others. Thatcher sent so many souls to their watery graves (Pisces on the cusp of the fourth house), during the Falkland Island conflict (Aries on the cusp of the fourth house). This violent antipathy was totally unnecessary, because it involved territories (Uranus), and land, which belongs to the Earth, and not to man. It could have been resolved diplomatically (Uranus adjustment to Neptune). In addition, the overall quality of the Uranus quincunx meant that her intellect, and her inner voice were powerful. Maybe, she should have listened more?

'Intercepted souls' have the greatest potential for soul transformation — personally and collectively. However, if they *stray* from their life mission, especially when it turns out to be disastrous for themselves and others, their highly-developed souls will be held to account, more than the conventional soul. It is regrettable perhaps, that the soul of Margaret Thatcher has placed itself in a very dire and precarious position — amassing cerebral karma. When in fact, all it needed to do was to *listen* to what its own supreme intellect was relaying — governed by Uranus and its quincunx to Neptune.

John Fitzgerald Kennedy

Uranus is concerned with situations that are deemed atypical hence *unforeseen* and *misfortunate*. Throughout the chronicles of history; particularly American history, a myriad of unexpected occurrences has taken place. However, one significant and tragic event, that was *unanticipated*, happened on the 22nd of November 1963. This was most definitely 'a date that will live in infamy.' [12]

This was the pivotal day, when the president of the USA, John Fitzgerald Kennedy (J.F.K), was assassinated. Thus, Kennedy was shot dead, by his mentally disturbed assailant, Lee Harvey Oswald.

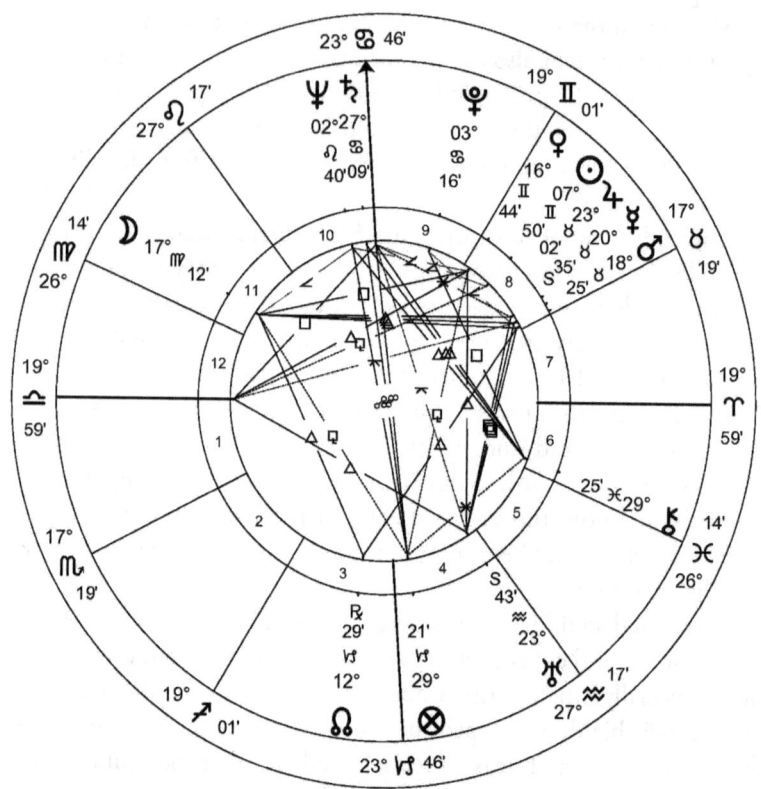

Natal Chart for John F. Kennedy, 5/29/1917, 15:00, Brookline, Massachusetts

Although Oswald initially denied assassinating Kennedy, it was believed that Oswald's involvement in the assassination was part of a bigger plot to assassinate the president [13].

At the time of the shooting, J.F.K had only been in office for three years. This Uranian *harbinger* is profoundly exhibited in the natal chart, as we shall see.

Necessary Uranian Adjustments

In the natal chart for John Fitzgerald Kennedy, lovingly referred to as J.F.K, Uranus tenants the fourth house of the grave, and makes an exact quincunx to the MC. Therefore, the 'no room for manoeuvre' adjustment, which is necessitated by the quincunx, is attributed to taking precipitous and unnecessary risks, which are all typically Uranus.

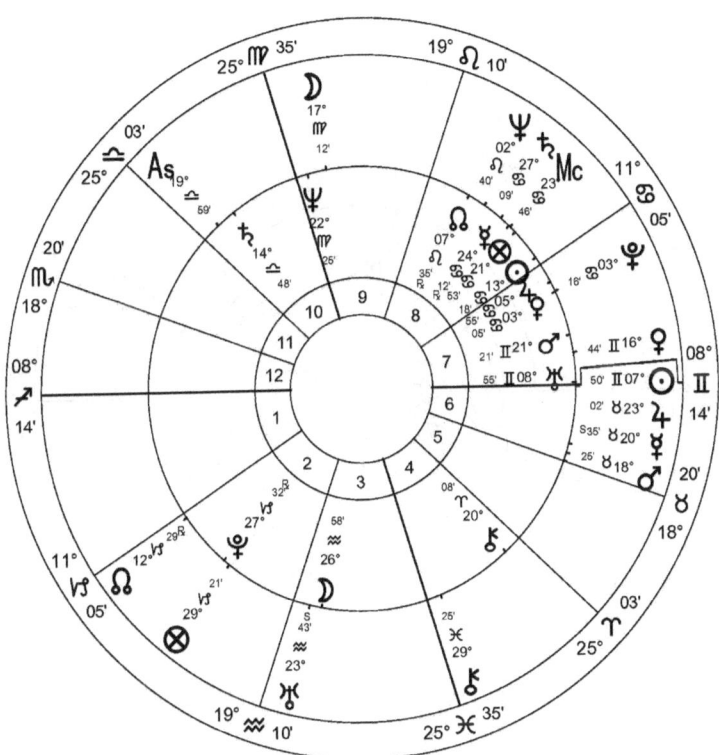

Inner Ring: Sibly Chart for USA, 7/4/1776, 16:50, Philadelphia, Pennsylvania
Outer Ring: Natal Chart for John F. Kennedy, 5/29/1917, 15:00, Brookline, Massachusetts

During his presidency tenure, the initial purpose of Kennedy's visit to Texas was to gain southern support for his anticipated 1964 election.

However, to begin with, he was advised by his closest advisors, to travel in a much safer and durable vehicle — one that would protect him from potential harm. But, because of his penchant for showmanship (Uranus), Kennedy preferred to travel in an open top vehicle, and in a motorcade. This was considered by his security staff to be reckless and dangerous. Taking these type of security risks was most likely the result of the Moon's square to security-orientated Venus.

Preferable, he should have exercised more common sense. Thus, he should have travelled in a covered top vehicle — symbolized by the hard and protective shell of Cancer in his chart. Therefore, the sign of Cancer governs his MC, and the elevated Saturn, and Pluto. Pluto tenants

Uranus the Awakener

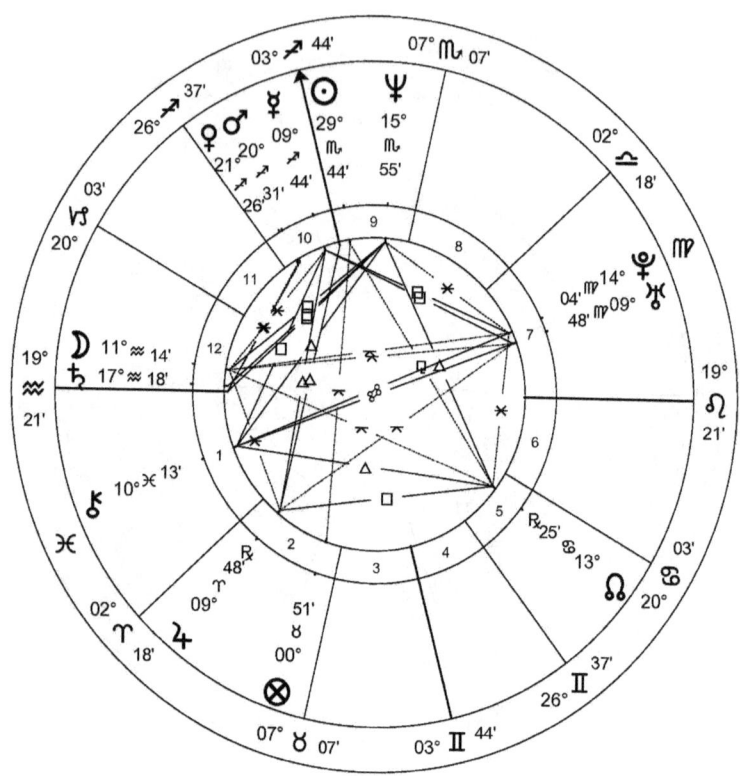

Assassination of JFK, 11/22/1963, 12:30, Dallas, Texas

the ninth house of travel. So, transformation where security issues are concerned, would be strictly necessary where matters of travel are concerned. Most significantly, there would need to be an adjustment from the dramatic (Uranus) — towards common sense (Saturn).

For President Kennedy however, it would have been difficult to comply, simply because of the position of Uranus in the chart, which is *inferior*. So, his need to 'stand out' and be recognized, would have been a crucial factor, especially when it came to reinforcing his posture over those he governed (Cancer/MC).

But, with Saturn closely conjunct the MC, Kennedy should have possessed *heaps* of common sense. However, on this occasion, he obviously preferred not to implement it. The trines from Uranus to Venus, and to the Ascendant, provided him with an ability to look directly into the face of his chosen adversary — followed by a traditional two finger gesture. Perhaps, these Uranus trines are another reason why he preferred to take unnecessary risks.

Uranus's domicile rulership of the fourth house, with its squares to Mars, Mercury, and Jupiter, does imply that Kennedy took unnecessary risks. Furthermore, the Sun occupies the eighth house of death, and is sextile Neptune. Moreover, the Sun's condition is *dark* and *malign*, according to Lilly. Therefore, when death eventually arrived, it would no doubt be swift, violent, but duplicitous. This was very much the case when Kennedy was assassinated.

Further Uranian Adjustments

If you compare Kennedy's natal chart with the US sibly chart in the book's Introduction, you will see Kennedy's Uranus is conjunct the Moon, and quincunx the elevated Neptune in the sibly chart — distinguishing that in order to avoid catastrophe a further adjustment to his life is crucial. Otherwise, this becomes a potential death, via unforeseen circumstances, alignment.

In effect, Kennedy would, at some point, have had the opportunity to *adjust* his schedule on that sudden fateful day. Obviously, he chose not to do so.

Uranian Misfortunes

Additionally, in the death chart for J.F.K, the transit Sun and Neptune square Uranus in the natal chart. The transit Sun is also anaretic; hence it lies at twenty-nine degrees; hence the degree of fate. The Sun and Neptune are also in elevation — executing Kennedy's Uranian (cerebral) karma. Kennedy was after all shot in the head. In addition, transit Saturn in the death chart conjuncts Uranus in the natal chart, which supports the execution conviction of his Uranian karma.

Meanwhile, the transit Ascendant at nineteen degrees of Aquarius is lame (deficient), according to Lilly. This debilitating effect polarizes Uranus in the natal chart — rendering it extremely vulnerable. Further debilitating significators include, transit Pluto, which squares Kennedy's Venus. Mars and Pluto are also squared in the death chart. Thus, this is a tricky combination of elements. Essentially, his life would have been in mortal danger on that unfortunate day. Also, with Mars and Pluto squared, death would have occurred via a weapon of some description.

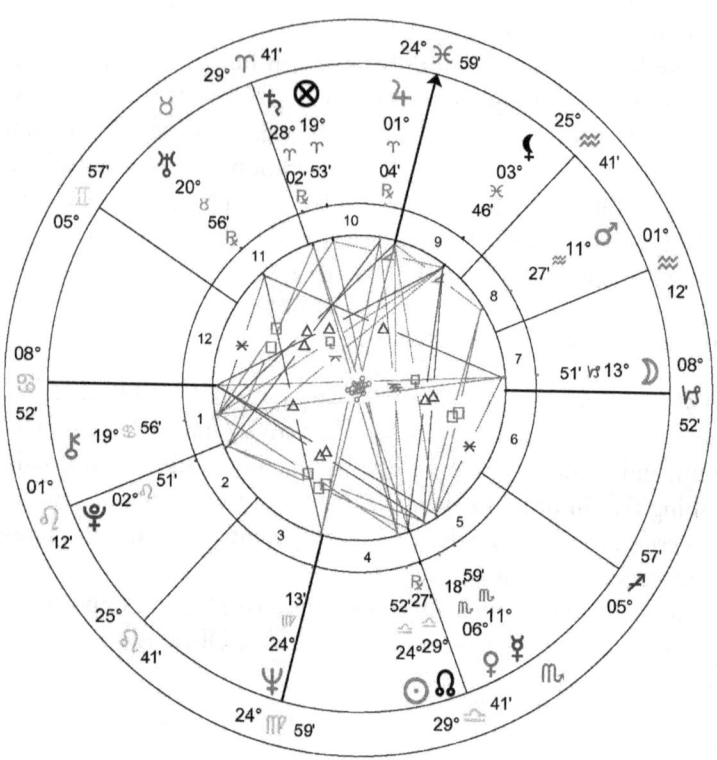

Natal Chart for Lee Harvey Oswald, 10/18/1939, 21:55, New Orleans, Louisiana

At Uranian Right Angles (Squares)

Moreover, the domicile Uranus forms triple squares to Mars, Mercury and Jupiter — inhabiting the eighth house of death, in the natal chart. Therefore, a further point of significance is that this triple conjunction signifies his 'three years in power' — with the eighth house symbolizing potency and power. Mercury is besieged; and its degree is void (deficient), according to Lilly. Thus, a deficient and besieged Mercury in the eighth house, which is square to Uranus, and conjunct its polarity planet Jupiter, implies that death would be sudden. In this case, death would most likely occur in transit — moving towards an unfortunate conclusion — underscored by Mercury's exact quincunx to the Ascendant.

Furthermore, the transit Sun and Neptune in the death chart square the triple conjunction of Mars, Mercury, and Jupiter — *volatizing* the

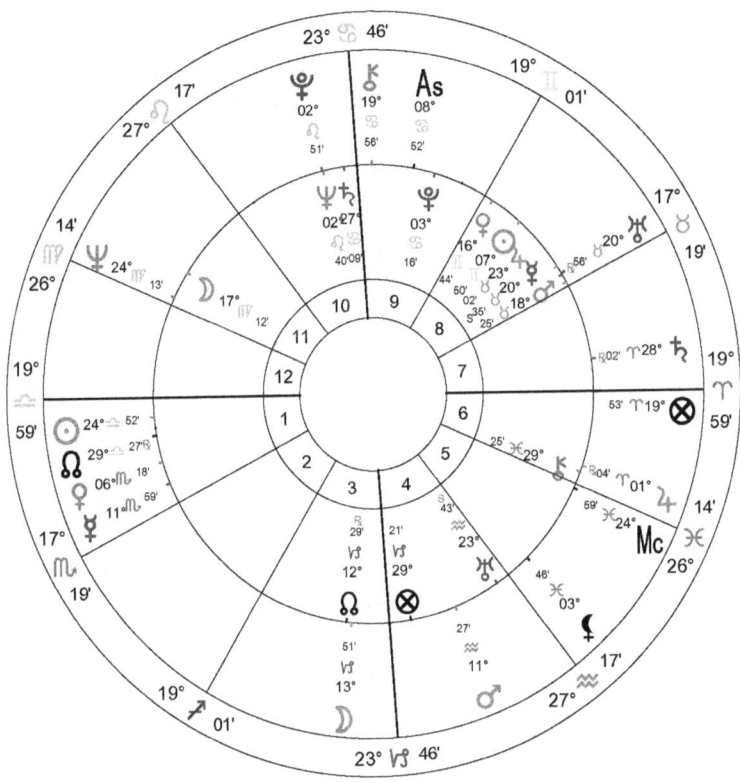

Inner Ring: Natal Chart for John F. Kennedy, 5/29/1917, 15:00, Brookline, Massachusetts

Outer Ring: Natal Chart for Lee Harvey Oswald, 10/18/1939, 21:55, New Orleans, Louisiana

very notion that danger might have been an issue of concern on that terrible day.

Lee Harvey Oswald

Lee Harvey Oswald was the prime suspect — accused of the assassination of President Kennedy. [14] During his life, Oswald was placed in juvenile detention at the age of 12, during which time he was assessed by a psychiatrist as 'emotionally and mentally unstable.' When he was 17, Oswald joined the marines. Oswald was court-martialled twice, while in the marines, and jailed.[15]

In the natal chart, Oswald's incarceration was most likely the result of Neptune's exact opposition to the MC. His emotional instability was most likely the result of the Moon's opposition to the Ascendant. However, his mental instability was most likely the result of the opposition between Mercury and Uranus.

The Uranian Insurgent

Uranus is domicile, in the eleventh house. The degree of Uranus is also *void* (deficient), according to Lilly. Furthermore, and as we have already determined, Uranus opposes Mercury in Scorpio; and Mercury squares Mars, which tenants the eighth house of death (Scorpio's natural domain). All of these potentially *unlit* components determine that Oswald generated dark thoughts of a malicious intent. Mercury has a powerful message from Scorpio, however when frictionally amalgamated with Uranus, the message can often be *tinged* with cruelty, especially as Uranus tenants the sign of its fall.

Mars opposes Pluto. Mars and Saturn are also in mutual reception. Overall, this is an extremely volatile combination, which denotes violent tendencies. Pluto's quincunx to the Black Moon however, implies that his violent propensities were *forged* in a previous life; but remained suppressed — until now.

In this life however, Oswald has been provided with the ability to *adapt* his temperament; whereby he possesses the ability to transcend his inherent dark thoughts. Primarily, these personal and intellectual transformations are highlighted by the trine between Uranus and Neptune. However, the necessary adjustments to his personality, and to his intellect, are highlighted by the Sun's exact quincunx the MC, and by the quincunx between the Ascendant and Mars.

Quincunxes are notorious for manufacturing violent emotions. When Uranus is involved in the overall composition of the quincunx however, a hot-tempered temperament can be expected, and even assured.

Uranian Synastry

Perhaps, the most striking configuration in the synastry chart between Oswald and Kennedy, is the fixed close square between Oswald's Uranus, and Kennedy's Uranus. Thus, this right-angled challenging influence orchestrates immense volatility within the often-unstable domain of this planet. Therefore, they could never be friends, even under normal circumstances. According to media reports, Oswald despised and abominated the politics of President Kennedy; and therefore, he needed to be subversively forced into an early grave. These habitual patterns are initially concerned with Kennedy's fourth and eighth houses.

Another distinguishing factor of upmost concern in a synastry chart, is the position of Oswald's Saturn, which closely squares Kennedy's Saturn, and the MC. In addition, Oswald's Uranus is exactly quincunx Kennedy's Ascendant. Therefore, there would have been absolutely no room for manoeuvre, concerning Oswald's loathing, towards President Kennedy. Moreover, Oswald's Uranus is besieged between Kennedy's Mercury and domicile Mars; and exactly conjunct Mercury in Kennedy's eighth house of death. At some point, Oswald may have become *confined* and *trapped*, especially in a mental capacity — brought about by the flamboyant and ostentatious mannerisms of President Kennedy.

So, in the Uranian mentally-compromised mind of Lee Harvey Oswald, there was no doubt that President John F. Kennedy had to die. The most popular theory of why Oswald assassinated Kennedy, was because of anger, and hatred towards the president. However, with all of this volatile Uranian influence between the two charts, this notion is substantiated.

Ultimately, Lee Harvey Oswald has no doubt amassed substantial amounts of cerebral (Uranian) karma in the afterlife, whereas J.F.K has only amassed moderate amounts of cerebral karma, which is mostly for taking unnecessary and dangerous risks — placing his own life as well as those around him in danger.[16]

Uranian Predispositions

Lesbians, homosexuals, bisexuals and transgenders, are regarded mostly as irregular preferences, which gravitate towards the curious and unorthodox rulership of Uranus. Traditionally, Mercury is considered to be the planet that is most associated with alternate gender types. But in my opinion, Uranus *showcases* these characteristics most astoundingly, and with highbrow precision. Interestingly, Mercury and Uranus are also without gender, because they are considered to be *neuter* — planets symbolizing emasculation. Thus, castration, or alteration of the genitals, is procedures often concerned with transgender types.

Additional relevancies that *elicit* these divergent qualities in the natal chart are when the Sun, Mercury, or the North Node is squared, or opposing Uranus. In this case, Uranus would progressively, and unexpectedly *convert* the personality, the mind-set, and the karmic circumstances of the individual — towards a more radical, extreme, and Uranian type of lifestyle.

Metaphorically speaking, Uranus often *reveals* a multitude of sins in the natal chart, especially when this planet receives hard aspects from personal planets. So, for example, if Uranus conjuncts, squares, quincunxes, or opposes the Sun, Mercury, Venus or Mars, the sexual orientation of the individual would most likely be *altered* in some way — shocking the more conventionalized souls.

Although, gender alteration 'does not' attract Uranian karma in the usual way, gender alteration still draws in a modicum of cerebral karma, which nonetheless has to be *balanced* throughout the course of Uranian evolution — either in physical incarnation — or in spirit. The choice however, in accomplishing this task, is entirely the soul's volition. An example of balancing Uranian karma is to commit the life to the challenges posed by scientific or humanitarian pursuits — raising the vibration of the Uranus archetype in the process.

Uranian Gender/Evolution

If Uranus radically impacts the thoughts, and the temperament of the individual, especially towards the practice of homosexuality and lesbianism, it generally means that the individual is *searching* for their alternate soul component. This represents the *masculine*, or the *feminine* segment of them, which we became divided from millennia ago. The soul is naturally *androgynous*. According to the *Akashic Records*, the soul divided during an evolutionary cataclysm of the Earth.

Meanwhile, gay males for example, are actually exploring their femininity. So, when they enter into a same sex relationship, *psychologically* they are attempting to *reconnect* with their own masculinity. Whether this transition occurs at an impulsive, instinctive, or a cerebral level of consciousness, is dependant entirely on the influence of the Sun sign in the natal chart — because the Sun oversees the impassioned side of the personality. In some cases, gay males *over express* their femininity, because of a Uranian imbalance within them. These unorthodox measures are in fact an important part of Uranian evolution, which functions purely as a 'visual impulse;' to which opens up the senses to other unorthodox possibilities.

Today, a generative dichotomy is apparent within all gender types. Thus, these evolutionary segregations actually began to unfold 'eons ago.' Initially, this disunity occurred as a result of Chiron being separated from Uranus. Today, this noticeable division is impacting the way we are physically attracted to the masculine, or to the feminine qualities within a human being. This is also why human beings display an *imbalance* between their heads, and their hearts.

Uranus and Neptune determine just how we can *reintegrate* this significant polarity shift. In essence, this karmic asymmetry, or inequity, means that most individuals possess, for example, considerably more male influence, than female in their overall makeup, for example. [17] Moreover, the imbalance between the masculine and feminine qualities, is determined solely by the qualities of the signs of the zodiac, in the natal chart

A typical example of Uranian gender alteration is displayed within the physical mannerisms of the now departed twentieth-century computer scientist, Alan Turing. In addition, the Uranian archetype is strongly portrayed most remarkably within the personality of the American acclaimed actor, Jodie Foster.

Alan Turing

Alan Mathison Turing was an English mathematician. Turing was also highly influential in the development of theoretical computer science; and he played a major role in deciphering the intercepted coded messages, which enabled the allies to defeat the enemy during the Second World War. Turing was prosecuted in 1952 for homosexual acts. He accepted hormone treatment — a procedure known as chemical castration — an alternative to prison.[18] Initially, Turing died from cyanide poisoning. An inquest determined that his death was the result of suicide.

Uranian Altruism

Perhaps, the most notable configuration in the natal chart for Alan Turing is the exact conjunction of Uranus to the MC. Perhaps this planetary/angular influence determines why he became a mathematician and a scientist. Initially, Mercury is concerned solely with mathematics, but Uranus is considered to be Mercury's cosmic administrator. The conjunction of Uranus to the MC is *compounded* by the adjacent quincunx from the Sun. The Sun's degree is *fortunate*, according to Lilly, which recasts the entire configuration, as a cosmic imprint, that symbolized a sympathetic genius.

Meanwhile, some military historians estimate that Turing's brilliance, especially with his ability to 'code break,' saved up to two million lives. Regrettably, this altruistic measure could have served as the catalyst for his acquittal; concerning his criminal conviction for homosexual acts. Turing was however, posthumously pardoned — long after his death — which obviously came far too late.

It is often said, that throughout astrological circles, Uranian measures often come to fruition in the hereafter. However, this evolutionary prognostication was, it seems, always going to be the case for Alan Turing. Hence, this Uranian afterthought, or the Uranian epilogue so to speak, was undoubtably the result of the elevated, domicile, highly technological, and profoundly humanitarian Uranus, in his natal chart.

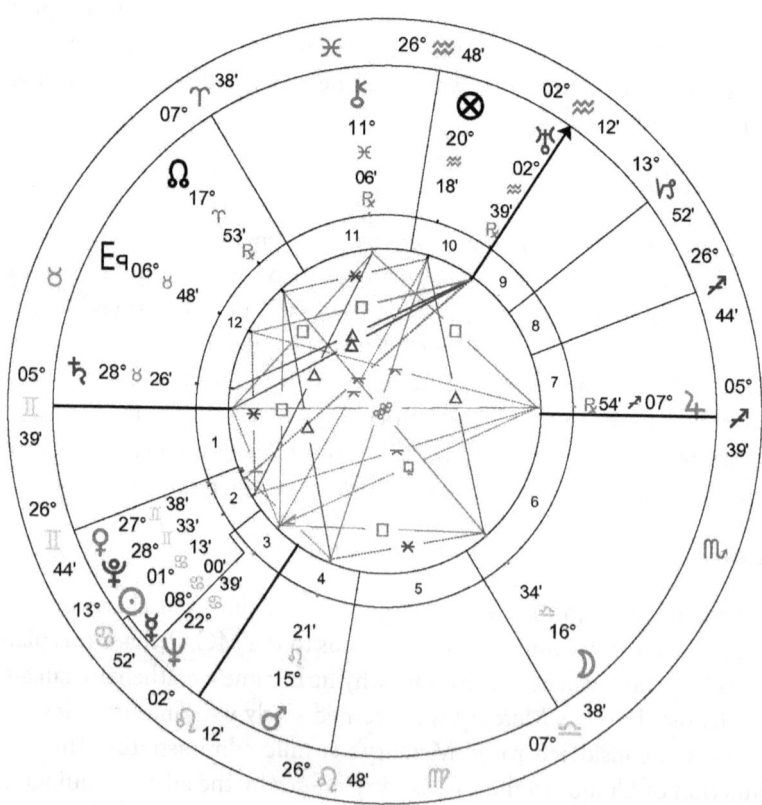

Natal Chart for Alan Turing, 6/26/1912, 02:15, London, England

The trine from Uranus to the Ascendant, may well pose as an additional testament to his scientific heroism. This is a characteristic he most likely acquired in a previous life. However, Saturn's tenure of the twelfth house, may well constitute as a slight 'throwback' to his life. It is often said, especially in esoteric circles, that when Saturn's tenants the twelfth house, the individual *shoulders* the karma of humankind. Well, it would certainly have seemed that way for Alan Turing. But, because of Saturn's trine to Uranus and the MC, he was 'karmically compelled' to save lives, no matter who they were.

Uranian Humiliation

In the natal chart, the Sun is in close conjunction to Venus and Pluto. Venus and Pluto are combust. Thus, this triple conjunction, coupled with the Sun's quincunx to Uranus, may well have spared him the public shame, and the humiliation, which was akin to being discredited at that time, for his shocking crimes. A combust Venus and Pluto may well have meant that the public didn't view his crimes in the same light, as the authorities did. Venus is after all a social planet. However, the Sun's quincunx to Uranus, may well have adjusted the public's perspective concerning his homosexual tendencies. Therefore, the shock of it all, might have been 'toned down,' due to Turing's heroics.

Uranian Homosexuality

To a greater extent, the quincunx from the Sun to Uranus, and the MC, would have most likely meant, that Turing had already adjusted his personality towards the notion of being *Uranian* in a previous existence; meaning that he was homosexual in a previous life. This is most likely connected to the Equatorial Ascendant (EP), in the twelfth house; and in Uranus's sign of its fall. There is no doubt that Alan Turing was a genius. However, genius can often be a characteristic, which comes to bear through inverted tendencies, which is the overall theme of his twelfth house. [19]

This distinguished characteristic of gay/genius is further exhibited with the quincunx between Mercury, and the domicile Jupiter. Jupiter is also pitted (incomplete), according to Lilly — indicating that an *imperfection* exists within his cerebral framework. Jupiter sextiles Uranus, and the MC. These are also representative as being an additional opportunistic catalyst for his homosexual inclinations.

Uranian Miscalculation

Jupiter is also significant in the natal chart; because, for the most part, it is the ancient ruler of the twelfth house — concerning past lives, and karma. Perhaps then, Turing preferred to reincarnate, in order to provide himself with an opportunity to subconsciously restore, and renovate this cerebral dichotomy of gender. However, with Saturn in the twelfth house, and Neptune's wide opposition to Uranus and the MC, it is quite likely that he *miscalculated* the appropriate time frame, in which he selected, as the relevant entryway for his return to physicality.

Uranian (Cerebral) Karma)

Unwillingly, Alan Turing accepted chemical castration, as an alternative to prison. He was most likely influenced by Neptune's opposition to Uranus, and the MC — Neptune having its rulership over toxins. Turing committed suicide, which was deemed the result of cyanide poisoning. This is also most likely the result of Neptune's opposition to Uranus, and the MC. Elevated planets, like Uranus, are the catalyst for the strength, and the specific type of karma, which is initially applied in spirit — preparing the soul, and the brain for reincarnation.

In the case of Alan Turing however, his Uranian karma was paramount — requiring an immediate resolution. The cerebral connections are clearly shown by the quincunx from the Sun to Uranus, and Uranus's opposition to Neptune. This karmic connection is strengthened further by the trine from Saturn to Uranus.

In a previous incarnation, it seems that Turing made similar choices with regards to his sexuality. Furthermore, it also seems that he died suddenly, as a result of strangulation, in that past life. This is displayed by the EP in Taurus, ruling the neck, in the twelfth house, and square Uranus. However, according to the *Akashic Records*, those who commit suicide, are sent straight back to Earth, in order to complete the life that they tragically 'cut short,' in which the law of attraction applies. Turing's big mistake was to commit suicide. He will return to Earth with heaps of cerebral karma, which is indicative to Saturn's connection to Uranus. In effect, the trine between Saturn and Uranus will be cancelled out.

The overall pattern of Turing's chart, coupled by his relatively young age (41), does suggest that his recent incarnation was the result of a sudden return to physicality, which is the result of Uranus on the MC, and quincunx the Sun. This being the case, Turing will no doubt have to return 'once again,' in order to complete the life, which he originally cut short, due to suicide.

But perhaps, he will find the transition much easier, due to the proximity of the Aquarian Age, and the tolerances that have now developed towards alternate Uranian sexualities. Perhaps also, he will no longer have to make his Uranian adjustments. Equally, however, he will be able to develop his powerful Uranian brain further in this technological age.

Jodie Foster

Alicia Christian Jodie Foster is an actor, director, and a producer. She is the recipient of numerous accolades — awarded for her outstanding achievements. Most notably, Foster has been acknowledged for her movie roles, which, for the most part, are very *Uranian*. In 2014, and after dating for just over a year, Jodie Foster married the American photographer, Alexandra Hedison.

Uranian Karmic Expression

In the natal chart for Jodie Foster, Uranus is broadly besieged; meaning that there is still plenty of *scope* for intellectual expression. In other words, we haven't seen the best of her abilities yet. Meanwhile, Foster's 'distinctive depth of intellectual expression' has hitherto been acquired in a past life. However, the oblique opposition between Uranus and Jupiter purports that somewhere throughout her extended evolution; Uranus *failed*, and to a greater extent, in its cerebral quest to further *radicalize* her development, and her contentment in a past life.

Contentment is a characteristic that seems to have evaded her for so long. This karmic *yearning* has been subconsciously expressed throughout many of her movie roles.

Uranian Interchangeable Gender

Oppositions symbolize *fusion* — blending the elements of the psyche. Unless the planets that comprise an opposition are *fused*, they will remain unfused 'indefinitely.' Thus, oppositions represent something we need to experience in life. In this case, Jodie Foster, for many years, has found it difficult to discover her true direction in life; as a result of the Uranus-Jupiter opposition in her chart.

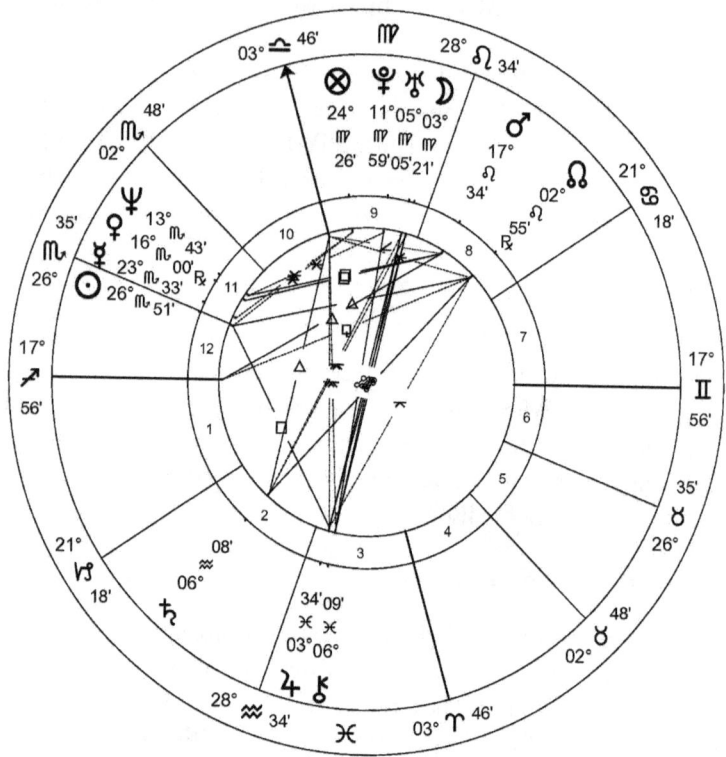

Natal Chart for Jodie Foster, 11/19/1962, 08:14, Los Angeles, California

She has however, radically transformed her ideas, beliefs and her innovative strengths — in the eyes of tremendous adversity and criticism — via this powerfully-infused opposition.

Regrettably, Jodie Foster has been the focus of enormous criticism, especially where her intentions are concerned. In essence, she has managed to *emerge* from her karmic hiatus so to speak, which is no doubt the result of the intercepted Uranus, opposing a domicile Jupiter. In addition, the Uranus-ruled opposition is partly responsible for her alternate gender preferences.

Thus, from its elevated and intercepted position, the accidental purpose of Uranus is to radically alter, the sentiments, the affections, the attractions, and the adoration, which are guided towards any Uranian-type (alternate) partner. In effect, with Uranus in such close proximity to the Moon, Foster favours a relationship, which the populace would consider to be *radical* in some way. However, because of the Moon's opposition to Jupiter; it might well mean that Foster is attracted to a partner who is extremely benevolent, charitable, and free-loving. Foster did remark previously that she 'keeps an open mind where her relationships are concerned.'

Ultimately, these committed and playful preferences are projected mostly via Uranus's wide conjunction to the intercepted Pluto; and Pluto's square to the Ascendant, which tenants free-loving Sagittarius — dragging in its ruler Jupiter. Uranus also connects to Venus by way of a quintile, which signifies 'the composer of scientific genius.' This is an extraordinary talent, or a karmic expression, which Foster acquired in a previous existence. In addition, the quintile between Uranus and Venus most likely means that she developed the capacity to alter her gender without seriously unbalancing her soul's plan for cerebral development.

Perhaps, the *unfortunate* downside here, is the degree in which Uranus frequents; hence five degrees of Virgo, which is *dark*, (deficient), according to Lilly. Because of this karmic degree, Foster has endured a volley of criticism in her work, and where her personal life is concerned. She once remarked "I continue to act to figure out who I am."

The Moon's degree is fortunate however, according to Lilly, which will greatly assist her in her ultimate pursuit for self-enlightenment. She will also be able to openly explore her extreme emotions, in order to acquire a resolution. Foster has been known for her sudden emotional outbursts over the years.

Uranian-Moon Exploratory Relationships

In 2018, Foster spoke openly and frankly, in an interview with the *Daily Mail* newspaper, about her fraught, complex and unusual relationship with her Mother.[20] Astrologically, these statements would be regarded as a typical Uranian complexity — impacting her Moon. Thus, when Uranus *nudges* a luminary, or Venus, the relationships we perceive as 'conventional loving relationships,' are anything but conventional. It was suggested however, that Foster's mother was a lesbian. In addition, when Uranus pokes at the Moon in this unfashionable manner, erotic and unusual dreams are often experienced in childhood. In time, these subconscious shifts can lead to self-experimentation, and self-questioning, as to one's gender.

When Foster was twelve years of age, she landed a role as a child prostitute in Martin Scorsese's film *Taxi Driver*. She later revealed that she had to undergo extensive psychological tests, in order to ensure that she would not be left completely traumatized by the experience.[21] This is most likely a further characteristic of Uranus's close conjunction with the Moon, coupled with the Uranian-type cerebral karma, which she most likely incurred in a previous life; and similarly, as a child prostitute.

The Unusual Depth of Uranus

Foster has been *hailed* a child prodigy, which, she says 'isolated her from the rest of conventional society.' This is yet another common characteristic — representative of an elevated and intercepted Uranus touching the Moon. Isolation is a characteristic, which is also emphasized in the natal chart by the heavy and powerful Scorpio stellium, and which tenants Uranus's natural domain; hence the eleventh house. Although there are no visible aspects between Uranus and the Scorpio stellium, except a very wide sextile to Neptune, this is nevertheless a powerful indicator of Uranian deep intellectual brilliance.

Foster's movie roles were mostly a combination of powerful, scientific, shocking, often unconventional, and undoubtably brilliant — boasting enormous depth and twists and turns at every inconceivable moment. This was very much the case for her role in *Flightplan*, which was tinged with lots of Uranian-Lunar moments. Her movies were also representative of a character that was isolated, or even ostracized, because of her beliefs or opinions (see final quotation). This was very evident in the movie *Contact*, in which she starred alongside Matthew McConaughey (see section When Uranus is Intercepted).

Added to this, Foster has a mutual reception between Mercury and Pluto, by which Mercury and Pluto are also in quintile formation. Essentially, she has a powerful message for humankind. However, it needs to be tempered with rationality and logic, to which the end result is intellectual transformation. This planetary combination denoting the 'iron fist and the velvet glove' provides her with an *edge* in all of her movie roles; meaning that she mostly has the upper hand, over and alongside, the character roles she ultimately selects to play.

Uranian Gender Transformation

In 2013, Jodie Foster *officially* announced to the world that she was a lesbian. The following year, she married Alexandra Hedison. Prior to this, transit Uranus had made quincunxes to the Moon, Uranus and Pluto, from the Moon's natural domain; hence the fourth house, in her natal chart. What followed was Uranian adjustment and cerebral transformation — *balancing* the cerebral karma her soul had amassed in a previous incarnation. Transit Uranus had effectively *readjusted* the natal quincunxes from the Moon and Uranus to Saturn — raining in the second half of her life. Thus, Foster had successfully *emerged* from her dark cerebral past, which is governed by Uranus's dark degree.

One thing to consider here however, especially with the Moon's influence in the natal chart, is that her preferred partner (Alexandra Hedison) just happens to be a Cancerian, the sign naturally ruled by the Moon.

Regrettably, the birth details for Alexandra Hedison are unknown. Therefore, no realistic comparison can be made between them both. However, it may be that Uranus connects them both in an intellectual, and a progressive capacity. If only it were possible to do a synastry chart, the results may have been staggering.

Uranian Powered Seclusion

It may be befitting to end with an appropriate Uranian quote; spoken by Jodie Foster herself, and which was uploaded to *Pinterest*. "Having a great fear of being alone, and having a desperate need for solitude and the solitary experience has always been a tug of war with me." This is very characteristic to the Moon/Uranus conjunction, and to the Scorpio stellium in the eleventh house of Uranus's natural rulership. Perhaps, her fear of being alone is an intellectual reflection to that past life, where she was coerced into child prostitution?

Uranian Natural Disasters

Earthquakes are perhaps, the most significant of all Uranian associated natural disasters. Thus, a very powerful, and devastating earthquake, which occurred without warning, took place in Haiti in 2010. Metaphorically speaking, earthquakes 'shake up' the brain of the Earth — allowing Uranus to survey the overall intellectual situation of our planet — and that of humankind. Primarily, this is to ascertain whether or not intellectual progression is ultimately transpiring, and at any given time.

A Powerful Uranian Earthquake

On the 12th of January 2010, a 7.0 magnitude earthquake struck the Caribbean island of Haiti. The epicenter of the earthquake was approximately twenty-five kilometres west of Port-au-Prince, Haiti's capital. More than 300,000 people were reportedly killed. By the 24th of January, at least fifty-two aftershocks measuring 4.5 or greater, had been recorded.[22]

In the event chart for Haiti, Uranus is in a commanding and dominating position. Thus, Uranus occupies the eighth house of death and transformation. Uranus lies at twenty-three degrees of Pisces, which is a masculine degree according to Lilly. Aside from the spiritual significance of Pisces, this may simply be an indicator that, more males perished in the earthquake than females.[23]

The idiosyncratic influence of Uranus in the often disillusioned and dichotomized sign of Pisces, may also be an indicator that the overall global practice of homosexuality caused the earthquake. According to Rabbi Yehunda Levin, spokesman for the Rabbinical Alliance of America in Brooklyn: Gays in the US military "we have seen the underground earthquake, tsunami, Katrina, and now Haiti. All this is in sync with a 2000-year old teaching in the Talmud that the practice of homosexuality is a spiritual cause of earthquakes." [24] Powerful words indeed!

Uranian Orchestrated Devastation

From this position, Uranus most definitely represents the watery brain of Haiti; watery as determined by an island — surrounded by water. Metaphorically speaking, the rest of the planets in the chart represent the brain's neurons. Effectively, it can be said that Haiti experienced a Uranian-type epileptic fit. Furthermore, Uranus's elevation, and its square to the Moon, is also a prelude to an international disaster. In addition, Mars's opposition to Neptune determines that Haiti's wealth and prosperity will be 'washed away' on a parabolic tidal wave. The death toll and the devastation that followed the earthquake are highlighted by the Pluto-ushered stellium in Capricorn — with the Sun opposing the Ascendant. Capricorn is the sign that represents infrastructure.

The psychological tension, and the apprehension following the earthquake, are determined mostly by Saturn's opposition to the MC, and Saturn's square to Pluto, and Mercury. The 'extremely high death toll' is displayed by Jupiter's close conjunction to Neptune. Both these plan-

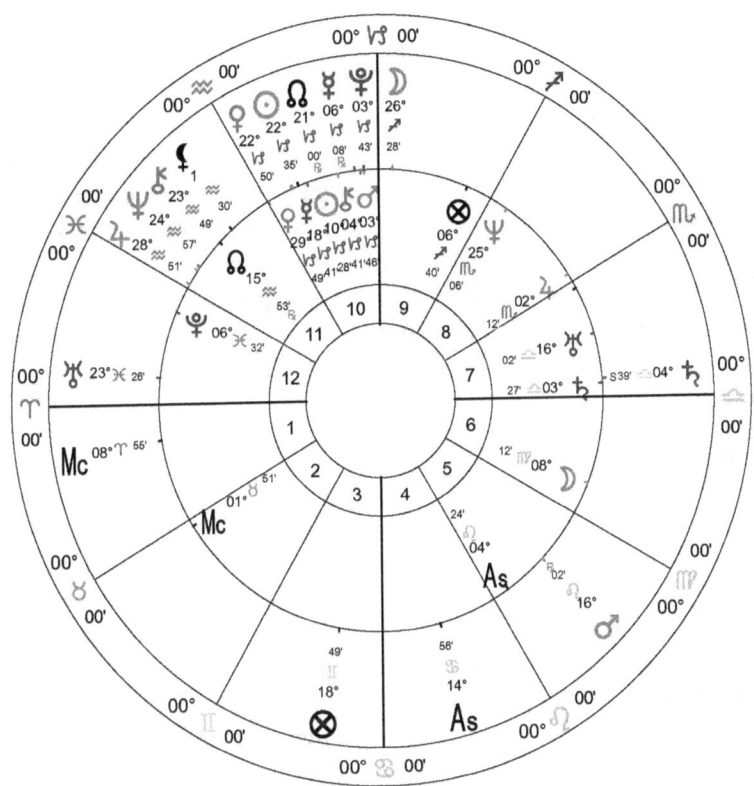

Inner Ring: Preferred Natal Chart for Haiti, 1/1/1804, 19:17, Gonaives, Haiti

Outer Ring: Event Chart for Haiti Earthquake, 1/12/2010/ 16:53, Port-au-Prince

ets tenant Uranus's traditional rulership sign of Aquarius. Because of this, there would always be an *abundance* of humanitarian aid on offer, although some of this aid will be in a state of corruption and disorganization. However, because Neptune's degree is *pitted*, according to Lilly, there would be severe consequences attached to this humanitarian aid (see next section for more information). This unruing notion is also confirmed by Mars's opposition to Neptune.

In any event, for the citizens of Haiti, a new chapter in the structural, and the social evolution of this island is about to written. This is confirmed by the exact conjunction of the Sun and Venus, which is sextile to Uranus. Thus, the islanders are about to embark on an entirely new journey, and one that involves the transcendence of the collective intel-

Uranus the Awakener   67

lect — from out of the watery ashes of destruction — a heightened form of realization could actually come to pass. This is despite the fact that Haiti is not recognized as a traditional developing nation.

Ten years on from this terrible disaster, Haiti hasn't really recovered from the trauma of it all. This is despite billions of dollars being spent on the rebuilding of the country's infrastructure. The primary causes however, are the weaknesses within the Haitian public institutions. [25] In addition, there has been an overall breakdown in communication. This may well be the result of the Jupiter-Neptune (weakness) conjunction, transiting Uranus's public sign of Aquarius. Furthermore, Neptune acts like a huge 'dampening field' — wiping out all forms of communication.

Uranian Evolution

Throughout the course of evolution, the terrible mistreatment of this small country, and its closely-linked inhabitants is vast, and with far reaching consequences. Thus, there are karmic-cerebral connotations attached to this nation. Primarily, this abstract idea is displayed by the Black Moon in Uranus's sign of Aquarius in the event chart. Moreover, the Black Moon lies at one degree of Aquarius, which is *pitted*, according to Lilly. This implies a country harbouring a problematic past. In addition, the Black Moon's semi-sextile to Pluto, which tenants Saturn's rulership sign of Capricorn, corroborates these underlying notions further. However, with the semi-sextile, there is a window of opportunity open to gradually redress the problem.

Perhaps, the 2010 earthquake occurred in order to set a new precedent in the evolution of the island? Furthermore, it may be that its citizens must learn to be more self-reliant, and privileged? Liberation however, often comes with a heavy price tag attached. Up to now, this is certainly been the case for this island nation. But for Haiti, and for its people, they have the innovative ability, and the intellectual will to ultimately survive, and more importantly, they have the capacity to orchestrate wealth and prosperity for generations to come.

Conclusion: The Profundity of Uranian Karma

When William Wallace, the Scottish noble, was being executed for treason, his reported last words were *"freedom,"* which was also portrayed in the excellent historical movie, *Braveheart*. An innovative word that is very Uranian indeed! Perhaps, freedom symbolizes an intellectual release from the confines of cerebral orientated karma? Whatever, the reason, freedom, holds the potential to *balance* Uranian karma, and consolidate more of the brain's capacity (see Part Three).

Throughout this first part of the book, I have examined a multitude of Uranian diversities — all of which have manifested some form of Uranian karma. Uranus is a self-analytical cerebral planet.

However, for the strong Uranian type, who can become 'cross wired,' especially when becoming too self-analytical. Thus, in some cases, self-analyzation leads to the long-term analyzation of others. Thus, to quote Peter Starstedt, looking inside their heads. This is a further basis for Uranian karma.

Unbalanced Uranian karma invariably leads to accidents, illness and disease, gender alteration, and even death, which has all been highlighted throughout Part One.

Chart Data

Natal Chart for Peter Starstedt, 10th December 1941, 04:00, New Delhi, India, Placidus Houses, Mean Node.

Natal Chart for Ted Bundy, 24th November 1946, 22:35, Burlington, USA, Placidus Houses, Mean Node.

Death Chart for Ted Bundy, 24th January 1989, 07:16, Gainesville, Florida, USA, Placidus Houses, Mean Node.

Natal Chart for Martha Stewart, 3rd August 1941, 13:33, Jersey City, USA, Placidus Houses, Mean Node.

Natural Chart for Kim Jong-Un, 8th January 1984, Pyongyang, North Korea, Mean Node.

Independence Chart for North Korea, 9th September 1948, 12:01, Pyongyang, North Korea, Placidus Houses, Mean Node.

Natal Chart for Margaret Thatcher, 13th October 1925, 09:00, Grantham, UK, Placidus Houses, Mean Node.

Natal Chart for Winston Churchill, 30th November 1874, 01:30, Woodstock, UK, Placidus Houses, Mean Node.

Natal Chart for John F. Kennedy, 29th May 1917, 15:00, Brookline, USA, Placidus Houses, Mean Node.

Event Chart Assassination of John F. Kennedy, 22nd November 1963, 12:30, Dallas, USA, Placidus Houses, Mean Node.

Natal Chart for Lee Harvey Oswald, 18th October 1939, 21:55, New Orleans, USA, Placidus Houses, Mean Node.

Natal Chart for Alan Turing, 23rd June 1912, 02:15, London, UK, Placidus Houses, Mean Node.

Natal Chart for Jodie Foster, 19th November 1962, 08:14, Los Angeles, USA, Placidus Houses, Mean Node.

Event Chart for Haiti Earthquake, 12th January 2010, 16:53, Port-au-Prince, Placidus Houses, Mean Node.

Preferred Natal Chart for Haiti, 1st January 1804, 19:17, Gonaives, Haiti, Placidus Houses, Mean Node

References
1. Telepathy is essentially a Uranus technique. Thus, telepathy is the purported vicarious transmission of information from one person's mind to another's, without using any known sensory channels, or even close physical interaction.
2. J.S. Zaveri is located at the Jain Vishva Institute, in Rajasthan, India.
3. Information source Wikipedia.
4. Information source Wikipedia.
5. Information source, www.townandcountrymag.com.
6. Information source, www.ninds.nih.gov.
7. Information source, www.britannica.com.
8. Information source, www.nbcchicago.com.
9. Information source, www.allthatsinteresting.com.
10. Information source, www.womenandhome.com.
11. Information source, www.womenandhome.com.
12. An excerpt, taken from a speech given by president Franklin D. Roosevelt, and with regards to the Japanese attack on Pearl Harbor, on the 7th December 1941.
13. Information source Wikipedia.
14. Lee Harvey Oswald was shot dead in a police cell by Jack Ruby. Unfortunately, the birth time information for Ruby is unknown, so no reasonable comparison can be made between Ruby, Oswald, and President Kennedy.
15. General Information source Wikipedia.
16. Karmic Information courtesy of the Akashic Records.
17. Evolutionary information source the Akashic Records.
18. www.pbs.org.
19. www.quora.com.
20. www.dailymail.co.uk.
21. www.news.com.au.
22. Information source, Wikipedia.
23. www.dec.org.uk.
24. www.salon.com.
25. www.theconversation.com.
26. www.washingtonpost.com.

PART TWO

Uranus is the Insurgent Silhouette of Chaos

(Chaos is the Principle Catalyst for Illness and Disease)

> *"The parts...that are rubb'd, do, in the Instant of Friction, attract the Electrical Fire and the same parts immediately, as the Friction upon them ceases, are disposed to give the fire they have received, to any Body that has less."*
> — Benjamin Franklin

Uranian Illness and Disease

Benjamin Franklin's proclamation is simply profound.
Yet, it also gives the appearance of Uranian-related illness and disease; but most commonly it gives rise to the existence of epilepsy — profoundly Uranian. This is because friction is the *pivotal* element associated with almost every type of Uranian disorder, including epilepsy. Uranian disorders are essentially typical of a dysfunctional electrical fire, which misfires — discharging sparks of fire. However, when biological components create friction, electrical impulses are released in much the same way as sparks are released.

To a much greater extent, when electrical (neurological) impulses build up and become fractured between the left and right segments of the brain, epilepsy, which is cerebral discord, is the neurological condition — generated by this 'frictional dissension.' After the onset of an epileptic seizure, there is often a 'cooling off' period, which is similar to the turning off of an electrical fire; because when an electrical fire is turned off, it takes some time before the element cools down. This cerebral rebalancing occurs before the brain *resets* its nonotological patterns to normal communicative functions.

In much the same way, the planet Uranus reboots our brain, so that we can function at a higher level of intellect.

Cerebral friction, which causes epilepsy, is a psychodynamic reaction, and it is very similar to the Earth's tectonic plates *shifting*, before the onset of an earthquake, which is also overseen by Uranus. Speaking figuratively, epilepsy is indicative to an earthquake in the brain. In this respect, we may refer to epilepsy as a *brainquake*. Thus, epilepsy, which is perhaps the principle of all Uranian disorders, is examined in great detail throughout this section. This is partly because of the ramifications associated with this shocking condition; and because it is a dis-ease that is on the increase. [1]

Unfortunately, there is still very little known as to the initial causes associated with this lightning-style neurological disease.

The Uranian Electrical Conductor

Uranian sparks of energy are indicative to neuro electrical impulses, which travel directly to, and from the brain — relaying necessary information. However, when these neuro impulses become *inflamed*, they produce a kind of 'holographical fire' within the body. According to the British National Health Service (NHS), the technical expression for this parody is *neuro inflammation*, which is defined mostly as an inflammatory response within the brain or spinal cord. This is an additional term of phrase for the condition epilepsy. It is also the catalyst for the popular turn of phrase called the 'nervous breakdown.'

Moreover, the brain is essentially one big electrical conductor, or an electrical charge carrier, which generates enormous amounts of neuro impulses. Sometimes these neurons collide in the body. This is yet another example of what happens to epilepsy sufferers. On occasion, neurons can misfire, thereby causing the explicit undertaking known simply as spontaneous combustion. This type of spontaneous combustion is not to be mistaken for the myth of when a person supposedly self-combusts. These are all further catalysts for the onset of Uranian type illness and disease, which is examined in detail throughout Part Two.

Internal Spontaneous Combustion

Misfiring neurons; hence this is when a group of neurons misfire all at once, are the primary causes for the onset of 'spontaneous combustion.' Thus, spontaneous combustion can also be the cause of epileptic seizures. Moreover, spontaneous combustion can cause other types of Uranian seizures — involving other involuntary actions in the body. Typically, this involves jerking limbs, and muscle spasms. However, severe cases concerning muscle spasms are commonly called myoclonus.

Unsurprisingly, the Sun/Uranus polarity has its rulership over spontaneous combustion. [2] The Sun/Uranus polarity acts, in some case, like a huge electrical (Uranus) fire (Sun). Tense aspects to the Sun or Uranus in the chart cause tension. As a result, neurons become inflamed in the body, or they misfire, thereby causing spontaneous combustion; and the onset of illness and disease.

Paradoxically, spontaneous combustion can be the 'symbolic trigger' for every Uranian-type illness and disease. Metaphorically speaking, this is because the sparks of Uranian infirmities ignite *suddenly* within the brain; or to be more precise, within either hemisphere. There is an old axiom, 'the fire that rages in the brain.' This is a typical expression for the existence of spontaneous combustion, and most particularly for the existence of epilepsy. Epilepsy is, strictly-speaking, a disorder that has its roots planted firmly within the left side of the brain, as the majority of Uranian infirmities do (see Part Three for more information).

Strictly speaking then, the notion of spontaneous combustion will only affect the left side of the brain. Frictional aspects to Uranus, particularly from the Sun, the Moon, Mercury, or the North Node in the chart can often present themselves as indicators, which determine that the individual is left-brained. Therefore, spontaneous combustion affects those individuals who are highly intellectual.

External Spontaneous Combustion

When Uranian lightning strikes from high above the Earth, hence external spontaneous combustion, it could very well be decided that the Earth is having an epileptic style seizure. But in my opinion, it is perhaps more relevant to suggest that lightning simply reflects the scale of Uranian disorders, which are currently prevalent upon the Earth. It could therefore be said that with every bolt of lightning, one more Uranian type disorder is diagnosed. Lightning is merely caused by friction in the atmosphere. Thus, it is also the spark of electricity that enforces the act of external spontaneous combustion — preceding to strike an infrastructure, or some tinder dry material — in order to reinforce combustion.

Curiously, individuals who are born with Uranus in combustion to the Sun (conjunct), or square to the Sun, are much more likely to experience combustible disorders, such as epilepsy (see section titled Uranian Collective Dis-eases). Furthermore, neuro conditions, such as epilepsy are spawned, as a result of neuro friction, which can occur when the Sun is conjunct, or square to Uranus, or even when Uranus afflicts Mercury, or the North Node. Interestingly, when Uranus afflicts the South Node, it just means that at some time in the long distant past, the individual was most likely an epilepsy sufferer; and therefore, has incurred cerebral karma, as a result. As I indicated in the Introduction, cerebral karma is dissimilar to other types of karma.

Meanwhile, neuro impulses that become inflamed can also be responsible for other types of Uranian-orientated disorders, such as deep vein thrombosis, heart attacks, and motor neurone disease, which are all examined further on in this section. Unfortunately, these infirmities are also on the increase. Therefore, I predict a sharp rise in all of these conditions, including epilepsy when Uranus's sojourn of Mercury-ruled Gemini begins in 2025.

The world is currently being bombarded by entirely new viral infections. Viral infections, which affect the central nervous system, are an additional cause of epilepsy. Uranus's tenure of Gemini (Mercury) will merely *personify* this alarming situation further.

Uranian Friction Exhibited

Benjamin Franklin was considered to be the father of modern-day science. Thus, he ascertained that Uranian electricity consisted of a common element, which he named 'electric fire.' [3] This notion may well be a testament to the position of Uranus in his natal chart, which is pronounced, and which opposes its natural polarity planet, the Sun. Furthermore, the Sun and Uranus are in mutual reception by house positions, which are the fifth and the eleventh house, hence a reverse polarity (see natal chart). These are essentially the segments of his chart that were responsible for generating Uranian friction. It is not clear however, whether or not Ben Franklin suffered from epilepsy.

Benjamin Franklin did however die from pleurisy. Thus, pleurisy is a condition that affects the lining between the lungs, and the ribs. Interestingly, pleurisy, which still exists today, is initially caused by internal friction between the lungs and the rib cage. This internal friction also causes, and can be caused by bronchitis. In the natal chart, Uranus op-

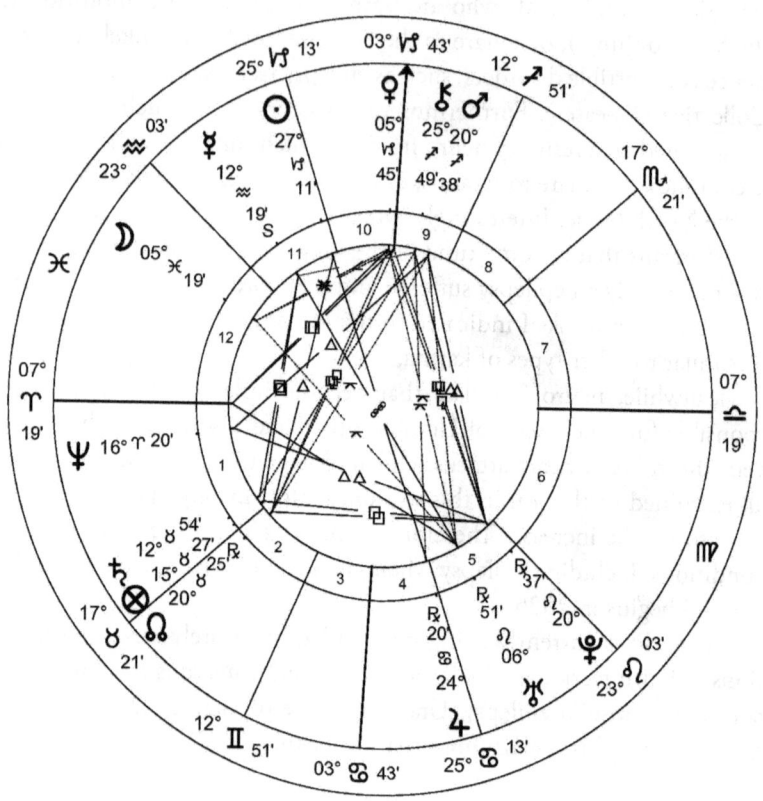

Natal Chart for Benjamin Franklin, 1/17/1706, 10:30, Boston, Massachusetts

poses Mercury (lungs), and squares Saturn (ribs) in the natal chart. This is a typical trigger for bronchitis. Furthermore, the degree of Uranus is pitted, according to William Lilly. In addition, the degree of Mercury is also pitted. The degree of the Sun is lame, according to Lilly.

This is all, in my opinion, a combination of Uranian deployed elements that infuse the chart, especially with the elements of air and fire — cornerstones of neuro energy — generating further friction. Air and fire are nonetheless natural significators of carbon-based friction. Pleurisy does however, cause 'burning sensations' in the chest, especially when the individual attempts to breathe deeply. This is perhaps indicative to the Sun's position in the frictional eleventh house.

I wonder, was Benjamin Franklin's demise from this world the perfect acronym to his reference, the electric fire?

The natal chart does consist of air signs — inciting the fire via natural friction — with Uranus acting as the sudden *spark* of electricity.

In essence, and by the very law of attraction, Benjamin Franklin succumbed to his illness through his own unique way of thinking.

As a further point of interest, when Uranus is elevated in the natal chart, the individual invariably possesses a powerful brain. However, if the brain isn't expanded sufficiently throughout life, the individual will be especially vulnerable to Uranian type illness and disease.

Uranian Collective Dis-eases

Throughout this particular section, we will examine the impact, and the underlying significance of Uranus-orientated illness and disease — collectively and individually. We will begin however, by examining the

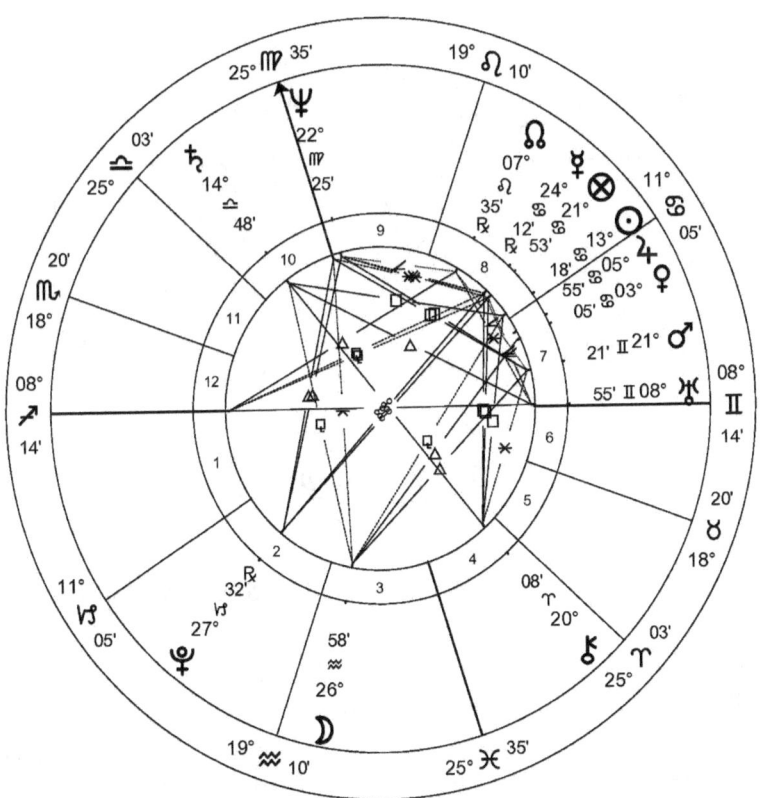

Sibly Chart for the USA, 7/4/1776, 16:50, Philadelphia, Pennsylvania

natal chart of the collective US; determining why this magnanimous and expansive nation has a profound history of mental health problems. The US is currently number two on the world's contemporary listings of electrically-charged psychological dis-eases. Perhaps, Benjamin Franklin was referring to the US, his natural homeland, as being an enormous 'electric fire.' Today, the US has an immeasurable proportion of neuro and electrical problems to contend with.

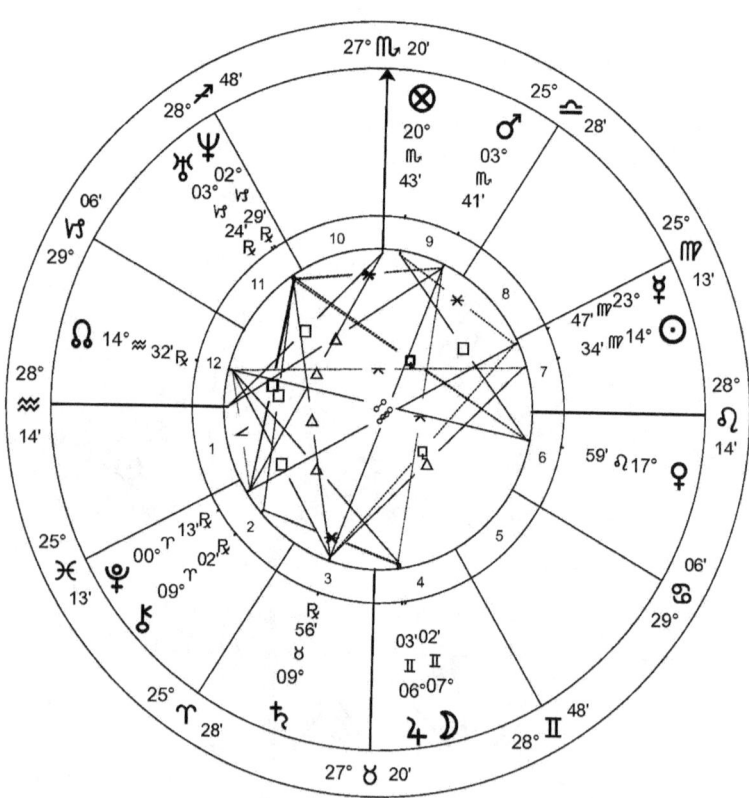

Natal Chart for Brazil, 9/7/1822, 16:35, Sao Paulo, Brazil

As I previously stipulated in the Introduction, there are roughly 3.4 million people with the dis-ease epilepsy in the US — comprising of approximately 3 million adults and 470, 000 children. [4] Considering the land mass of the US, this percentage is not considered as being particularly high. Nonetheless, these figures are still *shocking*. Ironically, Brazil also has a high percentage of epilepsy sufferers, which is interesting because Brazil is number one on the world's list of most lightning strikes, with the US as number two. Interestingly, in the natal chart for Brazil, Uranus is pronounced (see natal chart). This is interesting, because Brazil have just become the ninth largest and fastest growing intellectual economy in the world. [5] Uranus is also trine to Saturn, and quincunx to Jupiter — planets that are also concerned with the overall intricacies of the economy.

Meantime, in the chart for the US, the position of Uranus is *unequivocal* in relation to its mental health problems — tenanting the sixth house of health — opposing the Ascendant (see Sibly chart). The US Ascendant, at 12 degrees of Sagittarius is pitted (blemished), according to Lilly. Some software calculations give the US Ascendant as eight degrees of Sagittarius, twelve degrees however seems to be the most prevalent degree. Thus, a blemished Sagittarian Ascendant would most likely determine an overwhelming influx of foreign nationals into the country, due mostly to compromised border controls, which are caused by staffing problems.

Furthermore, a pitted degree weakens the Ascendant's ability to withstand the radical and electrical influence of Uranus, via the opposition; hence the imminent lightning strikes upon the nation. Moreover, and because Uranus is a collective planet, its extreme negative impact, displayed via the opposition upon the adaptive Ascendant, is far reaching. In essence, the omnidirectional arrows of Sagittarius would therefore carry a raft of mental health problems, which encroach upon a significant number of states within the US.

Furthermore, the US Ascendant represents the *fire* that ignites the nation's soul. Americans are considered to be very passionate about their collective causes. Unfortunately, the US Ascendant is vulnerable to extreme *manipulation* and *falsification* by Uranus. This is partly why its citizens become easily mortified and disheartened when life takes an unfortunate turn. In addition, Uranus lies close to the midpoint of the Moon, and the fiery North Node. Ordinarily, this would exacerbate the overall situation of the nation further, especially with matters close to the heart. Thus, Uranus on this particular midpoint would generate a nationwide outbreak of seizure related disorders — conditions which are karmic by design.

Interestingly, and according to statistics, in a high percentage of US states, where lightning strikes are particularly prevalent, epilepsy is a common factor.

So, for example, in the state of Mississippi, epilepsy is considered as 'disproportionately high.'

Mississippi does by comparison; experience more lightning strikes than most other US states. [6] This statistic in relation to its health concerns is, it seems, hardly a coincidence.

Further, with the Moon's North Node occupying Leo in the eighth house of karma — Leo being the polarity rulership sign of Uranus, the US continues to shoulder a heavy burden of mental health karma. I am wondering whether or not this is because the forefathers of America invaded these lands centuries ago; and its citizens are now paying a heavy price for the occupation. The US's heavy burden of karma is exemplified considerably by Mercury's opposition to Pluto — Pluto being the natural ruler of the eighth house. Pluto's degree is also lame (deficient), according to Lilly — debilitating the natural power of Pluto. Simply, Pluto doesn't have the power to *contain* the spiralling levels of mental health problems.

Ironically, epilepsy does affect a higher percentage of the white population, than it does with the black inhabitants. It also affects the Native American Indians. Thus, epilepsy is particularly active throughout the Navajo population. [7] These are shocking statistics. Unfortunately, epilepsy is endemic of its karmic roots.

Uranian Colonization

Perhaps then, and as I previously referred to, the burden of karma was inflicted initially at the point when the Europeans began invading North America. Perhaps, the white inhabitants transmitted, and thereby inflicted this inherent dis-ease, as a result of their penchant for greed, conquest, and colonization. With them they inflicted disease. Uranus is after all concerned with the invasion of another country, particularly when the planet opposes the Sagittarian (foreign) Ascendant. In this case, conquest and colonization are displayed by Uranus's opposition to the Ascendant.

Within each cornerstone of this nation, the Sagittarian Ascendant does determine that the foundations of the US were constructed solely by multi-national influences. Perhaps then, and because there are very little natural bloodlines left in this country, mental health has been allowed to subconsciously proliferate. This is a case in point, because mental health, particularly epilepsy, is beginning to proliferate across Europe, and the UK.

Further Uranian Ramifications

Epilepsy, within the US, has become more apparent and ostensible since transit Uranus squared the US North Node in 2020. Unfortunately, this condition may well become more widespread, especially when transit Uranus squares the US Moon in 2025. This configuration will also be in mutual reception, which will further reflect the physical/psychological *outspread* of this shocking dis-ease.

Uranian Epilepsy

In antiquity, epilepsy was regarded as a sacred disease that had been inflicted by the Gods— particularly by the Uranian God, *Ouranos*.

I would now like to examine four 'individual' case studies, where the cause of epilepsy is due, in the main, to a pronounced and afflicted Uranus in the natal chart. In most cases, these well-known and hugely respected US citizens have died from this related disease. My individual case analysis begins with the 1980s record setting American track and field athlete, Florence Delorez Griffith Joyner. Lovingly known as 'Flo Jo,' an autopsy confirmed that Joyner died from suffocation in her sleep, caused initially by an epileptic fit. At the time of her death, she was only 38 years of age. [8] Epilepsy is a condition representative of extreme 'internal Uranian combustion.'

Florence Griffith Joyner

In the natal chart for Florence Griffith Joyner, Uranus is most definitely a dominant planet symbolizing — breakthroughs and breakdowns. Thus, Uranus oversees most, if not all, of her distinctive and injudicious capabilities. First and foremost, Uranus lies at twenty degrees of Leo, which, according to Lilly is a smokey degree (see natal chart). Principally, the infrequent 'smokey degree' implies, and particularly in this case, that Joyner was originally spawned from ethnic origin. [9] 'Uranus's square to Venus in its fall is a further consideration and perhaps a testament to her natural background.

Unlike lame and deficient degrees, smokey degrees are *not* detrimental influences, according to Lilly. They merely *highlight* a specific and definite constituent in the chart. In this case, Uranus's azimine degree was more likely to emphasize her creative and athletic skills. Thus, her sporting abilities are emphasized further by Uranus's trine to Mars, and Jupiter, which is in essential dignity — tenanting competitive and go-getting

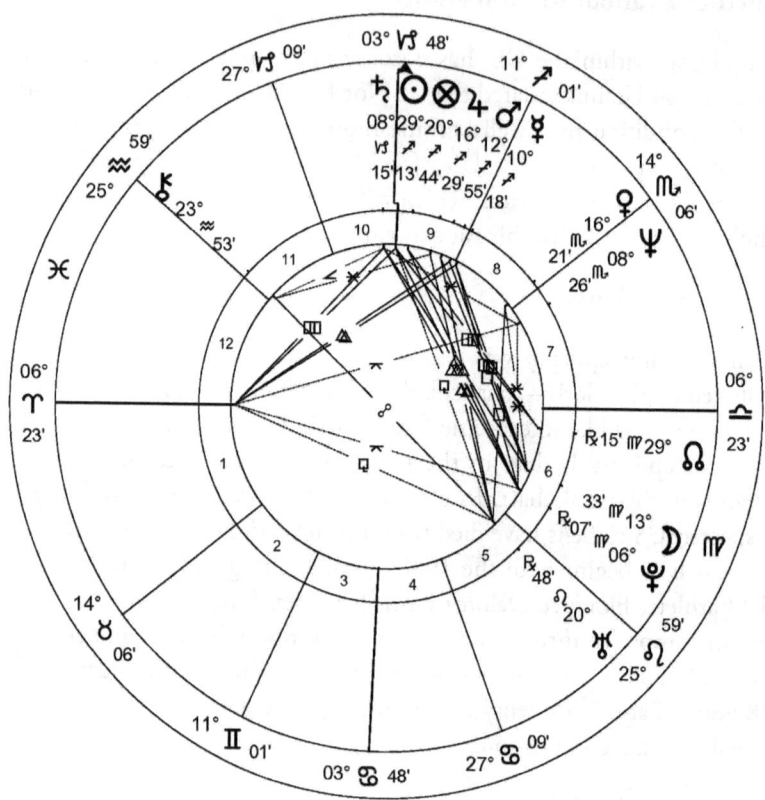

Natal Chart for Florence Griffith Joyner, 12/21/1959, 12:11, Los Angeles, California

Sagittarius. Ironically, Sagittarius is the sign that is most concerned with citizens, whose origins lie oversees, from their country of residence.

It was however, reported throughout her short, but successful life, that Joyner had endured periods of victimization, mostly because of her gender, and because of the color of her skin. [10] The square from Venus to Uranus may very well have had a lot to do with the discrimination she had endured in life. In addition, she was victimized for being a victorious female, which most likely can be attributed to the Mars-Jupiter conjunction, and with Venus overseeing the female gender. Joyner was also known for being a strong, but sensitive personality, which was the result of the Venus-Uranus square.

But despite her outgoing personality, Joyner was a *Vox Sola*; hence a lone voice in an endless sea of controversy. This can also be attributed to

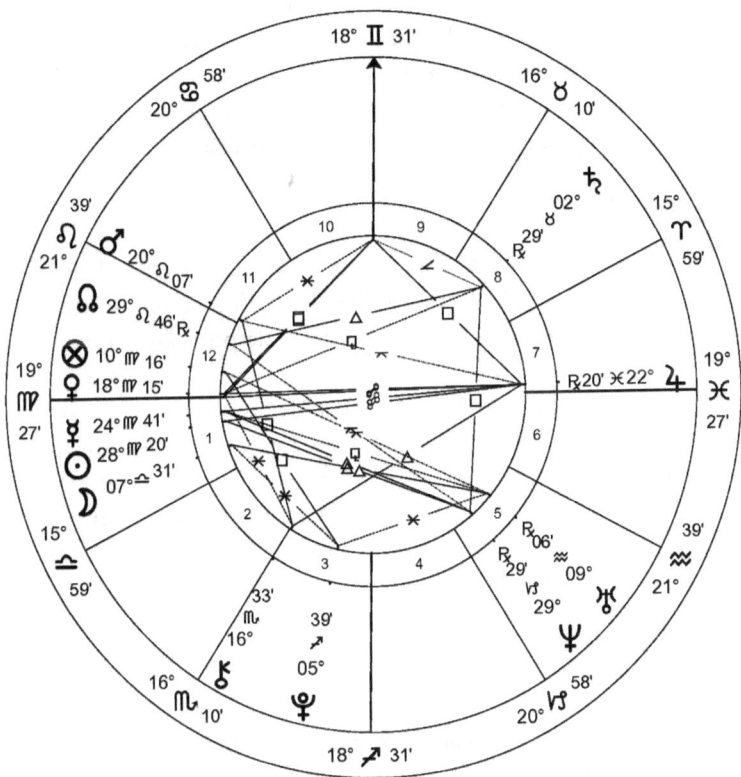

Death Chart for Florence Griffith Joyner, 9/21/1998, 06:00, Mission Viejo, California

the Venus-Uranus Square, and the wide conjunction between Venus and Neptune. It is also connected to the trauma she endured in her childhood (Moon-Pluto conjunction). [11]

Uranian Altercations

Controversially, Joyner was perhaps best known for continually speaking out about the use of performance enhancing drugs where other athletes were concerned — circulating in the competitive world of athletics. She was even accused of taking drugs to enhance her performance. But the allegations were never proven.

Perhaps, the allegations were never proven because Neptune (drugs) receives no hard aspects in the natal chart, even though it just falls short of a square to Uranus.

Neptune's exact sextile to Saturn, may have been her redeeming influence, despite the fact that Neptune's degree is void (nullified). Nullified degrees tend to 'cancel out' the major influences of the planet concerned — rendering them *neutral*. However, with Uranus domiciled, Joyner was always going to be singled out as a 'controversial personality.'

A Uranian Disorder

According to the results of an autopsy, Florence Griffith Joyner died from a massive epileptic seizure in her sleep. Near to her death, transit Uranus was still opposing its natal position, despite being in retrograde motion. At the point of her death however, transit Uranus was closely squared Neptune. Transit Uranus was also quincunx her natal Moon and Pluto (see death chart). Quincunxes are notorious for showing up in death charts. There were rumors that drug abuse contributed to her death (Neptune). But once again, these allegations were never proven.

The evidence here is quite compelling — pointing to the fact that death (Pluto) occurred in her sleep (Moon) — caused by an epileptic seizure (Uranus).

Danny Glover

Danny Lebern Glover is an American actor, and film director. He is also a political activist. [12] As a child Danny Glover suffered from epilepsy, and seizures. However, like so few with this dis-ease, he actually overcame it — recognizing the symptoms early enough in order to do something about it. [13]

In the natal chart for Danny Glover, Uranus is prominent. Thus, its position becomes obvious to the observant eye — conjunct the Moon's North Node — opposing a deficient (pitted) Ascendant. The pitted degree is in accordance with the precise teachings of William Lilly. Most significantly however, Uranus closely squares the elevated position of Mars (see natal chart). These difficult, but inviting configurations were most likely the cause of Glover's epilepsy. I say 'inviting' because there is most definitely room for manoeuvre with regards to any impending health condition, which may arise throughout the course of life; meaning that this is a healing chart. This is mostly determined via Chiron on the MC; and close to fortunate Jupiter.

However, the sextile between Mercury and Uranus clearly *signifies* that an opportunity is present, which will permit Glover to overcome this

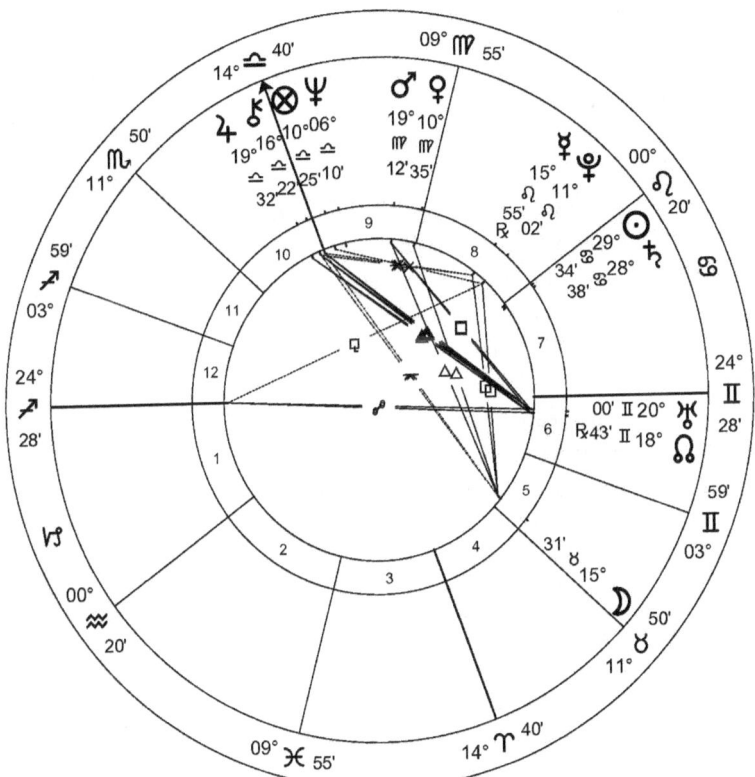

Natal Chart for Danny Glover, 7/22/1946, San Fransisco, California

debilitating dis-ease. This is further exemplified by the partial mutual reception between Mercury and Uranus, which recognizes Uranus's accidental rulership of Gemini; the sign that Mercury naturally rules. Further, Mercury accidentally rules Leo; which is the polarity sign of Uranus.

Despite Mercury's afflicted degree, which is also pitted, according to Lilly, Mercury tenants the eighth house of transformation. Mercury is also conjunct Pluto, which is the natural ruler of the eighth house. These are all exceptional significators that possess the ability in assisting with the gradual mitigation of the cerebral condition epilepsy.

Uranus the Awakener

Further Uranian Significators

During his childhood, and the early part of his extraordinary life, Glover began to endure focal onset epilepsy. [14] It wasn't until 1977 however, that he had a breakthrough with regards to this brain debilitating condition. [15]

In the chart, there are further significators to the onset of epilepsy, especially in childhood. In particular, the Moon is quincunx the MC. Thus, the Moon is unduly concerned with adolescence; hence childhood. This is significant, because it implies that an adjustment (quincunx) can be initiated around the first Saturn return, which is also discerned by the quintile between the Moon and Saturn. Generally speaking, quintiles provide a much greater emphasis on the purposeful manifestation of one's talents. However, in this case, the quintile was no doubt applied to his chart for the purposes of recalibrating his brain (Mercury/Uranus), from the damaging affects of epilepsy. This is also determined by the conjunction between Uranus, and the North Node.

Glover may well have endured this condition in a previous life. This is determined solely by the South Node in Sagittarius, and in the twelfth house of karma. Jupiter, the natural ruler of Sagittarius lies close to the MC, and Neptune, the natural ruler of the twelfth house is in elevation, thus highlighting potential past life disorders. Glover was 31 years of age when he finally overcame this condition. This was shortly after his first Saturn return. When multiplied 31=4. Interestingly, four is Saturn's number in numerology.

Meanwhile, the Moon is exalted in Taurus; meaning that its gentle effects are most likely *personified* — depending on the Moon's overall awareness in the chart, and its links to other planets. The Moon also trines the ruler of the MC, Venus, which is in its fall in Virgo; and which weakens its effects somewhat. Ordinarily, this meant that Glover wasn't able to completely *balance* this condition until later life, as determined by the MC. I have always considered the MC to be connected with the second Saturn return.

Furthermore, the conjunction between the Sun and Saturn (later life) secures his overall fate. However, Saturn's condition is *imperfect* — debilitated in Cancer. The condition of Saturn's degree is *light*, according to Lilly, which lets the light in, so to speak. Therefore, there is every chance that Danny Glover *should* overcome the ramifications, which are associated with epilepsy.

Venus lies on the cusp of the eighth/ninth house polarity — accompanied by the propensities of both transformations, and wholly new directions. The Moon also trines Mars; and Mars also tenants the ninth house of new directions, and life journeys. Thus, Glover possesses the determination, and the gritty intelligence, that would ultimately provide him with an ability to *resolve* this serious health problem. Hence, a condition, which also posed a serious risk to his overall health — preventing him from being 'fully ambulatory' in a previous life — perpetuated by Uranus's opposition to the South Node. Danny Glover has always been noted as a 'Uranian soul.'

Uranian Mitigation

There are additional significators in the natal chart, which establishes his ultimate resurrection — regarding the prospect of fortunate (Jupiter) and perpetual health (Saturn) — especially throughout later life. Uranus, which initially caused the epilepsy in the first place, and the North Node, which determines the eventual outcome, lies at the midpoint of the Moon, and the Sun-Saturn conjunction. Without going into too much detail here, this would imply that his condition started in adolescence (Moon). It is important to remember that adolescence symbolizes the 'closest juncture' to the soul's previous life. At which point, he would be nurtured (Cancer) back to good health, especially in later life, determined by the Sun-Saturn conjunction.

First and foremost, however, and in all likelihood, Glover had developed the capacity to overcome his epilepsy in previous lives. This is shown by the trines from Uranus to the MC, and Jupiter, which is the accidental ruler of the twelfth house. Trines do, after all, signify talents that have been *honed* in past lives. Jupiter tenants the tenth house, which is naturally ruled by Saturn. Jupiter also sextiles the Ascendant. Jupiter, Uranus, and the North Node are the trailing planets in this 'bucket style' chart, with Pluto at the midpoint. Thus, Glover possesses an ability to discover an unexpected breakthrough, which would 'give rise to' advantageous, and long-term transformation. This was most certainly the case for this accomplished Uranian-style actor.

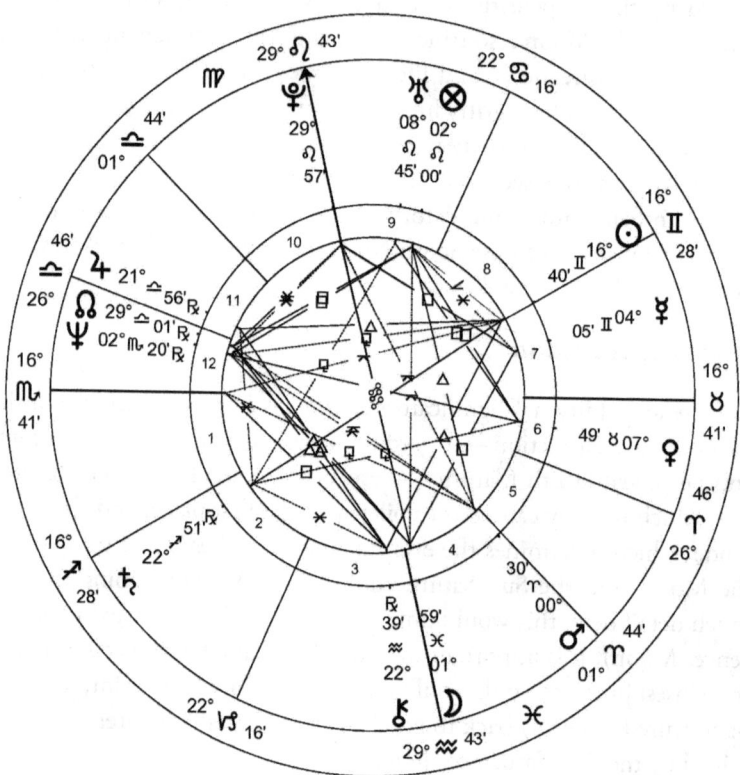

Natal Chart for Prince, 6/7/1958, 18:17, Minneapolis, Minnesota

Prince

Prince, whose real name is, Prince Rogers Nelson, was a singer/songwriter, a musician, and a record producer. He was the recipient of numerous awards, and nominations. Prince was widely-regarded as one of the greatest musicians of his generation, but needless to say, Prince was born with epilepsy. [16] He died in 2016. The cause of his death was given to an overdose of drugs.

In the natal chart for Prince, Uranus is positioned at the top of the chart (elevated). However, Uranus is debilitated in Leo, which weakens its overall effects *slightly*. Uranus widely squares the North Node, and shadowy Neptune, which is domicile in the twelfth house. Uranus also squares Venus, which is lame (deficient) according to Lilly. However, Venus is exalted in Taurus; meaning that its euphonious effects are *unas-*

sailable. Therefore, with Uranus residing at the apex of a T-square with Venus and Neptune, the energy that is being transmitted through the T-square from Venus is wholly *encouraging*. It is particularly heartening for Prince however, because Venus resides in the sixth house of health. In contrast, Uranus makes a sextile to a dignified Mercury. These impassive configurations do symbolize the act of mitigation.

Furthermore, they can be considered as exceptional significators — highlighting a highly mitigating chart. However, in an alternate sense, this is, in real terms, a *successful* natal chart. Prince's overall success however, was no doubt the result of Uranus's quintile to Jupiter, denoting an individual who exhibits uttermost talents. The Sun-Jupiter trine, and Jupiter's sextile to Saturn also played major roles in his success. Jupiter's degree is *fortunate*, according to Lilly. Jupiter tenants the eleventh house, which is naturally ruled by Uranus.

Prince was always considered to be eccentric, with an unconventional, but brilliant style. He could successfully entertain an audience. Later in his career, Prince became an icon, hence a *symbol*.

Uranian Speculation

There has always been much controversy surrounding Prince, and epilepsy. The most common conjecture suggests that Prince overcome epilepsy around the age of seven. However, it has not been completely ruled out that Prince *lived* with this condition, until the day he died. Thus, an elevated Uranus at the apex of a T-square does suggest that Prince lived with this condition all the time he was alive. The square from a debilitated Uranus to Neptune in the twelfth house implies that he managed to keep it a secret. However, because of the heightened 'benefic' influence of Venus within the T-square, Prince may have endured only a relatively mild form of the disease. Furthermore, the trine from Uranus to Mars may have *lessened* the severity of his seizures somewhat.

In an alternate scenario however, it has been suggested that Prince overcame epilepsy, around the age of seven. Significators in the natal chart do however point to this possibility. First and foremost, the Moon signifying adolescence is just in the fourth house; and therefore, it is considered to be domicile. The Moon also opposes the MC and Pluto — suggesting that an early onset virus caused his epilepsy in adolescence. However, he may well have mastered its effects via a life transformation. This would have been around the time when he underwent the first major Saturn transit (square). However, with transit Saturn con-

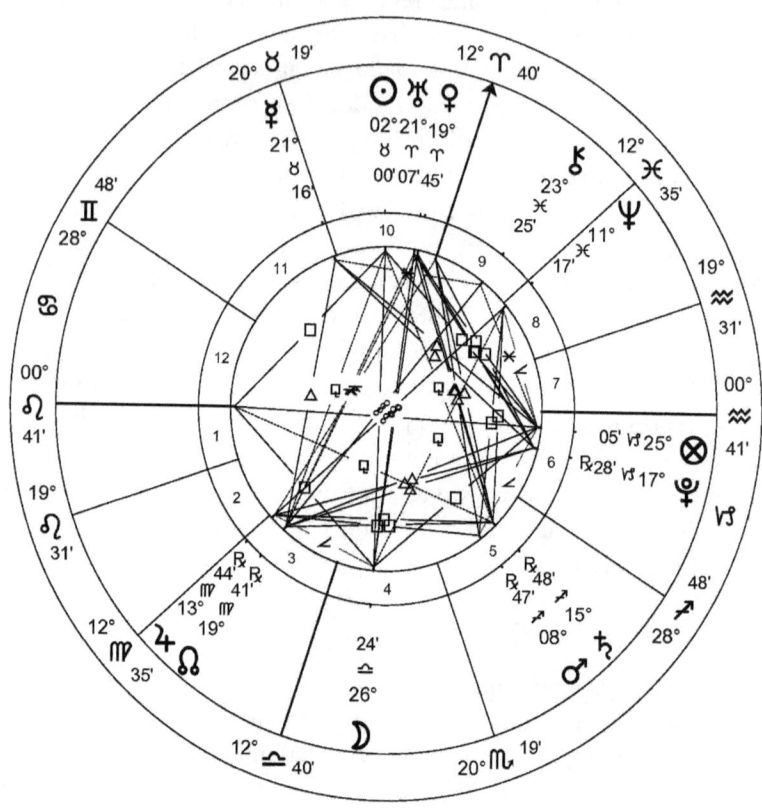

Death Chart for Prince, 4/21/2016, 12:00, Chanhassen, Minnesota

junct his Moon, and opposing the MC, and Pluto at that time, Prince may well have been forced to 'grow up' early. Possibly, this cosmic event symbolized the life transformation.

Further, the Moon partly connects to Uranus via its accidental sign of Pisces. Thus, Pisces is naturally ruled by Neptune, which squares Uranus. Unfortunately, the MC, and Pluto lie a twenty-nine degrees, which is anaretic. This implies that there is *uncertainty* regarding this early life hypothesis. The Moon's square to Mercury does suggest however, that the epilepsy continued long past adolescence. It may also be that Prince actually *believed* that he had overcome epilepsy.

Realistically, his ordinarily sharpened intellect may have been blundered — *cast* under a cloud of illusion, which is more relevant, especially when we take into consideration the unchallenging and illusionary effects of the trine between the Moon and Neptune. Moreover, the Moon and Neptune are also in mutual reception. Here, the Moon tenants Neptune's rulership sign of Pisces, whereas Neptune tenants the Moon's dignified sign of Scorpio, in its fall.

In my humble opinion, I believe it's more credible to believe that Prince shouldered this debilitating disease throughout his relatively brief, but nonetheless illustrious life.

A Uranian Style Death

Prince died *suddenly* of a fatal overdose, from the drug fentanyl. He was 57 years of age. Death in this manner would always be a consistent factor, especially when attributing the square between Uranus (sudden occurrences), and cloudy Neptune (drugs). Leading up to his death however, Transit Neptune would have squared his Sun and Saturn — forming a T-square — from the fourth house of the grave. Transit Neptune was also quincunx Uranus. Transit Uranus was opposing Jupiter, and the North Node.

Prince's unforeseen death was nevertheless imminent. His tragic death also represents an enormous loss, especially within the music industry. To this day, Prince is sorely missed. Yet, his death continues to make more than doves cry.

George Gershwin

George Gershwin was an American composer, and pianist. His compositions spanned popular, jazz, and classical genres. [17] Gershwin died in 1937; and the cause of his death was attributed to a malignant (cancerous) brain tumor.

At the time, it was widely believed that he actually died from an epileptic seizure, because the neurological symptoms associated with this disease, first appeared on that same year.

Extreme (Uranian) Predestination

In the natal chart for George Gershwin, the point of syllabification is unsurprisingly, Uranus, which lies sufficiently close to the Ascendant — *trademarking* the planet of heightened intellect as a recondite cosmic entity of great importance and significance. Furthermore, Uranus tenants the twelfth house — symbolizing karma, and current and past life end-

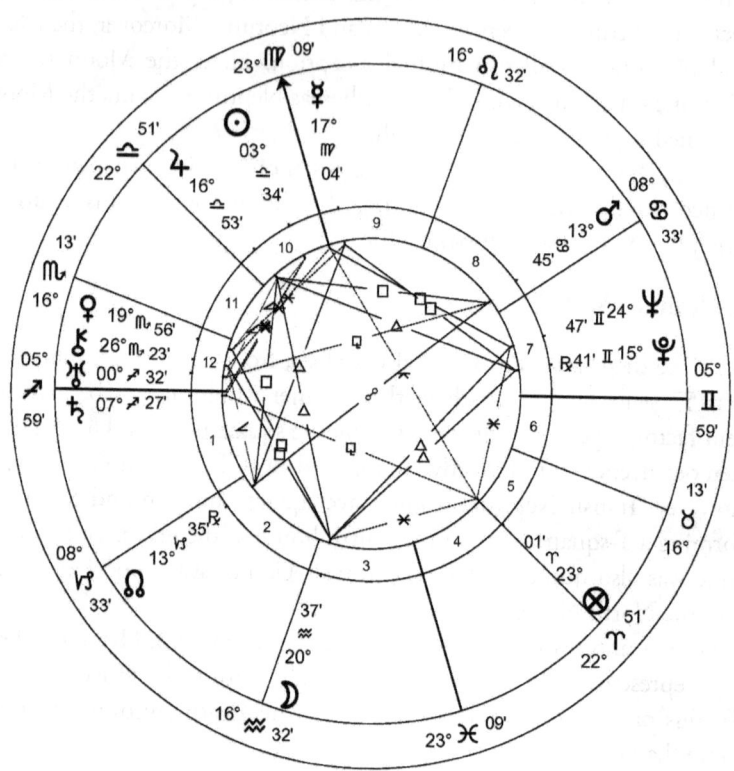

Natal Chart for George Gershwin, 9/26/1898, 11:09, New York, New York

ings. Speaking in a medical capacity however, when Uranus tenants the twelfth house, its presence implies that the personage most likely suffered from a brain disorder, or something very similar in a previous life.

For Gershwin however, this notion is further illustrated by Uranus's wide-ranging conjunction to the Ascendant, and to karma-orientated Saturn.

Presently, Uranus's position in the twelfth house implies that Gershwin's life may well be 'cut short' — due to sudden karmic implications. In which case, the significator most likely corresponds to a past life cerebral disorder. For that reason alone, if the past life karma isn't sufficiently *balanced*, in this case by pacifying Venus, death will most probably be instantaneous. Thus, the rough and stormy waters of Gershwin's twelfth house Uranus, demands to be *appeased*; particularly by the close and placating presence of Venus.

Twelfth House Karma

Inherently, the twelfth house acts as the 'inner radar' — *honing* our deeper predestined impediments; hence our karma. In most cases, the essence of preordained karma seems *fathomless* by its very nature. The effects of this would be similar to losing our bearings underwater. Metaphorically speaking, planets posited in the twelfth house are indistinguishable to 'drowned entities;' meaning they can appear as lifeless bodies. However, planets in the twelfth house are very much alive, and *saturated* with knowledge, and higher awareness, which are the cornerstones of karma. Moreover, planets in the twelfth house can often appear to be *surreptitious* — becoming *withdrawn* from the psyche — appearing to be *submerged* in a vast ocean of secrets — until we remember them — in which case we are able to access their hidden gems. Using a metaphor here, would be to imply that uncovering our wealth of twelfth house planets, is like discovering a shipwreck full of treasure.

Therein lies the paradox of the aqueous twelfth house; because planets in the twelfth house need bringing to the surface of this deep ocean, for fundamental scrutinization and dissection (remembrance). Eventually, the dissolution of their negative energies must take effect; particularly if they are frictionally aspected to other planets. This is particularly relevant if the past life karma is pathological. Pathological past life karma is symbolized chiefly by the outer planets, and their imperceptive effects upon the twelfth house.

Furthermore, if the negative energies of the outer planets are not *dissolved*, illness and disease will most likely return.

Moreover, the twelfth house *transcends* past life karma into spiritual realization. But in most cases however, the hazy portrayal of past life karma translates as nothing more that a collection of vague and obscure images, and timeless story lines — cast away on some elusive, and unfathomable underwater abyss. Gershwin's twelfth house karma is most definitely *pathological* — constituted in a cerebral capacity by Uranus.

Meanwhile, in the natal chart for George Gershwin, Uranus links to Saturn, in a wide conjunction. Saturn is often connected to cancerous tumors. Saturn's degree is pitted, and also lame (deficient), according to Lilly. Uranus links to Jupiter by way of a half square. Jupiter is often connected to the expansion of tumors. These configurations strongly imply that Gershwin *did* previously suffer from a homogeneous brain disorder — possibly a brain tumor in a previous life.

As we have previously established, Venus also tenants the twelfth house. Forming a vibrational confluence with Neptune, as the natural ruler of the twelfth house, Venus and Uranus are also concerned with the arrangement of music. Thus, this socially intellectual twelfth house pairing also implies that Gershwin was musically-minded in a past life. But perhaps, he encountered unforeseen difficulties, because of poor health for example, or from a similar disposition. Venus's accidental rulership of Scorpio in its fall accounts for this impending karmic consideration. In addition, the degree in which Venus tenants is *lame* (deficient). This further implies the presence of an impropriety in a past life.

Karmic Melodies of the Twelfth House

Planets in the twelfth house *mirror* our past life karma — reflecting it onto what seems nothing less than a vast and mysterious ocean. Ultimately, the quintessential ethos of karma is vast and inexplicable. Thus, it is a timeless argument that generates enormous amounts of mixed interest. However, when planets tenant the twelfth house, the very nature of our karma, and its emergence, is transmitted chiefly via our *fluidic* (liquescent) dreams. Thus, we are granted a lifetime by the soul (God) to cleanse our past life karma of all its illusionary impurities — for the purpose of spiritual transcendence.

This is a timeless predetermined melody that, according to the *Akashic Records*, resonates throughout both the evolutionary and spiritual universe (spheres). In the natal chart however, the vibrations of the evolutionary, and the spiritual universes, pulsate via the eighth (Pluto), eleventh (Uranus), and twelfth (Neptune) houses of the chart. In the case of George Gershwin, he possessed the ability to transcend its very essence into conceptual (Uranus) and sweet-sounding harmonies (Venus). Therefore, the twelfth house represents the karmic platform for his intellectual brilliance.

Meanwhile, the musical showpiece *Rhapsody in Blue*, is a testament to George Gershwin's predestined twelfth house karma.

Rhapsody in Blue

Perhaps, the most familiar, and outstanding composition, that was at the pinnacle of Gershwin's overall success, is *Rhapsody in Blue*. Composing this musical masterpiece — combining themes that are equally jazzy, inspiring, and melodic (all rolled into one), is synonymous with the mellifluous twelfth house in the natal chart. The opaline tone of the twelfth house is *blue*, which is also synonymous with Neptune. So, in my humble opinion, Gershwin wrote this composition in order to 'instinctively balance' his past life intellectual (Uranus) karma. Although, this composition appeared (twelfth house) to have had little effect on him, especially on his pathological wellbeing. Writing it nonetheless, may well have contributed to balancing his intellectual karma, especially in spirit, which is also representative of the twelfth house.

Thus, the many diverse *euphonies* within this modern piece are connected to the divergent and depthless influences of the twelfth house — with Uranus at the head of operations so to speak. For example, Uranus governs its jazz arrangements. Contrastingly, Neptune, as the natural ruler of the twelfth house, is attributed to its ability to *inspire* an audience; particularly when we consider its position in the social-orientated seventh house. Inspiring audiences is also concerned with Uranus. Venus however, takes care of the composition's melodic overtones.

Thus, *Rhapsody in Blue* is a karmic and timeless combination of boundless diversities, and never-ending counterpoints — climaxing in an apogee of soulful melodies — which are identified as being at the very heart of the twelfth house. However, Neptune's close proximity to Pluto in the chart also implies that Gershwin can *transform* his intellectual karma, via written music.

A Uranian Master Stroke

Moving aside from these conceivable muted twelfth house influences, what other cosmic gems are contained within the chart? Furthermore, which are perhaps significant to George Gershwin's overall success? Broadly speaking, the most prominent is Uranus's sextile the Sun, which lies in its fall in Libra. The Sun's degree however is *fortunate*, according to Lilly. This *clement* but *thundering* solar configuration to Uranus depicts, in part, why Gershwin was a modern-day (Uranus), celebrated and gregarious composer. Thus, Gershwin brought harmony and goodwill into the lives of others (Sun in Libra). Harmony and goodwill is synonymous to the sign of Libra.

However, the question remains, as to whether George Gershwin brought essential harmony into his own life? Maybe not! Had he had accomplished such a feat, it is likely that he would not have died so early in life from a cerebral disorder, that tormented his life in times past.

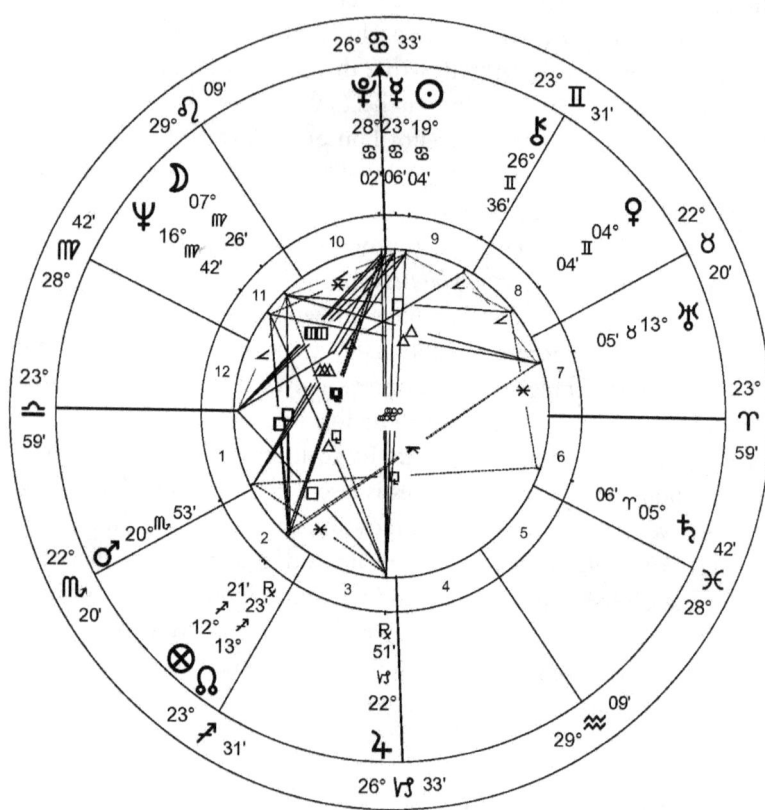

Death Chart for George Gershwin, 7/11/1937, 12:30, Los Angeles, California

In effect, his highly-intellectual brain was indeed the *source* of his karma.

A Sudden Uranian Style Death

In the natal chart, Jupiter, the natural ruler of the Sagittarian/Uranian stellium, squares Mars, which tenants the eighth house of death. Mars's degree is also lame (deficient). Thus, with Uranus at the apex of the Sagittarian stellium; and in the twelfth house of chronic health disorders, implies that the onset of a cerebral disorder is almost assured. This was particularly the case during the second part of his life — following in the wake of the first Saturn return. Thus, Gershwin was only 38 when he died.

In the death chart, expiration was precipitated by the transit Nodal influences. Thus, the transit North Node opposes Pluto (death), with the transit South Node conjunct Pluto. Transit North Node also squares the elevated Mercury. Moreover, transit Mars squares the Moon. Transit Jupiter, which is pitted, squares its natal position. Transit Saturn in its fall opposes the natal Sun. Transit Neptune, which is pitted, closely conjoins Mercury, and widely conjuncts the MC, and squares Pluto, and its natal position. All of these configurations would determine poor health. But perhaps more importantly, transit Uranus in its fall in Taurus opposes Venus in the twelfth house would determine that death from 'unbalanced pathological karma' is assured. It seems that George Gershwin never married. [18] He died a lonely man.

Marriage (Venus) would have brought about a resolve to his overall life situation. It would appear however, that having Uranus in his twelfth house, George Gershwin remained an uppermost individual — whose gentle soul was entirely celibate. However, he chose to incarnate solely to *purify* his brain. Unfortunately, because of this lack of purification (balance), the electrification of his brain (Uranus) became far too extreme — generating internal spontaneous combustion — giving rise to an evolutionary tumor of absolute cerebral proportions.

This completes my detailed analysis concerning the principle Uranian disorder of epilepsy. I will now continue my Uranian analysis — outlining a concise compendium of further indispositions — beginning with bipolar disorder.

James Dean

James Dean was an American actor. He is best remembered as a cultural icon of teenage disillusionment, and social estrangement. [19] Throughout his life, James Dean was subject to very 'erratic behaviour.' In today's medical world, James Dean *would* have been diagnosed with bipolar disorder, hence manic depression. [20] According to those who were closest to him, James Dean was a 'little boy lost.' In 1955, James Dean died in a traffic accident. The car he was driving impacted another vehicle — when travelling at over 65 MPH.

Extreme Uranian Behaviour

In the natal chart for James Dean, Uranus is unmistakably pronounced — rising exactly on the Ascendant. In addition, Uranus squares the MC, and Saturn, which is in essential dignity. Furthermore, Uranus Squares Jupiter, and Pluto. However, Jupiter's degree is lame, according to Lilly. But Jupiter is exalted, which softens the hammer blow — dispensed by Jupiter's afflicted degree.

Notwithstanding, with Uranus (bipolar), and the Ascendant, at the apex of a powerful T-square, it is reasonable to suggest that this configuration is the principle cornerstone for Dean's bipolar disorder. Jupiter's diverse energy is however the *impetus* that augments Dean's bipolar, which manifests via his intellectual (Uranian) personality. Furthermore,

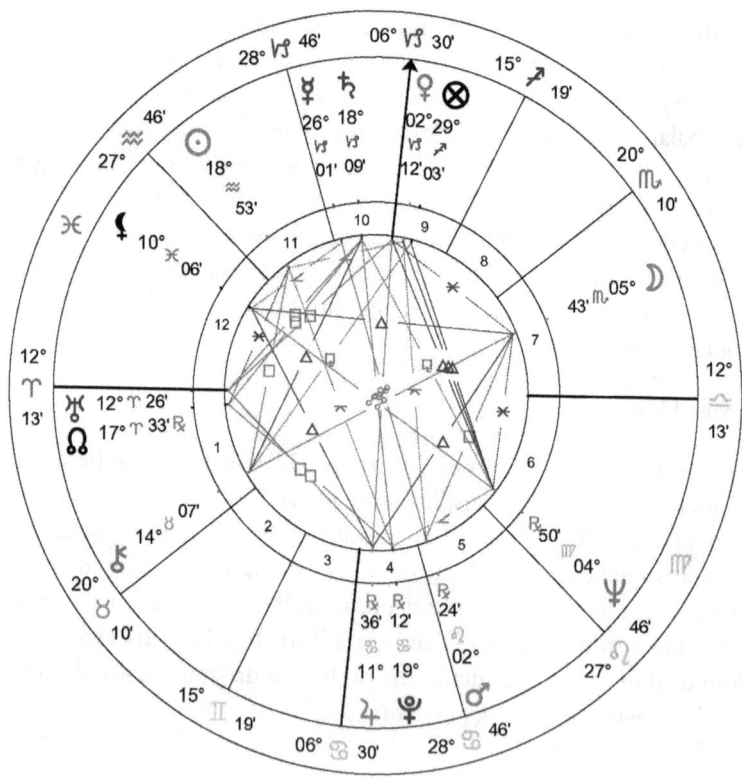

Natal Chart for James Dean, 2/8/1931, 09:00, Marion, Indiana

the bipolar disorder is *projected* through his social personality, via the Ascendant. It was reported that Dean was often 'scornful' of his fellow actors — mocking them whenever his need was aroused. Those who worked with him actually disliked him. [21]

Bipolar disorder is classified as a mental health condition that swings from one extreme to another, which is very Uranus. Thus, bipolar consists of furthermost highs and lows. These mood swings are displayed in the natal chart by Jupiter (highs), and Saturn (lows), which all manifest via Uranus, at the apex of the T-square. Moreover, his moods swings are further exemplified by the Moon in its fall, which is also square Pluto. Regrettably, there are *no* soft aspects to Uranus, or the Ascendant. Had there had been, it would have lessened the effects of the bipolar disorder. Mercury's degree, which is also afflicted, according to Lilly, was also a principle measure towards the onset of his bipolar disorder. Mercury is also concerned with mental health conditions, especially when the planet is elevated, as it is in Dean's chart.

Collectively, it was said that working with Dean was difficult, at the best of times. It is unsurprising then that this was the case; considering all of the Uranian-influenced energy in his chart. Dean was unpredictable, challenging, and often demanding, which are typical characteristics of Uranus. Moreover, Uranus ostracizes. Perhaps, this was the reason why he was known as the 'little boy lost'

Dean did however, believe he was *superior* (Uranus) to others. Thinking you are superior to others is a primary characteristic of bipolar disorder. According to Louise Hay, bipolar occurs when there is no emotional support, and there is a feeling present of being unloved.

James Dean always felt unloved. This was his *raison d'etre*, especially with Uranus rising.

Further, Neptune (love) is intercepted. However, because Dean was only 24 years old when he died, I doubt then whether he would have had 'complete control' over his diverse Neptune influences, as the outer planets tend to affect us more in later life. James Dean was however notorious for *gambling* with his life; hence taking unnecessary risks (Uranus). This trait was no doubt increased by the square from Jupiter, to Uranus, and the Ascendant in his chart.

Those who knew him very well, said that there was often a 'darkness that enveloped him.' No doubt, this shroud of darkness is mostly attributed to the Sun's close connection to the Black Moon, and Pluto's square to the Ascendant, and Uranus. Regrettably, had he had lived longer, and with the condition of Uranus in his natal chart, James Dean would have become an 'ambassador' for bipolar disorder.

James Stewart

James Maitland Stewart was an American actor. Known for his distinctive drawl, and his everyman screen persona, Stewart's acting career spanned decades — from 1935-1991. Stewart died in 1997.

The cause of his death was attributed to a heart attack; or in medical terms, a myocardial infarction. However, a thrombosis (blood clot) formed in Stewart's right leg beforehand — initializing the heart attack. Heart attacks are invariably *sudden* occurrences — befalling the unfortunate victim without any forewarning. Thus, the *suddenness* of a heart attack is concerned solely with Uranus; because a myocardial infarction can often *start* in the brain. Thus, inter cranial hypertension, as it is called, can lead to cardiac dysfunction, lung damage, and heart failure. Heart attacks can also cause a decline in mental processes. [22]

Try to imagine a thunderstorm (Uranus) as a huge Earthly brain infection, such as meningitis, where fluids build up in and around the brain. In this case, the rain clouds represent the fluid. Pressure then builds around the brain, which distorts the brain's electrical impulses. Lightning (Uranus) occurs when the thunderstorm builds up too much pressure. Thus, lightning pulses release the storm's pressure, but they cause serious damage to other parts of the Earth, such as trees (the Earth's lungs). In the case of the infected brain however, heart attacks occur when the infected brain sends out distorted neuron impulses, similar to lightning strikes, which help to release the pressure around the brain. Unfortunately, these distorted neuron impulses cause blood clots, which are the initial catalyst for a myocardial infarction. In the cause of James Stewart, it was a thrombosis that caused his heart attack.

Medically speaking, a thrombosis forms when there is a sudden and compressed build of plaque in the artery walls. The plaque will then *suddenly* rupture (Uranus), causing a blood clot. A thrombosis is therefore indicative to Uranian internal combustion.

Uranian Circumspection

In the natal chart for James (Jimmy) Stewart, Uranus is a sizeable 'focal point'— residing in the seventh house of social interaction, and important partnerships. Stewart always considered his marriage to be one

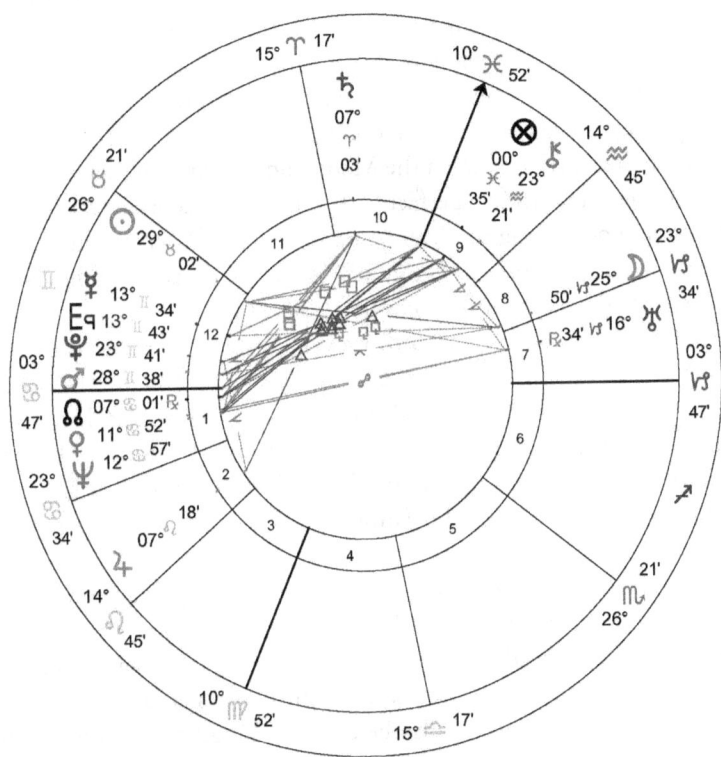

Natal Chart for James Stewart, 5/20/1908, 07:15, Indiana

of great importance. Stewart died three years after his wife. Throughout the media, it was said that he couldn't manage without her.

Essentially, his heart was broken (Uranus). So, it's no wonder he suffered a heart attack. The sweetness (Venus) had disappeared (Neptune) from his life.

Compellingly, Uranus opposes the natural ruler of the seventh house, Venus. Uranus also opposes a debilitated Neptune in Capricorn. These are perhaps the reasons why Stewart couldn't cope without his wife. Ordinarily, Uranus symbolizes *independence*. However, with Uranus in the seventh house, and opposing Venus, he chooses a partner who was independent. Venus and Neptune also tenant the first house, which is a medical zone.

Aside from the obvious health imbalance created by these oppositions to Uranus, which lead to his health implications in later life, Stewart had to work extremely *hard* to achieve a successful career, which was a mix of popular and his fundamentalist ideals. In addition, he had to work *hard* to transcend his dreams into concrete reality. The Christmas classic, it's a Wonderful Life, which starred James Stewart, conveys many messages beyond having faith (Neptune) in one another. Interestingly, the mutual reception between the Moon and Neptune in Stewart's natal chart depicts this notion perfectly. The mutual reception is displayed by Neptune occupying the Moon's natural sign of Cancer, whereas the Moon occupies Neptune's fall sign of Capricorn. Thus, all of these characteristics had become *refashioned* by altruistic Uranus.

Ironically, the bulk of Stewart's movies involved, for the most part, definitive perceptions, that were all humanitarian in nature. Moreover, Stewart was also frank and straightforward in all of his roles. Many who knew him, referred to him as a rebel with a cause (Uranus). However, Stewart had to overcome a multitude of obstacles and obstructions in his life, in order to achieve his familiar assertive and often judgemental reputation.

Being over assertive and judgemental however, is perhaps one reason why he developed thrombosis, which is considered by many in the medical profession to be the ultimate life-threatening blockage. According to the teacher and lecturer Louise Hay, thrombosis is caused by feeling unsafe *psychologically*. It can also be cause by judging the emotions too harshly. It is hardly surprising then that Stewart felt like this with Uranus (feeling unsafe) opposing Venus (the need for security), and Neptune (emotions).

Another vital point of consideration here is that there are no soft aspects to Uranus in the chart, except maybe for a very wide sextile to the MC, which had little or no effect upon his life. Ordinarily, a lack of soft aspects means that Uranus wasn't sufficiently safeguarded. Therefore, he would have been susceptible to Uranian type illnesses and disease; because soft aspects act as the *medicine* for the ailment concerned. The wide sextile from Uranus to the MC does however draw Mercury into the illness equation — because Mercury links to Uranus (thrombosis) through the MC, via a square. Moreover, Mercury is in essential dignity in Gemini, which is the sign that rules over the legs; and Stewart developed a thrombosis in his leg. Furthermore, Mercury is exactly conjunct the Equatorial Ascendant (EP) — both occupying the twelfth house of karma. This means that Stewart endured a similar health disposition in a previous life. This is also determined by the MC in Pisces; the sign that naturally rules the twelfth house. Pluto (judgement) is also in the twelfth house.

Meanwhile, in esoteric astrology, Uranus is considered to be the 'higher octave vibration' of Mercury. This is also significant; because it means that the dis-ease (thrombosis) was most likely incurred in a previous life. This notion is highlighted further by Mercury's position in the twelfth house.

Meanwhile, other factors include, Uranus's tenure of Saturn's natural sign of Capricorn — increasing the likelihood that the dis-ease was karmic. Saturn is also elevated in the chart. But ironically, Saturn is in its fall in Aries. The natural ruler of Aries, Mars lies in the twelfth house. Saturn is also squared to the Ascendant — increasing this karmic characteristic. The Ascendant also conjuncts the North Node (future). Hence, the term 'future' relates to Uranus.

It would seem that Stewart was destined to die from the same, or indeed a similar health condition as he did in a previous life, which in this case was a heart attack caused by a thrombosis. Thus, this Uranian condition brought the final curtain down on his illustrious, idiosyncratic, and intellectual life. The 'final curtain' is symbolized by his twelfth house; and Uranus's link to the Sun via a sesquiquadrate.

Ordinarily, sesquiquadrates represent controversy. However, when this type of aspect connects to the twelfth house via a lead planet, as it does in this case, the controversy surrounding Stewart's karmic dis-ease, turned out to be more than a storm in a teacup. Indeed, it turned out to be an unexpected storm in a desert, which is indicative of his twelfth house, where the Sun (heat) and Mars (dryness) both reside. Traditionally, the twelfth house is an ocean.

Metaphorically speaking, Stewart's twelfth house is also impacted by frequent lightning strikes — discharged by the sesquiquadrate — increasing the risk of further neurological-based complications. Equally, it is no coincidence that the thrombosis (Uranus) formed in his right leg (Gemini), considering that Uranus resides in the right side of his natal chart.

The Uranian Bell 'Sounding Out' the Twelfth House

James Stewart's twelfth house is encompassed by a multitude of angelic hosts — embodied by the four planets that tenant it. Uranus connects to it via a sesquiquadrate to the Sun — symbolized by an old-fashioned alarm bell. There is a famous line in Stewart's most prolific, and perhaps well-known movie, *It's a Wonderful Life*; and that is 'every time a bell rings an angel gets its wings.'

What a profound testament to the modern Uranian actor, whose natal chart was the purest reflection of spirit. It is unfortunate however, that Stewart concluded his life in such an impure manner.

Stephen Hawking

Motor neurone disease is another significant disorder; and one which is repeatedly associated with Uranus. This is mostly because of its unexpected impact on the brain. Therefore, throughout this particular section, I will examine two case examples, beginning with the esteemed professor of science, Stephen Hawking.

Stephen William Hawking was an English physicist, cosmologist, and author. At the time of his death Hawking was the director of research at the Centre for Theoretical Cosmology at the University of Cambridge. At the age of 21, Hawking was diagnosed initially with Amyotrophic Lateral Sclerosis (ALS), which developed into motor neurone disease — living with this condition for 55 years. On the 14th March 2018, Hawking died from complications caused by motor neurone disease. [23]

First and foremost, Stephen Hawking lacked spiritual faith. Thus, he was always considered to be an atheist by his peers. His final words were: "There is no God, no one directs the universe." Hence, in the scientific realm of Uranus, God is a concept, which is often *misconceived*. Intellectually, God represents higher reasoning; thereupon God reflects the higher mind.

In Greek mythology, Uranus (Ouranos) was the God of the sky. It can be said however, that the sky represents the Earth's higher mind.

Uranian Cynicism

In the natal chart for Stephen Hawking, Uranus conflicts with Venus via a square — causing emotional paralysis, and psychological imbalance. Maybe, this was the principle reason why Hawking had no faith in the divine; and towards a higher spiritual purpose. Yet, he had the potential to master this ultimate prospective, because Uranus and Venus are in mutual reception, and the degree of Venus is fortunate, according to Lilly. Thus, he could have balanced his affections (Venus) with his higher perspectives (Uranus/Aquarius).

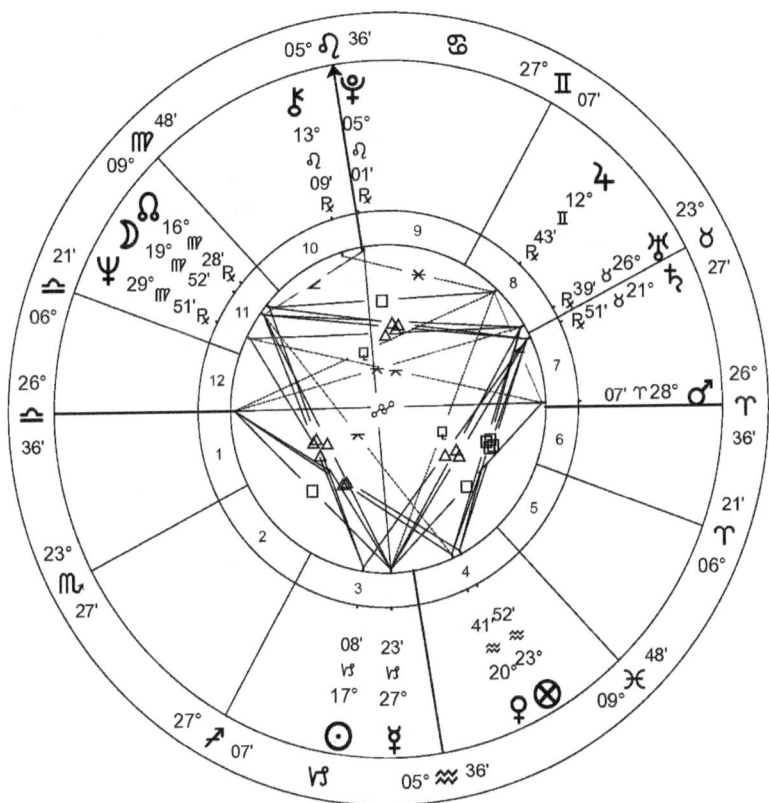

Natal Chart for Stephen Hawking, 1/8/1943, 02:29, Oxford, England

Intellectually, Hawking was deemed a collective and a social genius. However, from an emotional perspective, Hawking was inclined to be *disorganized* — demented by his emotions. Failing to embrace his emotions and deeper feelings in this manner may well have contributed to the onset of a Uranus-ruled disorder; hence motor neurone disease. According to the teacher and lecturer Louise Hay, the psychological cause of motor neurone disease is deep-set fear; hence a fear of not being able to love the self. This is typical of those concerns he had little control over, or what he didn't understand; such as embracing the God within.

Moreover, his 'nonacceptance of God' is highlighted further by Neptune's anaretic (uncertain) degree. In addition, Neptune, which is also debilitated, tenants the eleventh house; which is the natural rulership domain of Uranus. Neptune in the eleventh house often gives rise to

Uranus the Awakener   107

cynicism, with regards to matters of faith, especially when it is frictionally aligned to other planets. In this case, Neptune is quincunx Mars, which is in essential dignity. Thus, an adjustment is required here; and one that balances his long-forgotten faith, with his impregnable opinions, and brilliant scientific viewpoints.

Hawking needed to procure a reasonable degree of spiritual inspiration and guidance in order to remain in good shape. Unfortunately, his *disagreeable*, *agonizing* and *afflicted* Neptune in the Uranus-ruled eleventh house failed to provide these essential qualities. Thus, Hawking *lacked* the ability to realize that science is also a part of God. Furthermore, because of Neptune's position in the eleventh house, Hawking tended to blind the masses with scientific illusion — bound by his definitive convictions.

Uranus also conjuncts Saturn; and Saturn closely squares Venus. These configurations would make him very pragmatic. Thus, too much of the matter-of-fact person. Additionally, a lame (deficient) Mercury opposes the MC and Pluto; and with the MC exactly conjunct Pluto. Mercury also squares the Ascendant. This deep-set combination would create further imbalance and conflict within his mind; meaning that Hawking would dismiss anything he didn't understand.

Uranus trines Mercury. In effect, the trine *joins* the cosmic dots on these otherwise infirm configurations. Although, this opportunistic aspect had the potential to harmonize technology and specialized information into his daily life, it is still reasonable to hypothesize that all of these planetary aspects are the principle significators for the onset of Hawking's motor neurone disease. Motor neurone disease causes muscle (Mars) weakness, which is displayed by Mars's dissociated square to the MC and Pluto, and Mars's square to Mercury, and Mars's opposition to the Ascendant — followed by its quincunx to Neptune. Furthermore, motor neurone disease causes nerves (Mercury) in the brain (Uranus), and the spine (Saturn) to become *dysfunctional*.

Hawking was diagnosed with this ill-favoured condition relatively early in life. The Moon's quincunx to Venus is most likely the primary malefactor for his preliminary diagnosis. The Moon (early life) also tenants the Uranus-ruled natural eleventh house, in Mercury's rulership sign of Virgo — adding more analytical expression to this conflicted equation. In addition, Uranus tenants the eighth house of death, implying that Hawking would most likely die from a brain disorder. Gemini (Mercury) is the accidental ruler of the eighth house. Mercury opposes

Pluto; and Pluto is the natural ruler of the eighth house. Thus, when we connect the cosmic dots, the jigsaw for a cerebral infirmity becomes complete.

With that said, motor neurone disease is also indicative to Uranian internal combustion.

Its ironic however, that Hawking did not consider the divine to be anything of any consequence, considering that one of his famous quotes was to "remember to look up at the stars and not down at your feet." Nonetheless, this is a testament to Uranus. However, it seems that Stephen Hawking was more spiritually aligned than he realized.

Perhaps, Stephen Hawking was just too intellectually astute to actually realize this. In effect, it was Hawking's thoughts and beliefs that ultimately killed him.

Ronnie Corbett

Ronnie Corbett is the second of the case studies concerning motor neurone disease. Corbett contracted motor neurone disease in later life. This is indicative to Uranus (motor neurone disease), square to Saturn (later life) in his natal chart.

Ronald Balfour Corbett was a Scottish actor, a broadcaster, comedian, and a writer. [24] Corbett was perhaps best known for his long association with Ronnie Barker in the BBC comedy sketch show, *The Two Ronnies*. In 2016, Ronnie Corbett died from complications associated with motor neurone disease — previously being diagnosed with this dis-ease in 2015. Corbett was deemed a comedy genius (Uranus). Many said his timing (Saturn) was *impeccable*.

Uranian Straightedge Brilliance

In the natal chart for Ronnie Corbett, Uranus is at the apex of a diverse cardinal T-square, with Jupiter, Saturn, and Pluto. Uranus widely squares Jupiter and Pluto, and closely squares Saturn — with Saturn widely opposing Jupiter. At best, this is a dominant and dynamic T-square because of the Uranian theme, and is perhaps the main focus of attention in the entire chart. Thus, the T-square encompasses essential dignities; hence Jupiter is in its exaltation, and Saturn is domicile. For the most part, this *expansive*, *structured* and *energetic* T-square is *powered* by Pluto — despite Uranus's square to Pluto, which is very wide.

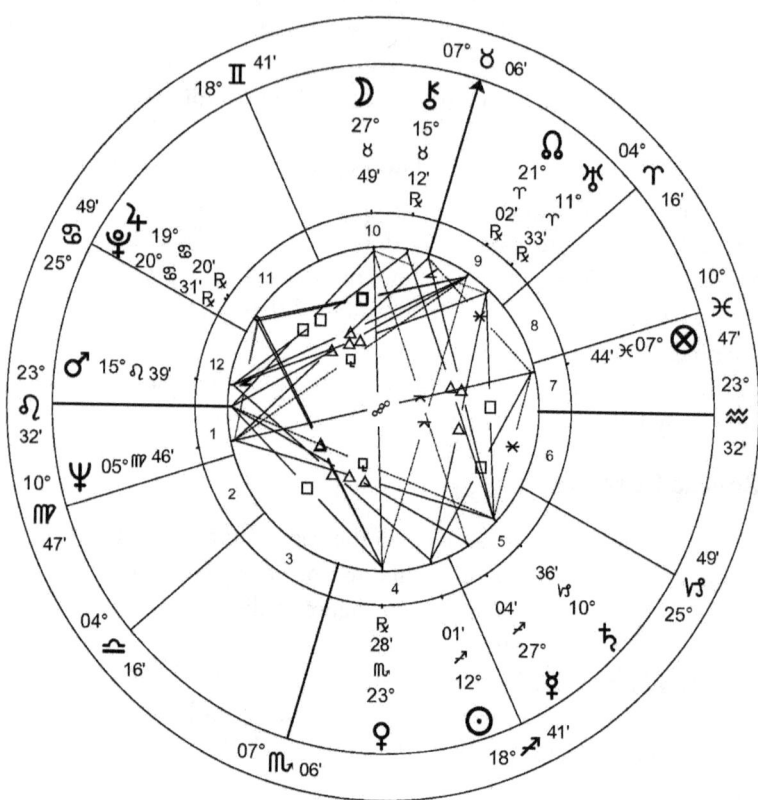

Natal Chart for Ronnie Corbett, 12/4/1930, 21:40, Edinburgh, Scotland

Nevertheless, Uranus is the presiding authority, which has overall command of the T-square — at its summit.

Alas, Uranus's degree is afflicted (pitted), according to William Lilly. This blemished indisposition does unfortunately throw a modest spanner into this 'Uranian mechanism,' which is representative of the T-square. Regrettably, the afflicted degree is likely to cause some Uranian health problems in later life (Uranus square Saturn), and which became apparent in 2015. What's more, Uranus tenants the sign of Saturn's debility; hence its fall. But because of Uranus's square to Saturn, Uranus's tenure of Aries also throws an additional cosmic spanner into the Uranian mechanism of the T-square, causing further health problems in later life.

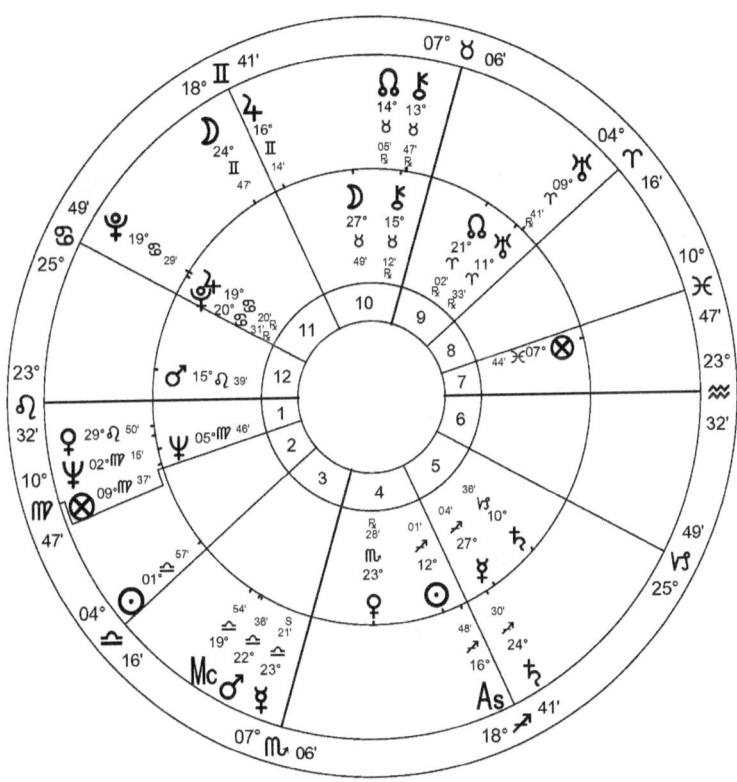

Inner Ring: Natal Chart for Ronnie Corbett, 12/4/1930, 21:40, Edinburgh, Scotland Outer Ring: Ronnie Barker, 9/25/1929, 14:00, Bedford, England

Notwithstanding, this Uranus-captivated T-square provided Corbett with the ability, as a comedian, to be 'quick witted' (Jupiter), and 'timely' (Saturn), concerning mostly his final delivery, hence the punch line of his humorous anecdotes.

Therefore, this dualistic, hence this cosmic/comic capability *moulded* Corbett into one of the ultimate straightedge comedians of his generation (Pluto).

As we have already established, Corbett's natal chart contains a multitude of essential dignities, which further *fuelled* his multiple talents. The sign of Jupiter's rulership, Sagittarius, is where Corbett's Sun and Mercury reside — adding even quicker wittedness to his comic genius persona (Uranus).

Uranus the Awakener   111

Although Mercury is in its detriment in Sagittarius, and Mercury's degree is pitted, according to Lilly, they nevertheless increase the risk of Uranian type illness and disease.

Moreover, Mercury intersects the T-square with a quincunx to the Moon, which is in its exaltation in Taurus; and the Moon's degree is fortunate, according to Lilly. In this respect, most of Corbett's jokes (Mercury in Sagittarius) centered on narratives that had an emotional connection to him personally (Moon). Perhaps, this was his adjustment (quincunx) — from straight man early in his life (Moon) — to becoming a quick-witted and reliable (Taurus) comic in later life.

His lightning quick-wittedness was most likely the result of having a mutual reception between Jupiter and Uranus. Hence, Jupiter resides in Uranus's rulership eleventh house, and Uranus resides in Jupiter's rulership ninth house. Corbett was also had the knack of playing (ninth house), to an audience (eleventh house).

Sadly, Ronnie Corbett was diagnosed with motor neurone disease in March 2015. In the natal chart, the North Node lies close to Uranus, and closely squares Jupiter and Pluto (death). This is yet another crucial factor, which adds further fuel to this overall Uranian disorder. The ruler of the North Node, Mars tenants the twelfth house; and Mars's degree is pitted (afflicted) according to Lilly. In addition, a debilitated Mars in the twelfth house of past lives implies that Corbett suffered from something similar beforehand, especially as Mars lies in Uranus's polarity sign of Leo. Moreover, the South Node tenants the third house in Libra, which is a medical zone. Furthermore, the natural ruler of Libra, hence Venus, squares the Ascendant. Venus also lies in its sign of detriment; hence Scorpio (death). These are all pivotal characteristics — implying that Corbett died from an autoimmune disease in a past life.

Ronnie Corbett died on the 31st March 2016 — a full year after he was initially diagnosed with motor neurone disease. Around the time of his death, transit Saturn in Scorpio (death), had previously made a quincunx to Uranus — symbolizing a death that was both drawn out, but swift at the end. Quincunxes are notorious for appearing, especially in death charts. However, at the time of his death, Saturn was converging on his Sun in the fourth house of the grave.

Transit Uranus had moved through his eighth house of death. Further, and around the time of his death, transit Uranus was conjunct its natal position in the ninth house — symbolizing the final journey — squaring the planets in the natal T-square. Transit Pluto (death) also squared natal Uranus. All of these cosmic convergences upon his natal Uranus meant that he could not survive this Uranian type dis-ease. It was time for Ronnie Corbett to finally hang up his jester's cap, and bow out gracefully (Jupiter, Saturn and Uranus).

A Uranian Testament

At Ronnie Corbett's funeral, his fellow long-time comedian and friend for over thirty years, Ronnie Barker, paid a final acclimation to him, by laying 'four candles' on his coffin. [25] This was a fitting tribute to the famous sketch, which involved 'fork handles' — the misinterpretation to one of their most memorable routines. Ironically, four candles signified the four planets that comprised the momentous T-square in Corbett's chart. Interestingly, when we delineate a composite chart, we see Corbett's Uranus closely conjunct Barker's Uranus. No wonder then, they were considered to be the utmost (Uranus) comedy and lightning duo.

Ronnie Corbett's death from such a terrible disease shocked (Uranus), the comedy world at large. He will be sorely missed, which just leaves me to say "and its good night from him." Those famous inevitable words uttered by Ronnie Barker at the end of their popular weekly comedy programme; *The Two Ronnies*.

May he continue to recite his humorous anecdotes in the Uranian spiritual sphere — denoting comic genius.

Orson Welles

Orson Welles begins the first of two case studies that examines the Uranian connection to 'sudden heart attacks;' hence myocardial infarctions.

Thus, George Orson Welles was an American actor, director, producer, and screenwriter. He is remembered mostly for his innovative screen work. Perhaps, his best-known work, in which he wrote, directed and starred in, was the tendentious and nominated film *Citizen Kane*. In 1985, Welles died of a heart attack. [26]

The Eccentric (Uranian) Uncle

Referred to affectionately as the 'eccentric uncle,' by the Australian journalist Stephen Mayne, Orson Welles was indeed nothing, if not controversial in the world of competitive show business. Welles was however, deemed a brilliant and inventive writer, and visionary.

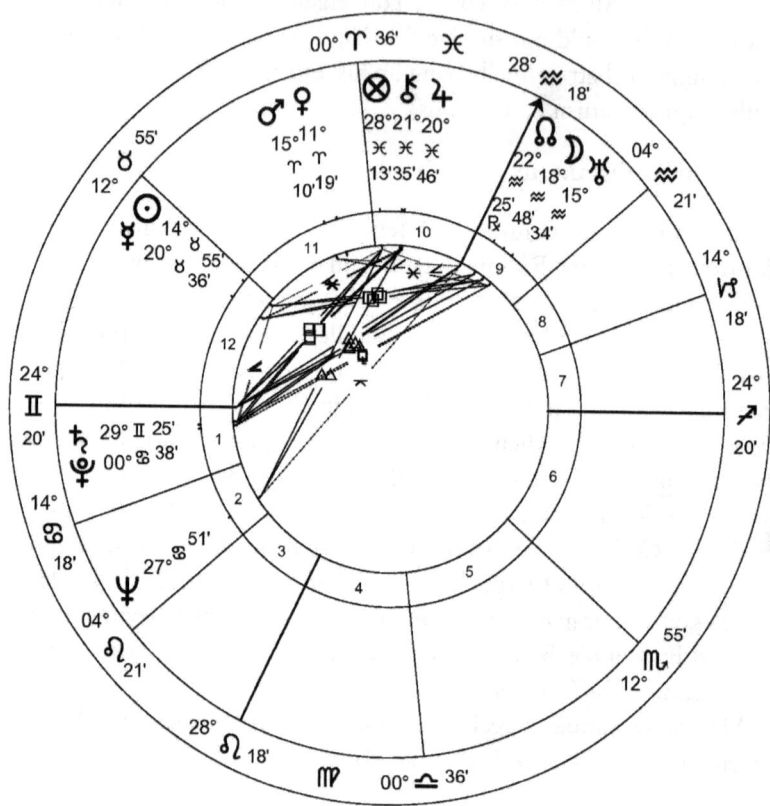

Natal Chart for Orson Welles, 5/6/1915, 07:00, Kenosha, Wisconsin,

But considering all of the Uranian influence in his chart, he could scarcely be anything but a prolific talent.

In the natal chart, Uranus is domicile — tenanting its rulership sign of Aquarius. Uranus squares the Sun and Mercury, making him a very controversial figure, and a brilliant writer. Welles was highly revered within his profession — undoubtably attributed to the mutual reception between the Sun and Venus. Here, the Sun tenants Venus's sign of Taurus, whereas Venus tenants the Sun's sign of exaltation, hence Aries. Uranus adds inventive flair to this mutual reception, with its sextile to Venus. Welles was also 'spontaneously creative.'

Uranus also conjuncts an afflicted Moon, to which the Moon's degree is lame, according to Lilly.

Furthermore, the Moon squares the Sun and Mercury, which would most likely make him emotionally, and psychologically *unstable*.

There were however, unconfirmed reports that Welles suffered frequent panic attacks. If so, this would be corroborated by Uranus's wide conjunction to a pitted North Node by degree. The North Node is also conjunct the Aquarian MC. However, all of these Uranian/Aquarian influences in his natal chart would no doubt contribute towards him being referred to as the eccentric (Uranus), uncle (the Sun).

Uranian/Moon Disorders

During his childhood, Welles suffered from a number of diseases. Among them were whopping couch, diphtheria, asthma, and sinus headaches. All of these infirmities can be attributed to the conjunction between Uranus and the Moon (children), and the squares between Uranus, and the Sun and Mercury. Welles also suffered from severe backaches, which were found to be caused by congenital anomalies in the spine. These disorders are attributed to the anaretic Saturn (spinal canal) in the first house, which is closely conjunct Pluto (congenital conditions). The Moon's square to the Sun was also responsible for his back issues (the Sun).

Uranian Convulsions/Cramps

Heart attacks are extremely Uranian by nature. Primarily, this is because of the 'suddenness,' of them, and their close connection to both convulsions and cramps, which fall under the medical rulership of Uranus. Metaphorically speaking, a myocardial infarction is representative of a heart cramp, or a rapid and rhythmic convulsion. They are also indicative of Uranian internal combustion.

For this particular assessment, I will ignore the cosmic triggers; hence the planetary transits, that were responsible for the fatal heart attack that killed Orson Welles. Instead, I will examine the chart to ascertain the 'medical natal catalyst,' which was always going to be responsible for the demise of this gifted actor. I for one believe that the troublesome patterns in our natal chart can be *refined* and *polished* for our own benefit. But first, we must know what they actually are, before we can take the appropriate measures to correct the imbalance.

If we remain *unknowing* however, life becomes a series of untimely risks and accidental calculations, especially when Uranus is at the cosmic helm of our natal chart so to speak. Thus, the popular and talented astrologer Alan Oken quoted in his brilliant book, *Soul Centered Astrology* that "The soul is born like an uncut diamond. The purpose of this life is to *polish* and *facet* the diamond, so it can return home to spirit, as the perfect jewel." Therefore, in the natal chart for Orson Welles, Uranus is without doubt the principle *agitator* for his unfortunate and unforeseen departure from life. Aside from the squares from Uranus to the Sun and Mercury, the sesquiquadrates from Uranus to Saturn, and Pluto (death) also played a major role towards a future (Uranus) demise — from a Uranus medical disorder. It was reported previously that Orson Welles did indeed incur a heart ailment long before his ultimate death. [27]

A Profound Uranian Testament

Today, Orson Welles is mostly remembered as the innovator (Uranus), of film and stage. Moreover, to quote a famous line from his distinguished film *Citizen Kane*, 'I don't think there's one word that can describe a man's life." Nothing could be farther from the truth, particularly where Orson Welles is concerned.

Carrie Fisher

The Star Wars actor Carrie Fisher is the second of the case examples, which examines the 'indispensable gravitas' associated with sudden, and fatal heart attacks.

Carrie Frances Fisher was an American actor and writer. She is perhaps best known for her portrayal of princess Leia in the Star Wars films. In 2016, Fisher died of a sudden cardiac arrest. She was just 60 years of age. Furthermore, Fisher died just four days after experiencing a medical emergency during a transatlantic flight. [28]

The Distinguished Sovereignty of Uranus

In the natal chart for Carrie Fisher, Uranus is 'profoundly debilitated.' However, its *enervated* influence can be a vital source for reclamation. Tenanting the regal sign of Leo, Uranus is in its detriment. Uranus is also pitted by degree, according to Lilly. But despite its debility, Uranus remains a highly creative influence in the chart. Moreover, Uranus squares the Sun and Neptune, which are both *elevated* influences in the chart. This Uranian configuration was most likely the primary authority, that both governed and directed Fisher into playing the fictitious (Nep-

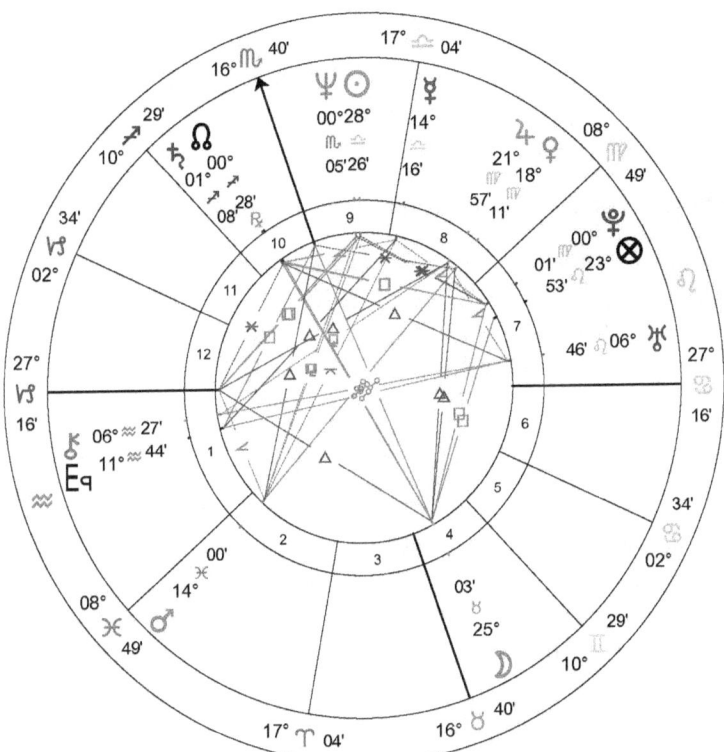

Natal Chart for Carrie Fisher, 10/21/1956, 12:49, Burbank, California

tune), princess Leia (the Sun and Uranus in royal Leo), in the science fiction (Uranus), film Star Wars.

Apparently, Carrie Fisher was not entirely the first choice to play this distinguished, but fictitious character. Being second best so to speak, was most likely the result of the debilitated Uranus in her chart, particularly with the squares to the Sun and Neptune. However, in an interview, she told Richard Wilkins that "she was impressed by the 'fairy tale' quality of the script, admitting that it was unlike any story she had encountered at the time." The composition of this statement is perhaps quintessentially typical of Uranus's square to Neptune; hence the 'fairy tale' quality of the script being designated to Neptune, and the story, which was unlike anything she had encountered before, being designated to Uranus.

Most likely, the catalyst that 'swung it' for Fisher to play this part was Uranus's trine to the anaretic North Node, and career-orientated Saturn. This was always going to be her role in life. When Fisher landed the role as princess Leia, she was much older (Saturn), than her predecessor, Jodie Foster. Foster couldn't play this part because of scheduling problems; hence confusion. In a composite chart Fisher's Uranus is however, square to Foster's Neptune, hence confusion, (see Part 1, and Jodie Foster's natal chart).

In Flight Uranian Incursions

Four days before her fatal heart attack, Fisher had incurred a serious medical incident on a flight bound from London to Los Angeles — suffering a massive myocardial infarction — in which she survived. Purely as a natal placement, this heart attack, which was not fatal, can most likely be attributed to Uranus's semi-square to Jupiter; with Jupiter having rulership over aircraft and long journeys.

One again, I am merely examining the 'natal triggers' that orchestrate potential medical incursions. Whether or not, the incursion is fatal is solely dependant on the nature of the transits at the time of the incident. However, with Pluto at the midpoint of the Jupiter-Uranus semi-square, it was always going to be 'touch and go' whether she survived the ordeal. Saturn's exact square to Pluto didn't exactly help matters. Saturn's degree is *deficient*, according to Lilly. However, Saturn's trine to Uranus helped to avert the inevitable.

Semi-squares are nevertheless deemed as *minor* aspects. In this case, it would be down to the *major* squares from Uranus to the Sun and Neptune, to complete the job in hand, so to speak — eliciting death via the onset of a Uranian type illness. Ironically, an additional impediment bringing about death, from a heart condition, is the dissociate mutual reception between Uranus and Venus. Suppressed within this cosmic scenario is Uranus, which tenants the seventh house; which is naturally-ruled by Venus. Venus however, tenants the eighth house of death, which is naturally-ruled by Scorpio; the sign of Uranus's exaltation. Venus's harmonistic conjunction with Jupiter in the eighth house of death most likely meant that Fisher wouldn't die forthwith from this onboard occurrence. Interestingly, Fisher suffered a sudden (Uranus), near-death medical condition in a social gathering (Venus in the eighth house), onboard an aircraft (Jupiter).

I am not normally one who believes in coincidences. However, Venus is approximately three degrees away from Jupiter by conjunction; and Fisher died three days later. Providence or not?

A Uranian Karmic Testament

Carrie Fisher's scientific movie career was always going to be short-lived. Uranus's very wide opposition to the lame (deficient) Ascendant is perhaps a testament to this unfortunate assumption. Thus, the wide opposition holds no worthwhile validity, or credibility. Moreover, the East Point (EP), in the first house, in Uranus's rulership sign of Aquarius; and to which Uranus opposes, is an indication that Fisher's scientific role in Star Wars was, in fact, formulated at the higher-minded level, in a previous life.

Mars's trine to the MC is a further testament to this 'fairy tale,' but irrational impression. Mars is the natural ruler of the first house, which contains the EP, and is the accidental ruler of irrational Pisces. Pisces is the natural sign rulership of the fairy tale twelfth house of past lives. In addition, Mars is sesquiquadrate Neptune; and Neptune is the traditional planetary ruler of the twelfth house. Neptune also connects to Uranus. Sesquiquadrates press us into working towards a solution, which in turn, help us to understand why the problem existed in the first place. Perhaps, she couldn't see her way forward very clearly, which psychologically (Uranus), may have led towards the sudden heart attack.

The fact remains that Carrie Fisher will always be remembered, as the original (Uranus) princess Leia, from the exceptional twentieth-century Star Wars trilogy. I hope that whatever spiritual domain she currently frequents, 'the force will continue to be with her.'

Conclusion

Throughout this section, I have examined *meticulously* the natal charts of a wide range of celebrity figures, who have unfortunately succumbed, like so many people, to Uranian health disorders. As I have repeatedly expressed throughout all of my publications, illness and disease have karmic implications. The spiritual teacher, Louise Hay, and so many like her, arrived at this same conclusion. Therefore, from my analysis of Uranus in a medical capacity, these hand-picked personages that are incorporated in the case studies have *unknowingly* and *inadvertently*, and without exception, failed to discover, with the exception of Danny Glover, a relevant conclusion to their cerebral karma, in their natal charts. Danny Glover however, balanced his epilepsy with the help of spiritual practices. Coincidentally, so did I, through powerful and continual meditation.

Although we cannot cheat death, as it were; we can greet it through a responsive and purposive approach. In other words, we can *choose*, via free will, how we meet that end. In most cases, we *unconsciously* and *ungraciously* select a conclusion to our lives, which is totally unmindful — induced by physical and mental impairments.

Simply speaking, if planets remain *unbalanced* in our natal charts, especially at the point of death, we will, in most cases, depart this Earth via poor health. Debilitations are connected to the inequitable planetary forces — paying particular attention to dominant, superior and elevated planets. Thus, it is vitally important that we remain *healthy* in life.

With regards to Uranus, we must keep the brain in good shape, by continually setting it intellectual challenges, which have a spiritual conclusion. We must also put some time aside each day to *silence* out thoughts, especially through breath meditation, and positive affirmations.

This represents the synchronicity of the mind, body and soul.

Chart Data

- Natal Chart for Benjamin Franklin, 17th January 1706, 10:30, Boston, USA, Placidus Houses, Mean Node.
- Natal Chart for Brazil, 7th September 1822, 16:35, Sao Paulo, Brazil, Placidus Houses, Mean Node.
- Sibly chart for the US, 4th July 1776, 16:50, Philadelphia, USA, Placidus Houses, Mean Node.
- Natal Chart for Florence Griffith Joyner, 21st December 1959, 12:11, Los Angeles, USA, Placidus Houses, Mean Node.
- Death Chart for Florence Griffith Joyner, 21st September 1998, 06:00, Mission Viejo, USA, Placidus Houses, Mean Node.
- Natal Chart for Danny Glover, 22nd July 1946, 17:03, San Francisco, USA, Placidus Houses, Mean Node.
- Natal Chart for Prince, 7th June 1958, 18:17, Minneapolis, USA, Placidus Houses, Mean Node.
- Death Chart for Prince, 21st April 2016, 12:00, Minnesota, USA, Placidus Houses, Mean Node.
- Natal Chart for George Gershwin, 26th September 1898, 11:09, New York, USA, Placidus Houses, Mean Node.
- Death Chart for George Gershwin, 11th July 1937, 12:30, Los Angeles, USA, Placidus Houses, Mean Node.
- Natal Chart for James Dean, 8th February 1931, 09:00, Marion, Grant County, USA, Placidus Houses, Mean Node.
- Natal Chart for James Stewart, 20th May 1908, 07:15, Indiana, USA, Placidus Houses, Mean Node.
- Natal Chart for Stephen Hawking, 8th January 1942, 02:29, Oxford, UK, Placidus Houses, Mean Node.
- Natal Chart for Ronnie Corbett, 4th December 1930, 21:40, Edinburgh, UK, Placidus Houses, Mean Node.
- Natal Chart for Ronnie Barker, 25th September 1929, 14:00, Bedford, UK, Placidus Houses, Mean Node.
- Natal Chart for Orson Welles, 6th May 1915, 07:00, Kenosha (WI), USA, Placidus Houses, Mean Node.
- Natal Chart for Carrie Fisher, 21st October 1956, 12:49, Burbank, CA, USA, Placidus Houses, Mean Node

References

1. Statistics courtesy of the World Health Organization (WHO).
2. Spontaneous combustion is a phenomenon in which a hydrocarbon substance unexpectedly bursts into flames without any apparent cause.
3. Benjamin Franklin was one of the leading figures of American history. He was a statesman, author, publisher, scientist, inventor, and a diplomat.
4. Statistics at, www.cdc.gov.
5. Statistics at www.pepsic.bvsalud.org.
6. Statistics at www. mafes.msstate.edu.
7. Statistics at, www.epilepsy.com.
8. Information courtesy of Wikipedia.
9. Christian Astrology by William Lilly.
10. www.ussporthistory.com
11. www.encyclopedia.com.
12. Information source, Wikipedia.
13. Information source, www.healthline.com.
14. Focal onset epilepsy (seizures) is the most common type of epilepsy.
15. www.blackdoctor.org.
16. Information source, Wikipedia.
17. Information source, Wikipedia.
18. Information courtesy of the New York Times.
19. Information source Wikipedia.
20. A testament from Dr. Ralph Cinque.
21. Information source, www.americanlegends.com.
22. Information source, Wikipedia.
23. Information source, Wikipedia.
24. Information source, Wikipedia.
25. Information source, the Guardian.
26. Information source, Wikipedia.
27. www.nytimes.com.
28. Information source, Wikipedia.

PART THREE

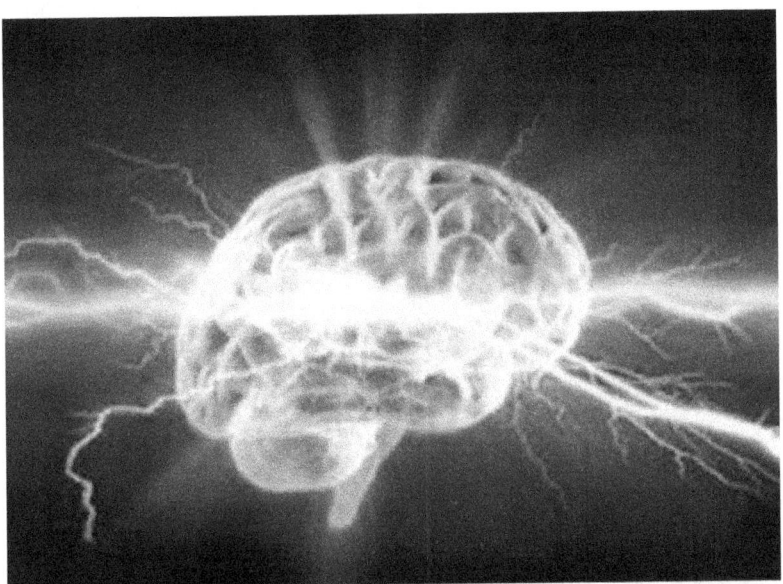

Uranus Represents the 'Unparalleled Movement' of Expression

(The Unparalleled Movement of Expression is an Essential Requirement for Supreme Liberation)

"Every moment, we create a new reality, and then the earlier reality loses its accountability."
Abhijit Naskar

Electrifying the Brain's Intellect

Mercury governs intellect, whereas Uranus governs 'inventive intellect.' This final section highlights a group of highly intellectual individuals; both past and present, who have orchestrated numerous 'master strokes' in their lives; and all within the Uranian field of experience, and expertise.

In a recent survey, which was conducted by *Britannica*, at least sixty-five percent of those who responded actually believed that human beings only use ten percent of their brain's intellect. In point of fact, we use all of our brain, all of the time. How is this information known? For example, and according to *Britannica*, 'if we only needed ten percent of our brain's capacity, the majority of brain injuries would have no discernible consequences — since the damage would affect parts of the brain that weren't doing anything to begin with.' [1]

However, it is how we avail oneself of the cerebral objectives, and the information, that is accumulated within our higher brain functions, that makes a difference to our evolutionary progression. Just as the soul accumulates physical karma, the higher brain functions *safeguard* the cerebral karma, which has been similarly amassed throughout previous incarnations. Ultimately, if the intellect is continually *electrified* throughout physical incarnation, it discerns the credibility, and the integrity of our higher brain waves. In other words, if we do not make full use of our higher brain functions to enlighten ourselves and others, it will appear that we are only using ten percent of our brain's potential. Therefore, we will lose the ability to function at a higher level of intellectual consciousness.

Today however, so many individuals have, *impaled* themselves with this inferior burden of irresponsibility, and intellectual stagnation. Life is continually comprised of unexpected changes (Uranus); which is what the neuroscientist Abhijit Naskar is referring to in his affirmation. It is these continual changes in life that ultimately infuse (electrify) the brain's intellect, which ultimately assists with our intellectual development. In essence, the brain needs challenges to decode, which is what Uranus, and its cosmic brother Mercury, were intended to do. Mercury however, is concerned solely with the conventional intellect, whereas Uranus is concerned solely with higher intellect. Therefore, when Uranus is *pronounced* in the natal chart, the individual is handed an opportunity to *electrify* the intellect further.

All of the case studies throughout this section are comprised of individuals who have, in different ways, *electrified* their intellect. Thus, they have become *masters* of their diverse and brilliant dispositions.

Uranian Chaos/Order

In a large percentage of cases, the higher brain functions are literally being 'set adrift;' whereby they become *perturbed*, and *disorganized*. Today, the higher brain functions, thus the elevated intellect of so many, is being 'dampened down' by unintelligent thoughts, and *brainless* gestures. These disturbing activities are occurring mostly because of the overall levels of non-cerebral progression — apparent within so many civilizations today. It's almost as if that intellectual bolt of lightning has nowhere to strike. Thus, so many individuals throughout societies are simply not progressing within the Uranian sphere of intellectual expertise. For that reason alone, Uranus is a planet that is continually misunderstood. For instance, the fact that we use technology to *manipulate*, rather than to *liberate*, is a classic textbook example of this 'Uranian lack of cerebral progression.' The *electrification* of the higher brain functions is what's required always; especially if we are to have any chance of becoming a more intellectual and enlightened collective. Otherwise, many individuals will still *appear* to be utilizing only around ten percent of the brain's intellect.

There are however, a handful of highly-evolved individuals, which are always present on Earth who incarnate — in order to raise intellectual awareness. Several of these highly evolved individuals, who operate specifically within the Uranian higher sphere of intellectual aptitude, are examined in detail throughout this final section. A principle example of intellectual genius was Albert Einstein, who we have already touched upon briefly. Einstein's revolutionary attributes, particularly on quantum physics, transformed science to a new level of intellectual understanding.

Similar scientific rulings also apply to Sir Isaac Newton, whose case example is scrutinized further on. Both of these individuals have previously *consolidated* their higher brain functions in previous incarnations. Thus, they have become intellectually superior in their unique disciplines — denoting inventiveness and innovation — and which is personified further in spirit. In addition, so many of these highly-evolved intellectual souls throughout this section have, and continue to implement astrology to further exemplify their cause.

Regrettably, many of the intellectually-evolved souls, who are examined throughout this section, have experienced a very difficult and arduous childhood. This is because they have taken it upon themselves to *rediscover* who they are in an intellectual capacity — redefining their ultimate purpose for incarnating.

Experiencing a gruelling childhood, so to speak, is mostly defined by hard aspects from Uranus to personal planets in the natal chart. Pronounced Uranian souls possess the ability to 'raise themselves' in adolescence, which invariably is what occurs.

Uranian Composition

Speaking within an evolutionary capacity, the brain divides into two halves, or to be more precise, it dissects into two hemispheres — intellect and intelligence. So, within each segment, specific regions manage certain functions. The two sides of the brain look very much alike; however, there is a huge difference in how they process information. Despite their contrasting styles, the two halves of the brain do not work *independently* of each other. This is referred to as the left-brain vs. the right brain theory. Primarily, the left brain is concerned solely with thinking, especially in words, whereas the right brain is concerned solely with feelings and visualization (see diagram below). Thus, the diagram below is a discernible representation of the planet Uranus, and its overall rulership of the brain. Furthermore, the indentation line at the center of the brain would undoubtably accommodate the planet's vertical ring system.

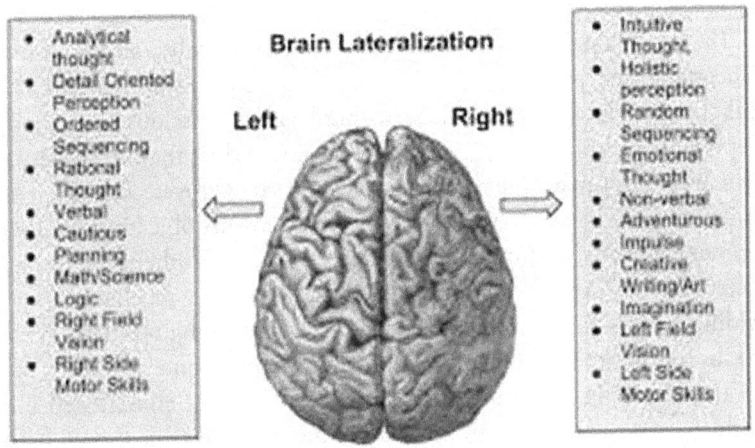

Uranian Proficiency

Albert Einstein was clearly left brained. However, like all intellectually-evolved souls, Einstein was attempting to *consolidate* the two hemispheres of his brain, in order to *electrify* more of his brain's intellect. Hence, this is a cerebral provocation, which we are all meant to undertake, once we incarnate. Uranus changes our perspective on life, in order that we may begin to realize the importance of this universal truth. Unfortunately, epilepsy, signifying the brainquake scenario, is a condition that is concerned solely with core cerebral management; hence cerebral *realignment* and *re-electrification*. Epilepsy occurs mostly because the brain wasn't electrified sufficiently in a previous incarnation.

Furthermore, epilepsy continues to exist, because we are no longer capable of *managing* both sides of the brain simultaneously. Unfortunately, this has become a habitual fact in our current state of non-evolution. Nowadays, we are all left brained, or right brained individuals, which severely *decreases* our intellectual capacity, as a collective. Epilepsy is a karmic cerebral disorder that will continue to impact the brain, until that is, we all successfully consolidate, and thus, *electrify* the higher functions of the brain.

In spirit however, we have the option to *consolidate* the brain's intellect; because spirit is a transcendental domain, where perception, and thought are the principle elements attributed to evolutionary progression. Ultimately, in spirit, there is no discord, or division present, like there is on the Earth plane. [2]

Uranian Intellect

The 'traditional purpose' of Uranus is to break rules, and to demolish established patterns or structures, thus creating sudden and radical change. However, at a much 'higher level of consciousness,' Uranus represents technology, innovation, discovery, and all that is progressive. This is the ultimate purpose of intellect — to innovate (electrify) the brain with higher reasoning. Uranus also represents objectivity, enlightenment, novelty, and ingenuity. Rebelliousness is another Uranus characteristic; however, there is nothing wrong with being rebellious — providing there is an innovative cause. In most cases, being rebellious means to 'break free' of the conventional; hence the status quo.

The following case studies, are prime examples of enlightened individuals, of past and present, who have innovated (electrified) their brains with the higher power of reasoning. Hence, they have elevated their brains with personalized creativity, which has both *influenced*, and *inspired* the collective (Uranus).

Ludwig van Beethoven

We begin this final component of the book with the first of the case studies, which spotlights the ingenious, and inventive German composer, Ludwig van Beethoven. Today, Beethoven remains one of the most admired composers. His works rank amongst the most performed of the classic musical repository. [3]

Uranian Intellectual Melodies

Before I examine the challenging but innovative influence of Uranus, in the natal chart, I would like to explore the astrological/physical agitators, which were the principle cause of Beethoven's deafness. Thus, Beethoven's deafness gradually developed throughout his relatively short life.

Primarily, Mercury has its rulership over the physical (corporeal) ears. But more importantly, Mercury rules over the ear's ability to listen to physical-orientated sounds. However, Uranus has its rulership over the inner (non corporeal) ears. Thus, Uranus rules over the inner ear's ability to listen to sounds at a much higher intellectual level; which simply means to discern beyond the conventional.

An example, would be to imply that each of us possesses the ability to hear sounds resonating within.

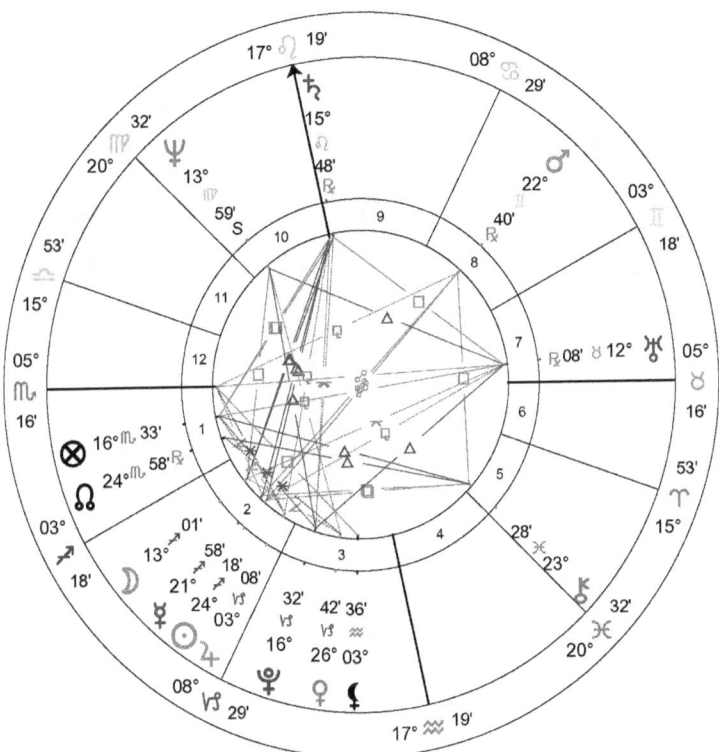

Natal Chart for Ludwig van Beethoven, 12/16/1770, 03:40, Bonn, Germany

Conceivably, it would be forearmed to refer to these resonations as, the 'melodies of embodiment.'

Spiritual practices, such as meditation, and yoga's; such as raja yoga, disclose these incorporeal, but intellectual convictions, and flawlessly, which we would refer to as the melodies of embodiment.

Uranian Inspiration

Throughout the course of his life, Beethoven became completely deaf; particularly around the time he began composing his major symphonies; hence his life works. Although he became totally deaf, Beethoven could still recognize the distinctive tones, which were vibrating within his higher intellectual self. This was to the point that he could *reorganize* them into coherent harmonies — reproducing tuneful expressions.

Uranus the Awakener

Ultimately, these were transformed into the beautiful and masterful symphonies, which we enjoy today.

In the natal chart, Mercury is in its detriment. In addition, Mercury opposes a domicile Mars, in the eighth house, which is the traditional rulership domain of Mars. Mercury is also combust; hence conjunct the Sun. Ordinarily, this would mean that the individual possesses a powerful brain, but has a tendency not to use it; particularly in the first half of life. Combustible planets are burnt by the Sun's rays. But they do recover in later life. The Sun's degree however, is *pitted* (incomplete), according to Lilly, which impacts the overall health of Mercury. This is most likely the cosmic reactant that caused his overall deafness. Metaphorically speaking, one can imply that a weak Mercury opposing a powerfully-placed Mars in the eighth house of death, meant the 'eventual death of his hearing.' Mars is also in Gemini, the sign which is traditionally ruled by Mercury, which in this case contributed further to his hearing loss. The fact he could still work was no doubt the result of Mercury's trine to the MC, and a closely conjunct Saturn.

Beethoven's loss of hearing was a *gradual* affair, and not sudden, as some would seem to think. In the interim, the transiting planetary catalysts for his impairment could well be attributed to Neptune and Pluto — frictionally aligned to his Sun, Mercury, and Mars — throughout a significant part of his life. Ironically, if these planets were involved, they would have transformed his musical intellect to a higher level of consciousness. Beethoven's symphonies (Neptune) were always very profound and deep arrangements (Pluto). However, in the natal chart, Uranus (intellect), is intellectually anchored to musical Neptune, and intense Pluto, via harmonious trines. Thus, Beethoven's symphonies were nothing short of 'intellectually profound' instrumentations.

A Classical Uranian Genius

Uranus is both pronounced, and deficient, in this constellated type chart. The degree of Uranus is *deep* and *pitted*, according to Lilly. This means that Uranus can still be *outstanding*, and *exceptional*, despite the existence of several perplexities, which may, or may not, impact its innovative and inventive style of temperament. Beethoven was no doubt a musical genius; a testament to his impaired abilities.

This sublime ability can be attributed to the close trine between Uranus and Neptune; whereby it transcends his musical intellectual genius. Doubtless, Beethoven *emulated* the internal musical melodies that resonated deep within his Uranian intellect, and which was doubtlessly the result of the exceptionally-powerful Uranus in his natal chart. Thus, Uranus is also trine to Pluto. Essentially, this is how he managed to *fabricate* his unprecedented symphonies.

Trines however, signify unsurpassed abilities, and expertise, that have been *sharpened* in previous lives, or in spirit. However, depending on how close the planets are to each other, within the traditional orb of eight degrees, is dependent solely on how much knowledge was actually acuminated previously. For example, an exact orb alignment would mean that a massive amount of knowledge, to the point of absolute perfection, was accumulated in a previous life, or alternately in spirit.

Uranian Altercations

The quincunx between Uranus and the Moon most likely meant that Beethoven had an unusually difficult childhood. [4] Thus, his childhood was dominated by his unruly father, which was also the result of the square between Uranus and Saturn (father). Moreover, the deficient degree of the Sun (also father) would also be responsible for the difficulties he incurred, as a small child. The Moon's exact square to Neptune made the situation worse, because his father was known to be a drunk (Neptune).

Beethoven's musical abilities were *procured* most unexpectedly (Uranus). One story implies that his drunken father would come home, get him out of bed, and force him to play the piano/harpsichord. This disruptive measure would also be attributed to the Moon's exact square to Neptune in its detriment; hence in Virgo — an unmistakable and unconventional form of practicing his musical art that would be deemed *antisocial* today. This classical idiosyncrasy is also the result of the deficient degree of Uranus — impacting the seventh house of social discourse. In effect, Beethoven learned his extraordinary musical abilities in the most unusual of circumstances (Uranus).

Beethoven's Pastoral Symphony; Hence his Ultimate Genius

According to research, Beethoven's pastoral symphony; hence symphony number six, is the most loved, cherished, and admired by his many devotees; including myself. Ironically, Uranus frequents the seventh house, which is naturally ruled by Venus.

In numerology, Venus's number is six, which, in this case, would symbolize his pastoral symphony. However, it would seem that its overall composition was not easy to accomplish. Thus, the dalliance between the composer, and the pen, was indeed fraught, at the time of its composition — most likely the result of poor health.

Remarkably however, the pastoral symphony became a testament to his higher intellect; hence his musical genius.

Unfortunately, Beethoven wrote so many of his symphonies — living in squalor — and in poor health. For the most part, Beethoven suffered from kidney disease, as a result of the poor living conditions, which he had to endure for most of his life. This was most likely the result of Uranus's square from the seventh house of the kidneys, to the MC, and Saturn. Beethoven also had to tolerate frequent bouts of diarrhoea, which was most likely attributed to the quincunxes between Pluto (bowels), and the MC, and Saturn. Quincunxes are often 'health hazard' aspects.

Additionally, Venus (kidneys) is virtually unaspected in the natal chart, except for a sesquiquadrate to Neptune (disease). In addition, Venus's degree is lame (deficient), according to Lilly. This configuration was most likely the root cause of his kidney dis-ease. Moreover, the seeds of this particular condition were most likely set in a previous life.

It was reported however, that when Beethoven wrote his pastoral symphony, he had entered a momentary period of joy. Rejoicing his accomplishments was however, a rare occurrence for him. Without indulging in the transit stimulants, the natal catalysts for his brief lapses of happiness was most likely concerned with Jupiter (joy) in its fall, in melancholic Capricorn; and its sesquiquadrate to the MC, and Saturn (gloom). There are no soft aspects to Jupiter; hence the bringer of jollity [5] except for a sextile to the Ascendant. In some cases, sextiles can be unfavourable.

Thus, Beethoven enjoyed only brief, but nonetheless sudden intermissions of pleasure, and excitement — under which he had to learn to be 'intellectually inspired' for such limited amounts of time (Saturn). These sudden intervals of pleasure and excitement can be attributed to Uranus (excitement) in the seventh house, which is naturally ruled by Venus (pleasure).

During these brief interludes, where he felt inspired and entertaining, Beethoven managed to compile his memorable pastoral symphony.

Beethoven's intellectual skills emanated no less, from a previous life. This is displayed primarily by Pluto's quintile to the Ascendant, and the

East Point in Scorpio, which is Pluto's rulership sign. It is also displayed by Pluto's trine to brilliant and inspired Uranus; hence the planet of intellectual genius. This intellectual genius however, is further conveyed by Aquarius, the natural rulership sign of Uranus, on the cusp of the third house of communication. Essentially, the intellectual soul of Beethoven has always *communicated* via music. There is no doubt that the initial idea for his pastoral symphony came originally from a past life — fine-tuned in spirit (Neptune).

I conclude this particular case study with a profound quote from Beethoven himself, *"don't only practise your art, but force your way into its secrets."* [6]

On the whole, this is an intellectual testament to the trine between Uranus (observation), and Neptune (secrets). Despite having to live through appalling conditions, Beethoven still managed to further *electrify* his intellect.

Uranian Noticeable Distinguishedness

'Intellectual genius' is a relatively common term that seems to be fairly prevalent, especially amongst the classical composers of the bygone era. In the case of Beethoven, being referred to as an intellectual genius may very well be connected to Uranus's opposition to the Ascendant — conspicuous in Beethoven's natal chart.

Likewise, it was also a distinguishable pronouncement in the natal chart of Beethoven's equivalent; hence the German composer Richard Wagner. Thus, Wagner was equally gifted — boasting an elevated intellect. Wagner was also inspired by Beethoven's work. It has been said many times that Wagner's most prolific piece of work was the musical drama, *Das Rheingold*, which is perhaps symbolic to an influential Uranus, and a partially autonomous Neptune.

Sir Isaac Newton

Sir Isaac Newton was an English mathematician, physicist, astronomer, alchemist, theologian, and an author. Newton was widely recognized as one of the greatest mathematicians and physicists, and among the most influential scientists of all time. [7] By far, his best achievement, was for having formulated the theory of universal gravity. Newton also contributed to the universal theory of calculus.

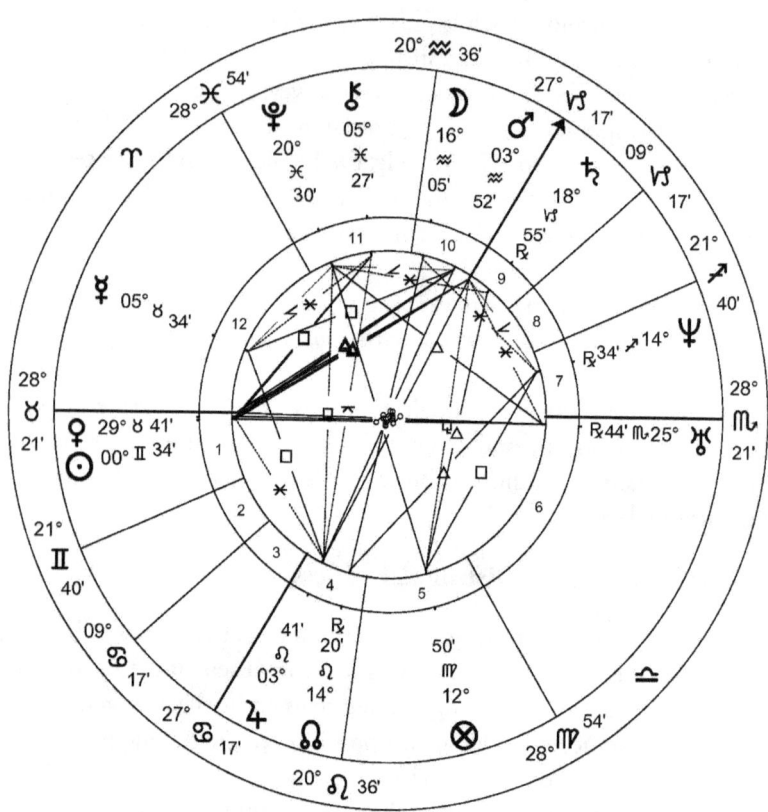

Natal Chart for Richard Wagner, 5/22/1813, 04:00, Leipzig, Germany

Uranian Tears in the Structure [8]

Sir Isaac Newton was born to a widowed mother, which was most likely the result of Uranus's sesquiquadrate to the Moon in the natal chart. Early in his childhood, Newton was sent to live with his grandmother, and was separated from his mother — a further consideration of the Uranus-Moon sesquiquadrate. But in spite of this, the Moon (childhood) is elevated, and domicile in Cancer. Moreover, the Moon's degree is *fortunate*, according to Lilly. Thus, the potentially favourable condition of the Moon meant that Newton most likely received ample nurturing and support, even though he was taken from his mother. Likewise, an abundant childhood would provide Newton with every opportunity to instinctively *focus* upon his futuristic objectives, which was most likely courtesy of Uranus in exaltation; and in the first house.

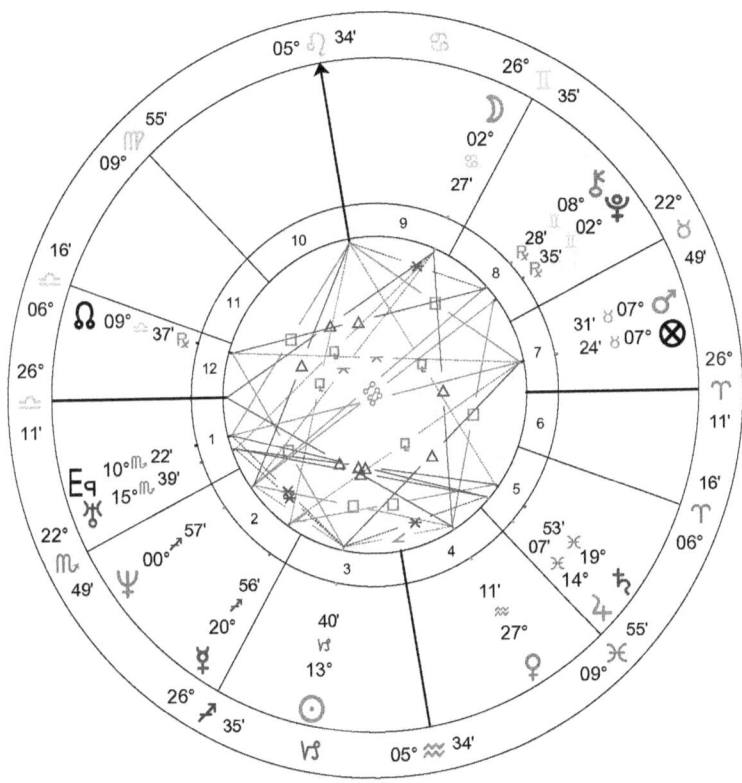

Natal Chart for Sir Isaac Newton, 1/4/1643, 01:38, Grantham, England

For the most part, Isaac Newton had been born to uncover a very important scientific truth; and to present his findings to the world at large. In the natal chart, the Moon is a significant part of a Grand Trine — fabricating the harmonious configuration with the Ascendant, and Venus. Thus, this advantageous Grand Trine would have also provided Newton with stability, and an instinctive sense of security — providing him with a good foothold on life. Essentially, the Grand Trine was his 'saving grace.'

The Uranian 'tear in the structure;' hence Newton's ability to eventually *conquer* the circumstances of his natal chart, is attributed mostly to the Moon's sesquiquadrate to Uranus. Such sequences would explain why shortly after his birth, Newton was *suddenly* taken away from his mother — quintessentially characteristic of this type of planetary alignment. The perpetrator for this misdeed was his stepfather. Ostensibly, the catalyst for this unkindly gesture, was Saturn's sesquiquadrate to the MC, which occupies Uranus's polarity sign. Thus, both of these difficult sesquiquadrates symbolized the tears in the structure of this otherwise ingenious, and inventive natal chart.

Meanwhile, the husband of Isaac Newton's grandmother, was a minister within the Anglican church; thus, Newton was to be *nurtured* in a house of God. However, Newton still had to learn to *adapt* to his new environment; a difficult task when there are sesquiquadrates present. In addition, this formidable characteristic is exhibited by the Moon's quincunx (adaptation), to Neptune (God). Moreover, the Moon and Neptune are in a partial mutual reception. Here, the Moon tenants the ninth house, which is naturally ruled by Sagittarius (religion). Sagittarius is Neptune's accidental sign. Neptune tenants the second house, which is ruled by the Moon in its exaltation in Taurus. Indeed, a refection of Newton's 'higher purpose.'

Newton's religious *upbringing* was embodied further by Jupiter, which is the natural planetary ruler of the ninth house. Jupiter tenants Pisces; the sign which is naturally ruled by Neptune. Possessing a scientific, and a somewhat rebellious brain (Uranus), Newton would no doubt have found his childhood difficult, but well within the boundaries of *acceptable*. This is because, Newton transformed himself into an 'unusual Christian;' hence an alternate belief. At some point in his adult years, Newton had dismantled the traditional bible teachings, for the doctrine of the trinity, whilst keeping his beliefs to himself. [9]

This rebellious mark on his otherwise untarnished character, symbolized another 'tear in the structure,' in Newton's natal chart. Newton's dismantling of the traditional bible teachings, is no doubt a final deduction to the close trine between Jupiter (religion), and Uranus (dismantling traditional structures). The fact that Newton kept his beliefs to himself can be attributed to Uranus's accidental sign; hence reticent Scorpio, the sign of Uranu's exaltation. In addition, the natural ruler of Scorpio, Pluto is domicile, in the eighth house, and opposes Neptune.

Therefore, Newton was not inclined to *openly* convey his spiritual beliefs. But they were no doubt a source of concern to him.

Meanwhile, all of these 'tears in the structure' within his natal chart, did, in effect, keep Isaac Newton on the alternate path — one that would eventually denote scientific genius. Predominantly, these tears in the structure *underpinned* the gravity field around his chart — placed there by Uranus in exaltation in the first house. Uranus would eventually construct the foundations for the making of a scientific genius.

Newton later founded the now familiar quotation, which is celebrated throughout the scientific community; "*to any action there is always an opposite and equal reaction.*" This prominent expression conveys the ultimate meaning and purpose of Uranus in his natal chart.

Uranian/Karmic Infirmities

Perhaps, the most significant mental condition that Newton endured in his life was the indisposition known simply as irritability (Uranus in the first house). The irritability was initially caused by his depression, which he endured for brief periods throughout his life. There were however, karmic implications attached to his short temperedness; hence irritability. Thus, the implications are displayed primarily by the South Node's position in the sixth house of health, and which is squared to the Moon.

A further karmic indicator is the North Node in the twelfth house of karma, which is squared the Sun. The accidental planetary ruler of the South Node, Mars (temper), opposes Uranus. This powerful opposition would bring about sudden temper tantrums. Not only did Uranus awake the intellectuality of Newton's brain to his scientific genius, but it awoke his subconscious to the karmic infirmities, which were evident in a past life.

Hitherto, Isaac Newton honed his scientific genius in a past life; which is consistent with the South Node (past lives) in the sixth house of work. However, he also *forged* his temper in a past life, as Aries (angry disposition), is the accidental ruler of the sixth house. This indignation is also displayed by Mars (the ruler of Aries), laying close to the midpoint between Saturn and Pluto. It was also claimed that Newton suffered from paranoid delusions.

This unfortunate characteristic is most likely reflected via his Pluto-Neptune opposition, which leaves me to conclude with another Newton quote, *"I can calculate the movement of the stars, but not the madness of men."*

Uranian Conquests

Generally, the world of science considers Isaac Newton to be a scientific genius. To confer this, in the natal chart, Uranus is both superior, and advantageous. It is also adept; in its propensity towards experimental and technological science. As we have already established, Uranus is in its exaltation in Scorpio, and rises in the first house. Thus, Newton was a person who was always ahead of time — innovative and unique in his thoughts and actions — determined to transform his ideas into unique perspectives. Newton was also *predisposed* to changing the world with his seemingly radical conceptions.

Newton theorized that the same force that caused an apple to fall from a tree was also the force that kept the Moon in place. Thus, Newton worked tirelessly (Saturn), until he had developed the law of 'universal gravitation,' which appeared in his book, *Mathematical Principles of Natural Philosophy*.

Further, in the natal chart, Uranus makes close trines to Jupiter (philosophy) and Saturn (natural law). In addition, Uranus sextiles the Sun. Moreover, the Sun's degree is *fortunate*, according to Lilly; meaning that Newton was given every opportunity to present his ambitious conjecture (Sun in Capricorn), to the collective of humankind (Uranus). Mercury (mathematics and writing), squares Jupiter and Saturn. However, Mercury's degree is *fortunate*. As a result, Newton was considered to be a brilliant mathematician (Mercury); which was also the result of having Uranus in the first house. Uranus does however, share its penchant for mathematics with Mercury.

With all of these Uranian fusions *electrifying* his natal chart, it is hardly surprising then that Isaac Newton became one of the greatest, and legendary scientists of modern times. Furthermore, Newton's chart is evenly balanced. Moreover, with an exalted Uranus in the first house, the gravity circling his chart, so to speak, is 'symmetrically synthesized.' The overall consistency of the chart's gravity, is maintained by the trines from Uranus to Jupiter, and to Saturn. We all have gravity,; hence a form of 'intellectual defence,' situated around our natal chart.

Its blanket stability however, relies solely upon the quality, and the strength of planetary aspects to Uranus.

To further highlight this remarkable 'Uranian creation,' — symbolizing Newton, and his natal chart, I would like to finish with another quote from the great intellectual himself. This particular expression wholly describes the scientific nature of Uranus in the natal chart. Thus, *"gravity explains the motions of the planets, but I cannot explain who sets the planets in motion."*

The latter, denoting spiritual scepticism, which is otherwise *consistent* within the chart; hence the 'tears in the structure.'

Uranian Perplexity

Newton could not explain who sets the planets in motion. According to the *Akashic Records*, the angelic host, who are the guardians of the physical universe, are ultimately responsible for the movements of the planets. In the natal chart, Neptune's dissociate square to Venus would no doubt be responsible for Newton's spiritual confusion. Newton was a brilliant scientist, mathematician, and a writer. But with an anaretic Neptune frictionally joined to a 'scientific-orientated' Venus in the house of the grave, and which tenants Uranus's rulership sign of Aquarius, any chance Newton had of resolving his spiritual perplexity *died* at his birth.

Indeed, Isaac Newton was deemed an intellectual genius, where understanding matters of an empirical nature were concerned. But for matters of faith however, Newton remained *inexperienced* — exhibited by Uranus's conjunction to the East Point. Perhaps, he was meant to somehow *transform* (Scorpio first house) his notion surrounding his flawed spiritual beliefs — coalescing his intellectual brilliance with a powerful prompting that echos through the internal embodiment of his soul — constantly reverberating the fact that the divine *does* exist. This is the ultimate purpose of the Neptune-Pluto opposition. However, with Venus sitting at the apex of the opposition, Newton's Uranian (Aquarius) impulses were 'electrically charged.' Thus, Isaac Newton was a *personification* of Uranian intellect.

Ada Lovelace

Ada Lovelace, otherwise known as, Augusta Ada Byron, was an English mathematician, and a writer. Lovelace was the daughter of the well-known English poet, Lord Byron.

First and foremost, Lovelace was best known for her work on Charles Babbage's proposed mechanical general-purpose computer; hence the Analytical Engine. [10]

In point of fact, the computer was never built. Nevertheless, her work on this project was considered to be outstanding. Today, Ada Lovelace

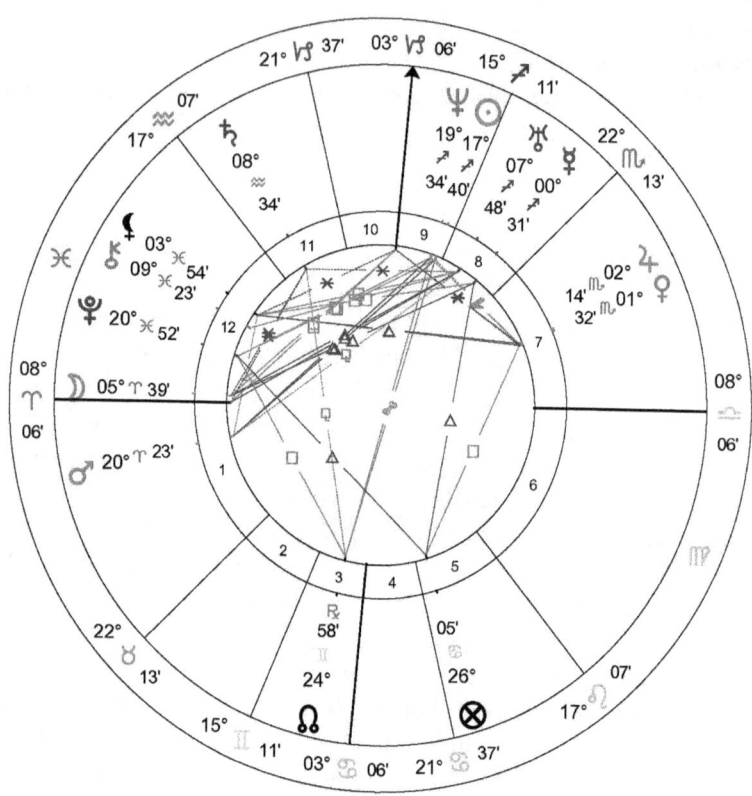

Natal Chart for Ada Lovelace, 12/10/1815, 13:00, London, England

is adjudged to be the world's first computer programmer. She wrote a series of books on the subject; the most popular being *Ada's Algorithm*.

Uranian Repressed Configurations

In the natal chart, Uranus's influence is, in some measure, *constricted*. This is because it stations between the Sun and Mercury — residing in the eighth house of death and transformation — loosely conjunct Mercury. Expressly, Uranus is not totally independent, which, ideally it should be, in order to be able to function correctly — relaying its ideas to the collective mind.

Throughout her life, Lovelace worked on many innovative creations, but they were not solely her own. In effect, and because the influence of

Uranus is *coalesced* in the natal chart, this planet therefore needs the assistance of other brains in order to function; in order to add to its own intellectual perfection. Having Uranus in the eighth house however, and with no major hard aspects to it, is perhaps the reason why none of her projects came to fruition. Thus, the intention, not the idea, *died* before it was assembled.

Integrated with other planets in the eighth house, and without having too much room to manoeuvre, Uranus would have found it somewhat disconcerting to successfully implement its innovative/transformational intention. Under normal circumstances, Uranus is a planet that is instrumental in the operations of its own unique style. Conventionally, the eighth house is illustrative to a zone of suppression; and Uranus doesn't recognize concealment in any form.

Typically, innovative transformation would be the ultimate purpose of Uranus in the eighth house; hence to *increase* its intellectual and technological perfection. However, because of its proximity to Mercury, its understudy, it has to relay on other minds to function. Lovelace was essentially an inventive utopian; which is indicative of Uranus in the eighth house. This notion is also symptomatic to an elevated Neptune in the ninth house.

Symbolically, with Uranus tenanting the eighth house, and adjacent erudite Mercury, the eighth house could have been *transformed* into the house of intellectual/technological modification, and conversion. Although Uranus receives no major hard aspects, the degree of Uranus is nonetheless lame (deficient), according to Lilly. Thus, the deficient degree is a further reason why Lovelace remained *unprivileged* in witnessing the construction of the Analytical Engine, in which she had invested so much of her time, and intellectual energy.

When we successfully apply intellectual energy onto a project we are working on, it is similar to *electrifying* it with an electrical discharge; which is similar to the effects of a lightning strike. Thus, we can either destroy it, or alternatively, it can proliferate. According to the UK Met Office, the extreme heat of lightning strikes upon the ground causes nitrogen to bond with oxygen to create nitrogen oxides, which combine with moisture in the air to fall as rain — helping to sustain natural growth. [11]

Persistence of Uranian Vision

After completing her work with Babbage, Lovelace continued to work on other projects. In 1844, she *voiced* her desire to create a mathematical model, which would calculate how the brain gives rise to thoughts, and nerves to feelings. Hence, this she would have named, 'a calculus of the nervous system.' Unfortunately, she never actually achieved this aim, which was mostly due to funding problems (eighth house). For the most part however, Lovelace had acquired her interest in the brain's functions from her mother. [12]

As we have already ascertained, Uranus loosely conjuncts Mercury. Thus, this methodical and structured conjunction, is perhaps a cosmic testament to why Lovelace worked alongside Charles Babbage on the Analytical Engine; hence Analytical (Mercury) Engine (Uranus). In addition, Mercury's degree is anaretic, and Mercury is in its detriment. Coupled with the lame degree of Uranus, Mercury's anaretic degree is perhaps another reason why she never got her projects 'off the ground' so to speak.

Furthermore, Mercury's wide conjunction with Uranus would have symbolized her open intellectual desire towards mathematical inventions. Moreover, the trine from Uranus to the Moon (mother), is representative of her inherent interests in the brain; which were no doubt karmic, as the Moon tenants the twelfth house of karma. The twelfth house is also intercepted, and domicile, which explains mostly why she acquired her abilities in a past life. Her past life intellectual abilities are also symbolized by Uranus's closely linked trine to the Ascendant; coupled by the intercepted Pluto in the twelfth house, which is square to the Sun and Neptune, which is the natural ruler of the twelfth house.

In practice, Ada Lovelace should have brought her scientific ideas into a world of concrete experience, and acceptance, and not into the usual dismissive backdrop of no creation. Her *solid* scientific ideas are also displayed by Uranus's encouraging sextile to domicile Saturn. But perhaps, Saturn's square to directional Jupiter and Venus placed a sweeping dampener on everything.

Jupiter is closely conjunct Venus, which would ordinarily represent a benevolent manifestation of good fortune. But, Venus is indisposed in Scorpio, which most likely meant that it failed to provide adequate benefic qualities, which were expected, especially being alongside Jupiter. Thus, Venus failed to support Lovelace in her vital Uranian work; even though Venus tenants the sign that naturally rules the eighth house. Venus is also domicile, but detrimental in Scorpio. In addition, Venus has only one soft aspect, which is a sextile to the MC. So, for sextiles to display 'potential,' these aspects do need support from other planets; particularly via the quincunx.

Essentially, the natal chart for Ada Lovelace is *unequivocal*, but remains relatively *unproductive*. Therefore, Lovelace's 'Uranian capacity' was to foster her intellectual ideas — until mankind was ready to receive them. This is often the purpose of possessing such a highly-intellectual, and technological Uranus — bordering on sheer brilliance.

Uranian Reminiscences

The Uranus-Mercury conjunction is reminiscent of past life karma — denoting potential intellectual superiority. In addition to this, we see that Pluto, which is the natural ruler of the eighth house, residing in the twelfth house of karma, and squares Neptune. The twelfth house also houses the Black Moon, which is squared to Uranus, and Mercury. Uranus is sesquiquadrate to Mars; and Mars trines a deficient Neptune, according to Lilly. Neptune is also the traditional ruler of the twelfth house. Mercury is the traditional ruler of the sixth house, which is the polarity of the twelfth. In this chart, the sixth house is domicile.

Unquestionably, these are all cosmic indicators that Lovelace *developed* her highly-intellectual brain in a past life, and possibly in spirit. In essence, Lovelace incarnated to *electrify* the advancing, and the inventive seat of humankind.

Unfortunately, Ada Lovelace died from uterine cancer in 1852. This condition also had karmic connotations attached to it. According to reports, Lovelace was often ill; initially beginning in her childhood. This is significant to the Moon in the twelfth house, square the MC. Death from uterine cancer was no doubt caused initially by Pluto's square to Neptune (cancer), and the Sun. Pluto receives no soft aspects in the chart — making the planet susceptible to fluid-orientated dispositions. Pluto is also in mutual reception to Jupiter. Here, Pluto is the traditional ruler of Scorpio, which Jupiter accidentally rules. Jupiter is the ancient ruler of Pisces, which Pluto accidentally rules.

This reflects an instinctive desire to leave her mark of wisdom upon a regressive, disenchanted and power-orientated world, which is backed up by her final quote, *"the more I study, the more insatiable do I feel my genius for it to be."*

So, to reiterate finally, the key to these karmic reminiscences is *electrified* and *intellectual* Uranus, which accidentally rules Sagittarius. Jupiter is the modern ruler of Sagittarius, and the traditional ruler of the twelfth house. Pluto in the twelfth, naturally rules the eighth house, which Uranus tenants. Simply speaking, Lovelace incarnated to hone her intellect, and was *guided* throughout her life by the arrow of modern invention.

Thus, the intellectual arrow of invention is 'powered' conversely by Uranian electricity in this coalesced chart.

Carl Jung

Carl Gustav Jung was a Swiss psychiatrist, and a psychoanalyst, who propositioned the postulation for analytical psychology. Overall, Jung's work has been most influential, particularly in the fields of psychiatry, anthropology, archaeology, literature, philosophy, and religious studies. Initially, Jung worked as a research scientist. [13]

Jung proposed, and later developed the concepts for the extraverted, and the introverted personality, archetypes, and the collective unconscious. Today, Carl Jung is recognized as one of the most influential psychiatrists of all time. [14]

Uranian Intellectual Artistry

In this 'intellectually-structured' natal chart, Uranus has the potential to be *artistically* commanding, innovative, ingenious, and highly creative. Yet, Uranus is in its detriment in Leo; but nonetheless it has taken a front seat — supremely in a *managing* and *originative* position in the natal chart. Uranus is also adjacent the Sun, which is Uranus's polarity planet. Both the Sun and Uranus tenant the seventh house of social consultation, and creative finesse. Jung was a skilled ambassador who enlightened the masses. Moreover, Uranus's square to a fortunate Moon, according to Lilly, and in exaltation, gave Jung the ability to *stimulate* and *revitalize* (electrify), the brains of his patients.

There is also a wide trine between Mars and Uranus; which meant that Jung most likely had the need to work independently of others — proceeding on his own volition — without any form of restraint. Jung did however, pioneer the concept of *individuation*. This represents a psychological process of differentiation of the self out of each individual's conscious and unconscious elements. Thus, Jung considered it to be the main task of human development.

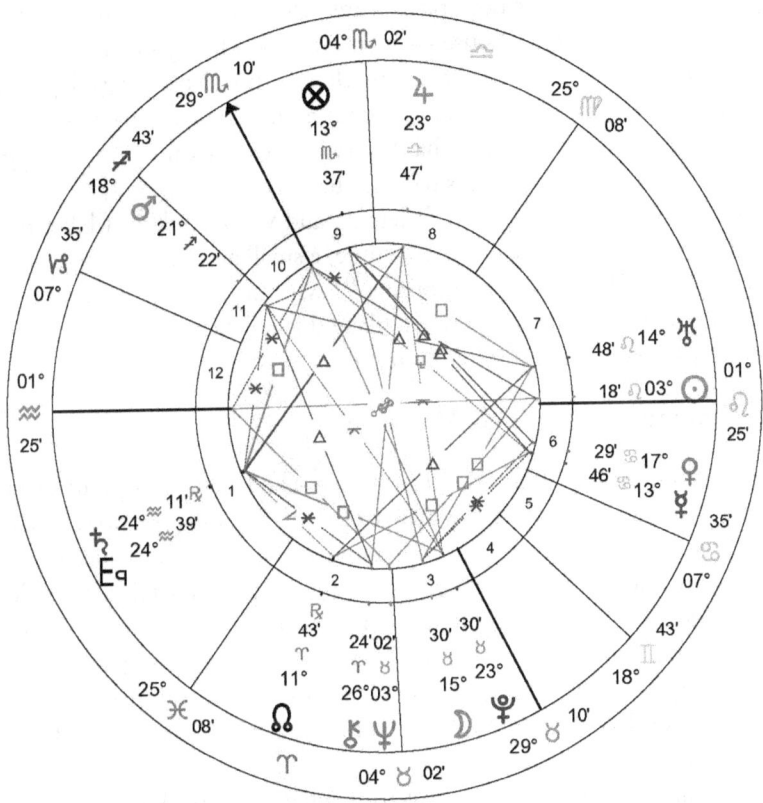

Natal Chart for Carl Jung, 7/26/1875, 19:24, Kesswil, Switzerland

This 'formative conjecture' is perhaps typical of Uranus in the seventh house. Jung also created some of the best-known psychological concepts, including the theory of collective unconscious; which is very Uranian, and Neptunian. In addition, his teachings relating to collective unconsciousness may also be applicable to Saturn rising in the first house — exactly conjunct the East Point. Saturn is also domicile in Uranus's rulership sign of Aquarius. It seems that his psychological/intellectual knowledge was acquired/honed in a previous life.

Carl Jung was adjudged to be a 'unique artist.' He was also a writer. However, the artist within him, is also admissible to Uranus, alongside the Sun, in the seventh house of artistry. Artistry may also be applicable to the closely linked conjunction between a domicile Mercury in its natural house, and Venus (art). Venus is also in mutual reception with the Moon. Therefore, the energy of the Moon/Venus mutual rulership *fuses*

Uranus. This is because both planets are *tethered* to Uranus's intellectual presence in the seventh house — with the Moon being squared — and Venus forming a wide semi-sextile to Uranus. Jung's paintings depicted lavish (Venus), abstract (Uranus), and unusual (Uranus), images — portraying the Sun and Moon. It has been suggested that his paintings represented the 'goings on' in his patient's brains.

Both the planetary degrees of Mercury and Venus are lame (deficient), and pitted, according to Lilly. Therefore, a small amount of Jung's written work is still awaiting publication. [15] Mercury's lame degree, and its sesquiquadrate to the MC, is most likely the malefactor in this scenario; hence the lengthy delay in publication.

A Uranian/Karmic Style Marriage

In 1903, Carl Jung married Emma Rauschenbach. As a point of interest, Rauschenbach was the owner of *IWC Schaffhausen*, which is an international watch company — manufacturing luxury timepieces.

Meanwhile, in the natal chart, Venus (marriage) is bi-quintile the domicile Saturn. Ironically, Jung was older (Saturn), than his wife (Venus). In my opinion, the conviction for this partnership was originally (Uranus), forged in a previous life. This is reminiscent of Capricorn, which is Saturn's rulership sign, and which accidentally rules the twelfth house of karma.

Bi-quintiles are said to possess karmic qualities and characteristics — honed in past lives. The very notion of a Uranian/karmic marriage is *exemplified* by the bi-quintile between Venus, and Saturn, which tenants Uranus's sign of Aquarius. This is coupled by Uranus's tenure of Venus's traditional rulership of the seventh house. Furthermore, and based on this evidence, Jung's intellectual abilities were doubtlessly forged in a past life.

Interestingly, Jung's marriage to Rauschenbach, also reflected these karmic connotations, which included her ownership of an international watch company — producing industrially advanced, and luxury (Venus in Aquarius), timepieces (Saturn).

A Brilliant Uranian Psychiatrist

Carl Jung was considered to be a brilliant psychiatrist. His unique and intellectual style (Uranus) of therapy, which is recognized solely as the 'Jungian treatment', not only improved the symptoms (Moon), it also increased the overall psychological wellbeing of his patients. This is most likely reminiscent of Uranus in the seventh house, and square the Moon. Moreover, Jungian psychotherapy has been proven to be effective, as well as being cost-effective. [16] Thus, being cost-effective is no doubt another characteristic of the Venus (cost/money), bi-quintile, to the Uranus-influenced Saturn ; Saturn personifies the notion of 'cost-effective.'

All of these Uranian natal influences leaves me to conclude this case study with a quote from Jung himself, which is indicative to his intellectual natal chart:

"Knowing your own darkness is the best method for dealing with the darkness of other people." This is very indicative to Saturn in the first house; and its close square to Pluto, which is in its detriment.

Bill Gates

William Henry Gates is an American business magnate, and a philanthropist. Gates is also the co-founder of *Microsoft*. During his career at *Microsoft*, Gates held the positions of chairman, chief executive officer, president, and chief software architect. He was a major entrepreneur of the microcomputer revolution of the 1970s and 1980s. [17]

Gates is regarded as being 'outstandingly intelligent,' and a 'computer genius.' He once said in an interview that *"his ambition was to make dreams come true."* [18]

Uranian Intellectual Innovation

Bill Gates has, for all intents and purposes, a very 'favoured' and 'intellectually-ingenious' natal chart. First and foremost, Uranus is stationed in a very commanding position. Thus, Uranus tenants the first house — rising on the Ascendant. Thus, rising planets are given a more direct channel of expression; especially in the personality. Even though Uranus is in its detriment in Leo, the degree in which it is placed is *fortunate*, according to Lilly. Principally, this means that his 'electrified and creative self-projection' is one that is tinged by a need to take risks; especially through unconventional means.

In addition, this chart implies that Gates possesses three-dimensional vision, and is very imaginative, especially within the field of scientific investigation, which is why he has succeeded in becoming a highly intellectual, and a prosperous entrepreneur. Above all else, Bill Gates is a person who 'gets the job done.' Those who are closest to him say he is a

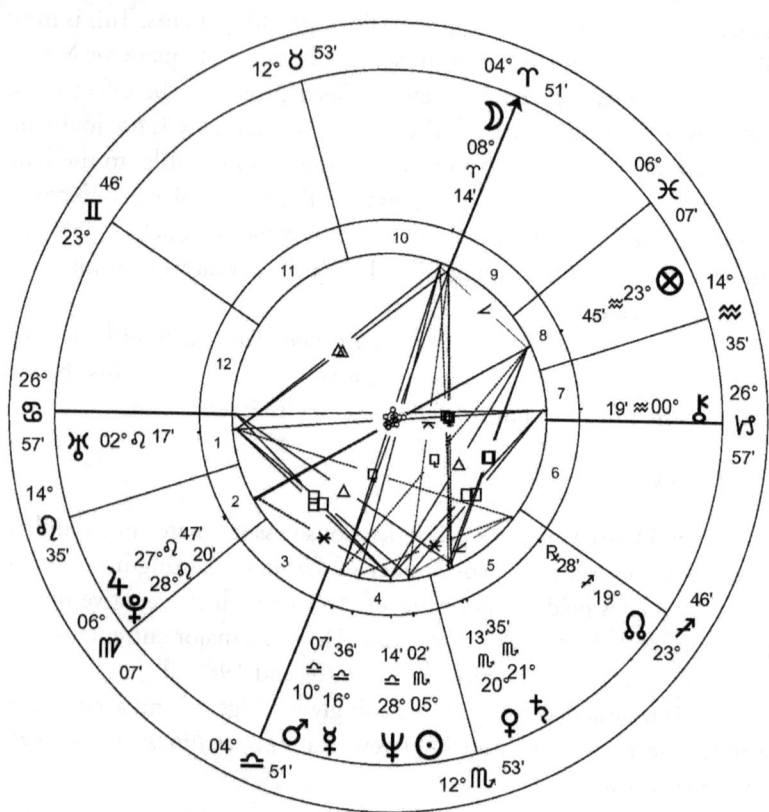

Natal Chart for Bill Gates, 10/28/1955, 22:00, Seattle, Washington

'modern-day genius;' especially within the field of Uranian technological innovation.

Uranus also squares the Sun. Some have argued that Gates is a very complex individual, which is a characteristic emblematic of Uranus squared to the Sun, and hazy Neptune. However, Gates has attracted controversy on more than one occasion; especially in the way he carries out his responsibilities, and obligations. Gates is extremely intelligent, and highly intellectual, which is also indicative to a Sun-Uranus square. Moreover, this configuration involves two planets that are a natural polarity, which increases self-awareness. Despite this however, a Sun-Uranus square can 'draw out' the worse qualities in other people. This is perhaps one reason why he has endured endless criticism.

Uranus also squares Neptune; which tends to leave him at odds with the world at large — a consideration that became relevant during the

Covid pandemic (see further on). Uranus also trines the Midheaven, and the Moon, which promotes diligence, and heightened feelings.

The Uranus trine to the Moon and MC, which are closely conjunct, are reminiscent of a decisive, but in some respects, *subtle* lightning strike in the natal chart. This configuration has the potential to introduce new and contemporary ideas into the cutting edge of his business. The Aries MC however, with the natural ruler Mars opposing it, was also the reason why Gates *launched* his ideas at knife point so to speak — thrusting them into the heart of the organization. Thus, for many years, *Microsoft* was at the leading edge of marketing and technological businesses. Some have said that without Gates at the helm, *Microsoft* would not have been as successful, as they are now. Moreover, Gates was responsible for creating miraculous, and unexpected breakthroughs in software innovation, which allowed *Microsoft* to remain at the top of the technological pile, in a manner of speaking.

Furthermore, with Uranus trine the Moon and the MC, Gates became *obsessed* in maintaining the overall optimism of his workforce — making sure that they were continually stimulated and infused — just as he was. Gates always commanded respect however, which he got, and he was often one step ahead of others in the company. Over the years, Gates has been accused of being unpredictable; especially where displaying his true feelings are concerned. As a result, many in the business world have accused him of being too eccentric and outlandish. This may be so, but his irregular style has led him to acquire and maintain intellectual brilliance in a very competitive arena of expertise. This is all courtesy of Uranus's square to the Sun, and Neptune.

In essence, *Microsoft* simply *thrived* in a world of cutthroat advertising, thanks, in part, to Bill Gates.

Uranian Interchange

During the whole of his time at *Microsoft*, Bill Gates's visual *image* has changed dramatically. This personalized characteristic is consistent with having Uranus in the first house, squared to Neptune, and conjunct the Ascendant. Gates was always perceived initially as being a *brilliant*, but *ruthless* 'robber baron.' [19] This depiction is also consistent with Uranus in the first house, and squared to the Sun.

However, after Gates departed *Microsoft*, he turned his attention to philanthropy — donating millions of dollars to causes such as public health, education and poverty. For the most part, this is all representative to Uranus being on the periphery of humanitarianism, and charitableness.

Thus, he later became known as the 'techno-philanthropist.' These 'master strokes' are all indicative to Uranus conjunct the Ascendant.

Additionally, Venus is closely conjunct Saturn, and squares the close conjunction of Jupiter and Pluto in the natal chart. Venus and Saturn also trine the Ascendant, which *colonizes* the comforting and nurturing sign of Cancer — promoting his need for charitableness. Philanthropy represents a desire to promote the welfare of others, which is perhaps also reminiscent of Uranus conjunct the Cancer Ascendant. In a good number of cases, philanthropy is expressed by a generous donation of money (Jupiter/Pluto conjunction), to good causes (Uranus).

Meanwhile, Gates turned to his attention to philanthropy — giving money (Venus), to the good causes, in later in life (Saturn). By employing Uranus, particularly via an intellectual standpoint, Gates successfully managed to hone not only the planets penchant towards technological expertise, but also its humanitarian disposition. Hence, to employ these methods is the mark of a true genius at work.

Uranian Controversy

Uranus and Neptune are the planets that symbolize *misunderstandings*; particularly when they square a luminary, such as in this case, Uranus squares the Sun. Moreover, similar differences can occur when Uranus squares Neptune, as it does for Bill Gates. Neptune is also combust in the natal chart — 'blocking out' the planets natural radiance — bolstering the potential for more misunderstandings.

A recent example of misunderstandings occurred in 2021. Gates, along with a fellow businessman, became the objects for various baseless conspiracy theories, which surrounded the Covid-19 pandemic. [20] Essentially, the Uranus-Neptune square can be considered as a *distorted* alignment, thus attracting, in part, embarrassing controversies. Because of the conspiracies against him, Gates became suspicious, and paranoid about the world, as a whole.

Today however, he continues to invest more money towards the eradication of diseases (Neptune combust the Sun); particularly with concerns for dementia.

Despite what people think about his true intentions, Bill Gates, seems genuine enough (Uranus).

He also comes across as a good Samaritan (Uranus trine Moon/MC), especially in a world, which is perhaps more rebellious and uncontrollable than he himself.

Perhaps, Uranus in the first house reflects his unique points of view in this way? Nevertheless, I conclude this section with an appropriate and fitting quote from this highly-intellectual and ingenious individual. *"The belief that the world is getting worse, that we can't solve extreme poverty and disease, isn't just mistaken."* Gates most definitely believes in the unexpected power of intellectual wisdom.

Garry Kasparov

Garry Kimovich Kasparov is a Russian chess grandmaster, former world Chess Champion, writer, political activist and commentator.

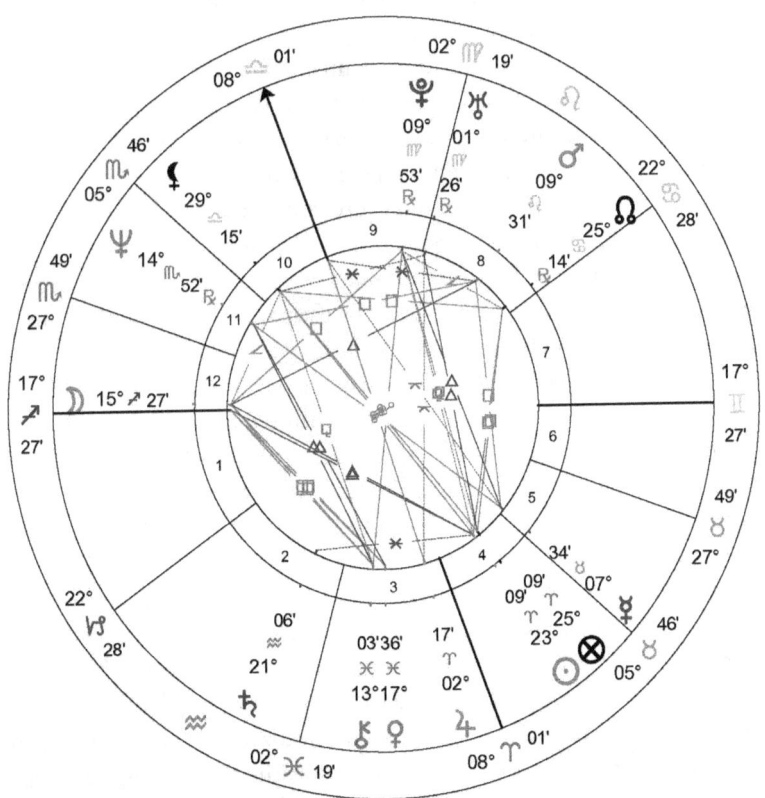

Natal Chart for Garry Kasparov, 4/13/1963, 23:45, Baku, Azerbaijan

Kasparov became the youngest ever undisputed Chess Champion in 1985, at the demanding age of 22.

Since retiring, Kasparov has devoted his time mostly to politics and writing. He formed the *United Civil Front* movement, and joined as a member of the *Other Russia* — a coalition which opposes the administration and policies of Vladimir Putin. [21]

Uranian Transfigurations

I wish to begin my initial analysis with a quote from Kasparov himself, which symbolizes the position of Uranus in his natal chart, which is *elevated*, and conjunct transformational Pluto. *"Avoid change for the sake of change."* This is a quote taken from his regular chess column, which illustrates 'transformational moves' in chess [22].

In the natal chart, this Uranian/Plutonian axiom is indicative to the wide conjunction between Uranus, symbolizing sudden change, and Pluto, which symbolizes long-term change; hence transformation. Notwithstanding, what Kasparov actually meant was before making changes, we should take the time to see what is working, and what is not, before we make the appropriate changes, which are necessary. This is also reminiscent of the Uranus and Pluto conjunction in his chart. Thus, Uranus brought about *awareness* from its eighth house tenure, whereas from the ninth house, Pluto *transformed* how the world at large viewed the game of chess. Pluto also *remodelled* Kasparov's perception of life.

Because of the highly progressive influence of Uranus in the natal chart, Garry Kasparov became the 'cutting edge' of competitive chess. In addition, the International Olympic Committee now considers chess to be a mainstream sport. [23] According to conventional astrological consensus, Aries and Scorpio are the signs, which produce the best chess players. Kasparov is a sun sign Aries; and the Sun trines an elevated Uranus. Therefore, Kasparov was always destined to be a competitive and brilliant chess player. But perhaps more importantly, he is always been responsive and amenable to new experiences.

Additional significators in the natal chart, which spotlight Kasparov's sporting propensities, are Jupiter's accidental rulership of Aries; in which Jupiter opposes the MC. Thus, Kasparov realized that he possessed the power and determination to do great things in his life. Jupiter is also trine a domicile Mars in the eighth house. Mars rules over competitive sports; and from the eighth house Mars is energetic and deeply enthusiastic — personifying a need to achieve great things. Moreover, Jupiter quincunxes Uranus. Ordinarily, this meant that Kasparov managed to *adjust* the public's perception and awareness of chess; therefore, *expanding* the overall interest towards the game.

Essentially, Kasparov somehow managed to *electrify* the game of chess; thus, making it more *exciting* (Uranus).

Developed Uranian Techniques

In a further, and perhaps *unusual* Uranian move, Kasparov took on IBM; namely the super-computer, nicknamed Deep Blue. This marked the ultimate Uranian engagement of man verses machine. In 1996, Kasparov managed to beat the super computer. This ultimate conquest appealed to both computer experts, and scientists alike (Uranus).

Most significantly however, Neptune, which is attributed as being the 'blue planet,' tenants the eleventh house in the natal chart. Thus, the eleventh house is Uranus's natural domain. Neptune is also in an esteemed mutual reception with Uranus. Here, Neptune occupies Scorpio, which is the sign that Uranus is exalted in, whereas Uranus tenants Virgo, the sign in which Neptune is in its detriment.

This is all significant to Kasparov's ultimate challenge with the IBM computer; particularly as Neptune loosely opposes Mercury, and Mercury trines Uranus, which *refines* the mutual reception — bolstering his artistic, imaginative and his idealistic side. In essence, Kasparov knew within his heart, that with perseverance, he could overcome his machine competitor. Furthermore, the trine between Mercury and Uranus personifies his inventive and original fluency; especially with his writing, and his shared commentary skills, which are evident today.

Kasparov's intellectual capabilities were no doubt honed in a previous life; which are, to a greater extent, indicative to the Black Moon's sextile to Pluto. Kasparov possesses a very high IQ, which adjudges him to be an intellectual genius. This is also determined by Saturn's accidental rulership of Aquarius, which is Uranus's rulership sign. His intellectual expertise is also exemplified by Saturn's sextiles to the Sun, and the Ascendant.

In this particular chart, Uranus most definitely signifies the unparalleled movement of expression.

Uranian Values

With a domicile Saturn in Uranus's rulership sign of Aquarius, and tenanting the second house, Kasparov had 'put down' scientific roots, which were strong and solid, and which had *emerged* initially from a past life. This is indicative to Saturn's square with Neptune.

Thus, a domicile Saturn linked to Neptune in this way, indicates someone who can profit the most — from investing the least.

Unquestionably, Kasparov's style was such, that he *invested* his Uranus intellect into acquiring his ultimate aspirations. In this life, he invested very little energy into attaining his objectives; because he had *honed* his electrified intellect in a past life. Thus, in this life, he reaped his Saturn/Uranus rewards — something he didn't achieve previously.

With that said, it just leaves me to conclude with a pertinent and karmic citation from Kasparov himself. *"Knowing is not enough; we must apply. Willing is not enough; we must do."* Hence, this is very much a 'must do' chart.

David Bowie

David Robert Jones, known professionally as David Bowie, was an English singer-songwriter, and an actor. Bowie was a leading figure in the music industry; and he is regarded as one of the most influential musicians of the twentieth century. Bowie was acclaimed by critics, and other musicians, particularly for his innovative work, especially during the 1970s.[24]

Uranian Imagery

Once again, I would like to begin with a quote from David Bowie himself; and which symbolizes the awesome power, and the intellectual influence of Uranus in his natal chart. *"I find only freedom in the realms of eccentricity."*

This testament is so characteristic of the sublime intellectual capacity — housed in the natal chart. Uranus lies in the northern hemisphere of the chart, near to the IC, and conjunct the North Node. However, the degree of the North Node is *fortunate*, according to Lilly; which is extremely auspicious for Uranus.

Essentially, Bowie incarnated with a view to 'breaking new ground;' hence changing the status quo, particularly within the music industry.

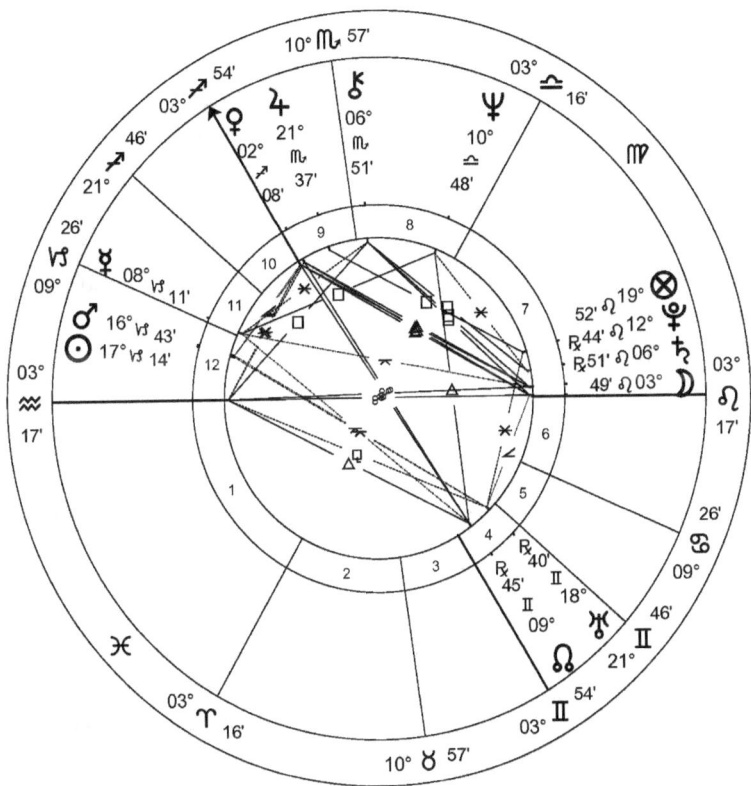

Natal Chart for David Bowie, 1/8/1947, 09:00, London, England

Thus, he managed to do exactly that; thanks to the North Node's fortunate degree — impacting Uranus. This contemporary conviction is also indicative to the wide trine between Uranus and Neptune (music). Bowie was unafraid to take chances, and he was always innovative in his approach to his work. In addition, he was much more progressive in his style of thinking, than the average musician, particularly during the 1970s. Bowie projected a personal image that was pleasingly divergent; a further characteristic of Uranus's conjunction to the North Node.

In much the same way, David Bowie continually *shifted* appearances from album to album; and he kept his fans and critics guessing about his next move. Within his era of intellectual eccentricity, Bowie helped to bring a *dramatic* sense of showmanship, and theatricality to the music industry. This is all indicative to the Uranian imagery that exposes his modern, and fashionable natal chart.

Uranus the Awakener

Bowie always exhibited a steadfast determination; wherein he was able to *adjust* the public's view towards his particular brand of music — displayed by the quincunx between Uranus and a domicile Mars — and the quincunx from Uranus to the Sun. However, Bowie did experience his fair share of problems with other people, particularly within the music industry — displayed by the Uranian-ruled Aquarian Ascendant's sesquiquadrate to Uranus. David Bowie was a person who did things 'his way.'

All things considered, Bowie always appeared to be a good-spirited and jubilant person, especially within the music industry. Today, David Bowie is considered to be a 'musical genius' — who changed the tempo of music forever.

The Uranian Space Oddity

Bowie was not an instant success with the public at large. It took him many years to *perfect* his unusual style. During the latter half of the 1960s, and the early 1970s, he moved from band to band, in order to acquire recognition. At the time, he considered this chopping and changing as an 'area of disappointment and frustration.' In the natal chart, frustration and disappointment are indicative to the sesquiquadrate between the Ascendant and Uranus. Sesquiquadrates demand that we develop persistence, and patience. Essentially, they require that we 'chill out,' which is what Bowie eventually did.

Bowie's initial success arrived when he released the single *Space Oddity*, in 1969. Thus, Space Oddity was Bowie's first major single release; and a major breakthrough towards his ongoing success. Furthermore, the title, and the lyrics of this song were very *Uranian*.

Hitherto, Bowie's earliest frustrations, were also the result of a deficient (pitted) Saturn opposing the Ascendant. As a result, Bowie always felt at odds with the world — no doubt the ramifications of such a tense and hard opposition. Moreover, these feelings of 'being at cross purposes' were indeed karmic; and emanate *equally* from the adjacent conjunction between the Sun and Mars, in Saturn's rulership sign of Capricorn — in the twelfth house of karma. In addition, the Sun and Mars square Neptune; thus, personifying his feelings of being at odds even more. However, with the Sun and Mars's quincunx to Uranus, Bowie needed to adjust his temperament — fitting in to a world he wasn't really a part of — a world which was not ready for him. Ultimately, he was the quintessential space oddity.

Furthermore, Bowie struggled with mental health issues throughout the course of his life — alcohol addiction and drug abuse. Before he died however, he became extremely vocal about these issues that plagued in his life. Thus, the Sun and Mars's square to Neptune; ruling drugs and alcohol addiction, was most likely the principle catalyst for these types of problems.

Moreover, the Moon and Saturn's oppositions to the Ascendant were most likely the catalysts for his mental health problems — coupled by Mercury's square to Neptune. Interestingly, Mercury tenants the house that Uranus naturally rules; hence the eleventh. Thus, an intellectual symbol, which *impresses* Uranus's interchangeable authority upon the natal chart even more. One could almost say that the Bowie's chart is *radioactive*.

Lazarus, a Multidimensional Image of Uranus

Lazarus is the title of David Bowie's final and classical song. Lazarus was intended to be a self-epitaph. Hence, Lazarus was released two days before his death; and it is very characteristic of his ultimate demise. Thus, Lazarus symbolizes a new multidimensional life — born from the ashes of a previous one. In the video, Bowie was initially performing this song from his death bed. [25]

Recently, Lazarus was interpreted as, a song referring to Bowie's prediction of increased fame, following his death. Furthermore, the lyrics to Lazarus are very Uranian indeed, particularly the verse. *'I'm so high it makes my brain whirl. Dropped my cell phone down below.'* Ironically, dropping his cell phone down below, could be an intellectual testament to Uranus in his chart, which is positioned 'down below.'

Regrettably, David Bowie passed away on the 10th of January 2016. This was two days after his 68th birthday. His final words were, *"it has been my doorway of perception and the house that I live in."* While it is not clear what he actually meant, we can assume that these words illustrate the higher meaning to the ancient fable of Lazarus. David Bowie was most definitely a soul who was versed within the Uranian field of intellectual aptitude.

The Sudden Passing of Lazarus

In the natal chart, Uranus is positioned in the fourth house of the grave; hence the point of physical departure. In effect, the fourth house represents the 'death bed.' Lazarus, which symbolized both Uranus, and Bowie's modern intellect lies in his death bed, reminiscing methodically about his life (Uranus conjunct North Node). Bowie's departure from liver cancer however, was precipitated principally by transit Jupiter's quincunx to Uranus and the North Node — with Jupiter overseeing the liver. In addition, Saturn's transit opposition to Uranus and the North Node secured his ultimate fate — with Saturn overseeing cancer.

Transit Neptune's square to Uranus, and the North Node, poured water over the infirmity — transcending the damaging effects of the cancer.

Lazarus, which was the 'metaphorical silhouette' present at Bowie's death *recapitulates* the concrete notion that eternal life *will* follow physical death. Furthermore, Uranus's sextile to Pluto in the natal chart implies that Bowie's life was a combination of intellectual planning — followed by sudden and long-term transformations. Perhaps, this notion was the basis for the arrangement of his song Ashes to Ashes, which is also symbolic to the emblematic life of Lazarus.

Bowie once said, *"the truth is of course is that there is no journey. We are arriving and departing all at the same time."* This leaves me to conclude that he had indeed honored the purpose of Uranus in the fourth house; and conjunct the North Node.

Within the course of his natural life, David Bowie *electrified* his musical brain's intellect — innovating his ultimate Uranian purpose. Long may he continue to innovate his unique intellect.

Bob Marley

Robert Nesta Marley was a Jamaican singer, musician and songwriter; and was considered to be a pioneer of reggae music. In addition, Marley *fused* the musical genres of reggae, ska, and rocksteady into his own original and unique harmonizations — communicated in his distinctive vocal and song writing style. [26] Thus, Marley's voice was considered to be an omnipresent cry in an expanding electronic world of intellectual arts and crafts. Furthermore, Marley's intellectual contributions have left an indelible imprint upon the overall music profession.

Bob Marley remains an important portrayal of genius within the world's collective musical consciousness.

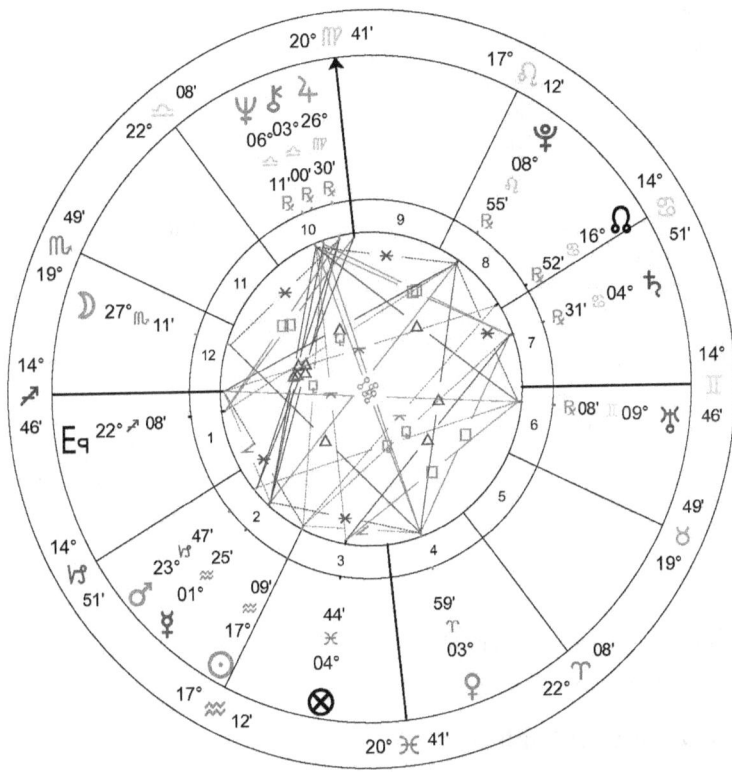

Natal Chart for Bob Marley, 2/6/1945, 02:30, St. Ann's Bay, Jamaica

A Dedicated Intellectual (Uranian) Genius

Throughout his distinguished life, and his eminent musical career, Bob Marley brought to the fore the importance of freedom, and the significance of liberation. These Uranian concepts were the focal point for many of his songs; the most popular of which was his Redemption Song.

"Love the life you live, live the life you love." This profound quote from Bob Marley is very symbolic of Uranus's *electrified* influence in the natal chart. Thus, in the natal chart, a particularly prominent configuration is Uranus's sextile to Venus. This symbolizes, in part, his love for humanity, which is essentially representative of this underlying expression. In point of fact, many of Marley's songs *highlighted* this exquisite perception.

Uranus the Awakener

However, his love of humanity was born from hatred, loathing, and suppression — dedicating his life to a higher intellectual cause, which is significant of the Uranus-Venus sextile.

"Don't gain the world and lose your soul, wisdom is better than silver or gold." Indeed, another profound expression from this humanitarian and magnanimous maestro. Be that the case, this particular expression signifies the Sun (gold, and the world), residing in the sign of Uranus's natural rulership; hence Aquarius. In addition, the Sun's degree is *fortunate*, according to Lilly. Moreover, the Sun makes a harmonistic trine to Uranus, symbolizing the ability to achieve the impossible; and for intellectual expansion.

The Uranian ruled Sun has also formed a sesquiquadrate to Saturn, symbolizing an ability to acquire wisdom through problematic adversity.

Uranus also sextiles Pluto; symbolizing an opportunity to overcome misfortune. Further, the Moon (silver), tenants Pluto's natural rulership sign of Scorpio, to which the Moon's degree is *deficient* (pitted), according to Lilly. The Moon's afflicted degree typifies Marley's early life struggles.

Uranus and Mercury are also in mutual reception — reflecting a polarized and abstract mentality — coupled by an intellectual genius.

Finetuned Uranian Karma

Both of these citations, combined by all of this Uranus influence, are the epitome for all of Marley's highly analytical songs. Marley's songs are also tinged with a measure of emotional regret, and perhaps despondency, which is also reminiscent of the Moon's imperfect degree. However, the trine between Uranus and musical Neptune most likely meant that Marley was in no doubt a melodious genius — born from the watery depths of conflict. Therefore, his dedication to his music stemmed from a past life, which is characteristic of the trine between Uranus and the Black Moon. His intellectual finesse is exemplified by Uranus's opposition to the 'finely tuned arrow' — representative of Marley's well-placed Sagittarian Ascendant.

The East Point; hence the Equatorial Ascendant, also lies in Sagittarius, which is also the accidental rulership sign on the twelfth house — denoting past life karma. Jupiter, the natural ruler of Sagittarius, is *elevated*; and lies close to the MC. This 'karmic and cosmically calibrated administration,' provided Marley with a likeable, and a conceptual temperament — necessary for honing his humanitarian attitude on life.

No Women No Cry

No Women No Cry is a *captivating* melody; and a *heartfelt* testament to Bob Marley's Uranus-Venus sextile. Moreover, No Women No Cry, is perhaps one of Marley's most well-known and celebrated songs. Primarily, the song is about Marley's upbringing, which is symbolic of Venus in the fourth house — portrayed in part by stories from his hometown. [27] The lyrics are both political (Uranus), and personal (Venus). Politically speaking, Marley despised governments and hypocrites. Personally, the song depicts a women (Venus) who Marley was talking to, and who was crying. Thus, Marley was telling her to forget the past, and look towards the future (Uranus).

Therefore, the sextile between Uranus and Venus represented an opportunity to relinquish the past — balancing the present with the future. Symbolically, the past is concerned with the Moon, and its natural rulership house; hence the fourth, which Venus tenants. Uranus has very little to do with the past. In this respect, Marley always defined himself by distinctions, which is very Uranian by design. All too often, he was accused of being overly controversial, which is indicative to Uranus opposing the Ascendant in the chart.

Meanwhile, No Women No Cry was Marley's *first* successful hit record. The multiple trines from Uranus to the Sun, Mercury and Neptune helped him to achieve this monumental accomplishment, especially during extremely difficult times. Marley's chart implies that he was however, assured of more success. Continued success so to speak was mostly the result of the trines from Uranus; but particularly because of Uranus's opportunistic sextile to Venus — even though Venus is debilitated in Aries.

Thus, the debilitated Venus may account for some of the difficulties Marley experienced with his Mother; particularly as it squares Saturn. However, it is also assumed that the influence of his mother became an inspiration for many of his songs — including No Women No Cry. No doubt, the result of the trine between the Moon and Venus.

A Uranian Reclamation Strategy

A further consideration of Marley's success, is that Marley's life *evolved* into being representative of a 'Uranian Reclamation Strategy.' Thus, his 1980 Redemption Song was essentially a protest against *discrimination* is a testament to this notion. The song also highlighted the need to be *free* from mental subjugation. The lyrics, *'emancipate yourself from mental slavery; none but ourselves can free our mind'* is also a testament to this notion. Uranus also tenants the sixth house, which is the polarity of the twelfth; representing prisons — both mental and physical.

In addition, being freed from mental slavery is indicative to the mutual reception between Uranus and Mercury — interfaced further by the wide trine between these planets.

The Redemption Song is indeed symbolic of a Uranian Reclamation Strategy, which became the ground-breaking assertion for Bob Marley's life.

Uranian Reclamation

Bob Marley was only 36 when he died from melanoma; hence skin cancer. Although, I don't believe in 'coincidental accidents,' it remains my opinion that he died long before he should have done. Thus, his death was purely by default. Maybe, his early death was linked to the arduous influence of the Venus square to Saturn. Venus does however, *characterize* the young generation; and was no doubt the overall *victor* in this challenging tussle, for karmic supremacy. Thus, it is believed that Marley's lifework has remained *incomplete*, thereby resulting in his early death. Uranus's tense opposition to the Ascendant no doubt played a crucial part in his sudden demise.

The cause of his death was initially due to the spread of the melanoma to his lungs and brain. Without taking into consideration the transits at that time, the most likely culprits in the natal chart were Saturn's square to Neptune — Saturn ruling the skin and cancer — Neptune ruling cancer. The Sun's sesquiquadrate to Saturn, and its opposition to a domicile Pluto in the eighth house, most likely contributed. Interestingly, in death charts, quincunxes and sesquiquadrates are often present.

Although mutual receptions can have a special connection, they can still become *fused* into metastasizing illness and disease. In this case, I believe that the heightened effects of the Mercury-Uranus mutual reception were somehow increased by a debilitating association with transiting planets. As a result, the cancer spread to his lungs (Mercury), and his brain (Uranus).

Unquestionably, Uranus was Marley's sole suppressor, executioner, and eventual liberator. However, his passage into spirit will no doubt be enhanced both *intellectually* and *symphonically*, because of the trine between Uranus and Neptune. Furthermore, as there are no hard aspects from the Moon in the twelfth house, Marley's future karma should be given over to destiny; meaning that destiny is what God chooses.

Be that the case, Bob Marley should no longer be 'Waiting in Vain,' to quote one of his songs, in order to finalize his Uranian reclamation. He can now do this seating firmly upon his intellectual seat in spirit. Thus, his Uranian style of music will echo throughout eternity — *electrifying* the intellectual brains of those souls who continue to listen to it on Earth. But particularly, in the musical halls of learning — sheathed in spirit. [28]

John Cleese

John Marwood Cleese is an English actor, comedian, screenwriter, and producer. In the late 1960s, he co-founded Monty Python; hence the comedy troupe responsible for the comedy sketch show *Monty Python's Flying Circus*. In the mid-1970s, Cleese and his then wife Connie Booth, co-wrote the sitcom *Fawlty Towers*; where he played the bewildered hotel manager, Basil Fawlty. In 2005, Cleese was ranked the second-best comedian in a channel 4 poll of fellow comedians. [29]

John Cleese is considered to be by many in his particular field of expertise, as a 'comedy genius.'

Uranian Showmanship

"And now for something completely different." This unforgettable expression became a well-known catchphrase in *Monty Python's Flying Circus*; and it is very relevant to the natal chart's modus operandi — powered substantially by Uranus.

So, in the natal chart, Uranus is elevated, and trine to the Ascendant. Uranus is also trine to idealistic and visionary Neptune. Accordingly, these moderate but influential Uranian configurations have prompted Cleese into becoming an open-minded, experimental, imaginative, and an innovative individual. Moreover, they are essentially the 'cosmic signatures' that have become the intellectual propulsions — masterminding his brilliance — making him the Uranian *showman* he is best known for. Hence, Cleese is considered to be a 'master of ceremonies' — complete with a Uranian twist ; wacky — becoming the basis for the creation of his *Ministry of Silly Walks* sketch. For this reason alone, Cleese's intellectual prowess literally knows no bounds.

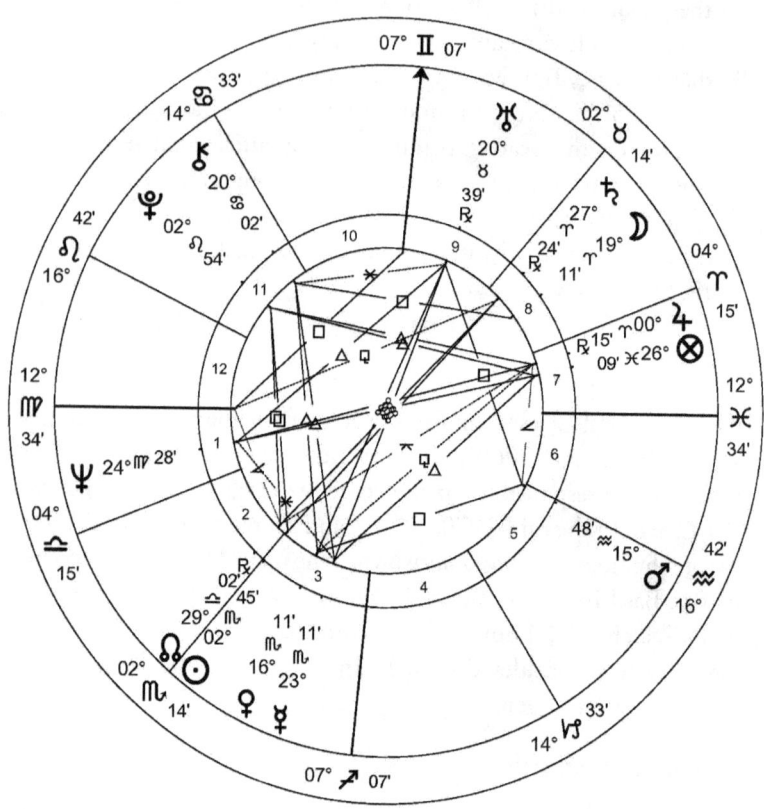

Natal Chart for John Cleese, 10/27/1939, 03:15, Weston-super-Mare, England

Meanwhile, Uranus opposes the capacious conjunction between Mercury and Venus, which is in its detriment. Mercury's degree is *afflicted* (pitted), according to Lilly. This accounts for the apparent 'mental demons,' which are displayed in Cleese's unique, but often unpredictable temperament — displayed throughout his comedy roles. Thus, John Cleese is a Uranian grandmaster, who continually walks that fine line between sanity and insanity. Hence, this is a classic Uranian idiosyncrasy — imposing sheer intellect.

Uranian Exhilaration/Rebelliousness

John Cleese once remarked that *"true love is a fish and three cats."* In this respect, his need for excitement are exhilaration are characteristics that have *snowballed* via his many marriages. This is perhaps the reason why he has been married four times, which is often a common theme, especially when Uranus afflicts Venus, as it does in the chart. Uranus is also square Mars. This difficult configuration makes him dogmatic and unbending. However, it does give him the drive and the determination towards honoring his creative achievements. Ideally, Cleese needs to strike a balance between his desire for a lasting, and balanced relationship; and his desire for excitement, change, and freedom from restrictive circumstances.

In other words, Cleese needs a marriage that remains *impartial*. It was reported that Cleese was *exhilarated* after he finally found true love in his life. It is my opinion, when Venus frictionally aspects Uranus, as it does in this chart, or alternatively when Uranus tenants the Venus-ruled seventh house, those concerned possess the capacity to 'love unconditionally.' However, these individuals often experience intellectual turmoil before they reach this heightened potential in their lives, which is what happened to Cleese.

Uranus is also in its fall in Taurus. Principally, this means that Cleese *rebels* against anyone in authority. This characteristic is portrayed in many of his acting roles; particularly in *Fawlty Towers*, where Cleese played a dominated, eccentric, but very intelligent hotel manager — who didn't suffer fools. The ninth house is however, a potentially good position for Uranus to be in. Furthermore, Uranus in the ninth house is significant to academic and intellectual brilliance, which Cleese has acquired throughout his life.

Once again, the catchphrase *and now for something completely different* comes to mind; because in 1999 Cleese became the 'ivy league professor' at Cornell University. Since then, Cleese has provided students with ideas — from script writing to psychology — religion to hotel management. This is all indicative to Uranus in the ninth house. Today, Cleese provides a unique view of his endless pursuit of intellectual discovery. This is perhaps a testament to his Uranian exhilaration.

Cleese's brilliant style of intellectual humor is also portrayed in the impressive movie, *Clockwise*.

Clockwise — an Orbiting Uranus

Interestingly, John Cleese described the movie as, *"the only time he was ever sent a truly wonderful script for a lead."* [30] Primarily, *Clockwise* is about a school headmaster, who is played by Cleese, and who is obsessed with timeliness, order and discipline. Furthermore, he is meticulously preparing for an educational conference, to which chaos naturally ensues. These are all characteristics predominantly connected to the position of Uranus in the ninth house — opposing Mercury and Venus.

Timeliness, order and discipline are in this case concerned mostly with Saturn's half-square with Mars. Mars also tenants Aquarius, which is the sign of Uranus's natural rulership. Saturn is in its fall in Aries, and is square Pluto. Thus, Cleese has the ability to *shift* roles by keeping hold of the same character, so to speak. This cleverly-timed attribute is also indicative of Uranus's trine to the Ascendant, and Neptune. *Clockwise* is essentially a 'one off' portrayal of *Fawlty Towers*; in which Cleese has made Basil Fawlty his own unique and timeless character. Since then, no one has ever managed to recreate Basil Fawlty. Thus, Basil Fawlty remains unique to John Cleese, which in this case, is indicative to an orbiting Uranus; hence elevated.

John Cleese's personality is essentially an *electrification* of pure intellectual genius. Furthermore, the film *Clockwise*, has been deemed 'an intellectual comedy classic,' by the British comedy board. This must surely be a personal and conceptual testament to Cleese himself, which is emblematic of Uranus; and its oppositions to Mercury and Venus.

Finally, it just leaves to finish with a befitting quote from the Uranian maestro himself. *"Creativity is not a talent. It is a way of operating."* This is Uranus operating at its maximum potential.

Arnold Schwarzenegger

Arnold Alois Schwarzenegger is an Austrian and an American actor, film producer, businessman, retired professional bodybuilder and politician, who served as the 38th governor of California, between 2003 and 2011. Time magazine named Schwarzenegger as one of the '100 most *influential* and *intellectual* people in the world,' in 2004, and 2007. [31] Hence, this must surely be a mark of a true genius!

A Seasoned Uranian Intellectual Grandmaster

"The worst thing I can be is the same as everybody else. I hate that." What a powerful testament to Uranus — karmically fuelling Schwarzenegger's natal chart — in the twelfth house — closely conjoining Mars. Thus, Uranus in the twelfth house conjoining Mars is most likely the catalyst responsible for his fighting (pussy cat) spirit, and unusual character portrayals throughout his movies. I use the remark 'pussy cat' because

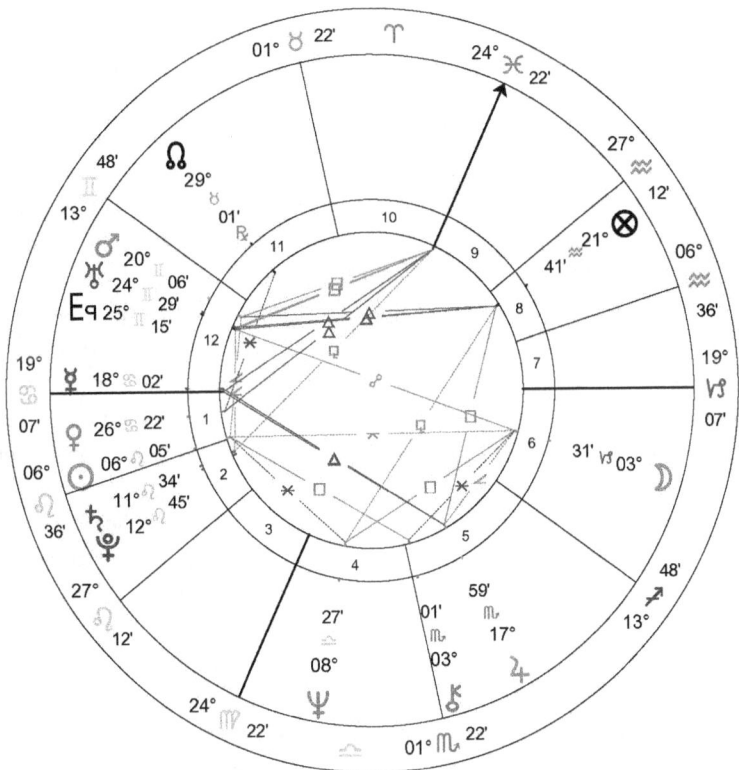

Natal Chart for Arnold, Schwarzenegger, 7/30/1947, 04:10, Graz, Austria

the twelfth house tends to 'dampen down' planets that occupy it. In addition, Schwarzenegger's Uranian powered twelfth house is both futuristic, and visionary. This would also account for the square between Uranus and the MC, which tenants Pisces. And, Pisces naturally rules the twelfth house.

However, with Uranus square the MC, Schwarzenegger is *committed* to leaving his unique signature — despite anyone who gets in the way. This distinctive character portrayal is very evident in the film T*erminator*; in which he comes from the future as a cyborg (Uranus) in order to get his man, so to speak, (see paragraph below titled I'll Be Back). Ostensibly, Schwarzenegger has always possessed the ability to 'think outside of the box.' This special characteristic is consistent with Uranus in the twelfth house. Uranus conjunct Mars however, reflects a dynamic confluence of creative energies, coupled with a steadfast determination, which produce unorthodox ideas. All of these Uranian characteristics are particularly evident in the movies, *Terminator*, *Conan the Barbarian*, and *Last Stand*. Some would argue that these are Schwarzenegger's finest projects to date.

Additionally, the North Node (future direction) tenants the eleventh house, which is Uranus's natural rulership house. This means that in this lifetime, Schwarzenegger must focus on how he can assist his community — to a much greater extent. Thus, contribution to society is an important keyword of the eleventh house. This is perhaps one reason why Schwarzenegger became the governor of California. Recently, Schwarzenegger was voted the most popular state governor of modern times, which is all consistent with Uranus. In March 2005 however, the Cato institute, which is an American think tank, issued a 'fiscal policy report card' for 2004. Here, it assigned an A grade to Schwarzenegger's performance as the governor of California. [32]

So many, who were interviewed at the time stated that Schwarzenegger was 'easy to approach,' and was always jovial. Jupiter's fortunate degree, according to Lilly, may also account for his good-humored personality. Jupiter tenants the *sunny* fifth house. Furthermore, Jupiter tenants Scorpio, which is the sign that Uranus is in exaltation; and connects to Uranus via a sesquiquadrate. It seems Schwarzenegger's 'chilled out' approach was genuine — emanating from the heart. Venus also rises on the Ascendant, and semi-sextiles Uranus. Chiefly, he is such a likeable character, whose intellectual charm is simply *measureless*.

Meanwhile, those with the North Node in the eleventh house are often entertaining individuals, with joyful personalities; and are fun to be around, which fits Schwarzenegger personal profile perfectly. Interestingly, with the Sun domicile in Leo (Uranus's polarity sign), in the first house, Schwarzenegger's tenure for governor had to be in a place where there is plenty of sunshine; hence California, the sunshine state.

Uranian Perception

Schwarzenegger's heightened intellect emanates from a previous life. This is consistent with Uranus conjunct the East Point — making him a seasoned Uranian grandmaster, of epic proportions. In a previous life, or in spirit, Schwarzenegger was most probably an innovative visionary, who was way ahead of his time.

I'll Be Back

Hitherto, I mentioned that Schwarzenegger's twelfth house is both *futuristic* and *visionary*. These are explicit notions, especially with regards to his movie, *The Terminator*. In all of his five *Terminator* films; Schwarzenegger came back to Earth from the future — boasting reinforced vision.

As a general rule, planets in the twelfth house indicate that the soul has reincarnated from the future with 'accentuated karma.' In this case, the future is highlighted by the spiritual cleansing spheres, whereas the past is determined by the Earth plane. With Uranus in the twelfth house however, Schwarzenegger has returned to Earth with a job to do, which is to *influence* the collective and the future in some way, by balancing his cerebral karma. Constitutionally, he has achieved this aim as the governor of California. Thus, he has *inspired*, and *liberated* so many souls.

Above all else, Arnold Schwarzenegger is an *entertainer* — a term that is relevant here to the Sun in the first house, and Jupiter in the fifth. *Terminator* spawned one of the biggest (Jupiter), and most lucrative movie franchises in history (fifth house). *Terminator* was a futuristic, and a visionary movie (Uranus). Therefore, producing this movie has helped to balance Schwarzenegger's cerebral karma, which is also indicative to a *deficient* (void) Mercury in his twelfth house, on the Ascendant. In my estimation, Schwarzenegger may *not* be back on Earth ever again. His title roles are now complete, on Earth, and in the world of sci-fi fantasy.

Currently, he has almost concluded his Uranian assignments; which included bringing California, and its people, into the *futuristic* twenty-first century. This leads me to conclude with yet another profound statement from the great man himself. *"And now, of course, this is another thing I didn't count on, that now as the governor of the state of California, I am selling California worldwide."*

Schwarzenegger's Uranus is essentially dominated by the light of the Sun, and the power of Mars; which is what Uranus is symbolized by in Greek mythology. Arnold Schwarzenegger is, most definitely, a representation of upstanding *electrified* intellect.

Conclusion

All of the individuals I have precisely selected throughout this section, are and were, trailblazers, and forerunners within their communities — combining extremely electrified intellects. In esoteric astrology, Uranus is considered to be the higher 'octave vibration' of Mercury; another planet which also governs intellect. However, in Greek mythology, Mercury was a messenger to the Gods; which leads me to conclude that Mercury is concerned mostly with the nerves in the body, which carry messages to and from the brain — to whatever place they are required — sustaining the body's autonomic system. Uranus governs 'heightened intellect;' hence brainpower.

In addition, all of the individuals throughout this section, are extremely innovative, and have invented a substance of some description, or a particular object, or they have created an alternate reality; especially for the collective influence of humankind. This is because of their unique Uranian abilities — characterizing their innovative accomplishments, which resonate throughout the collective like a bolt of lightning — computing them as 'compelling intellectual souls.'

An image of Uranus's intellectual genius emanating from the center of the brain

Chart Data

- Natal Chart for Ludwig Van Beethoven, 16th December 1770, 03:40, Bonn, Germany, Placidus Houses, Mean Node.
- Natal Chart for Richard Wagner, 22nd May 1813, 04:00, Leipzig, Germany, Placidus Houses, Mean Node.
- Natal Chart for Sir Isaac Newton, 4th January 1643, 01:38, Woolsthorpe Manor, UK, Placidus Houses, Mean Node.
- Natal Chart for Ada Lovelace, 10th December 1815, 13:00, London, UK, Placidus Houses, Mean Node.
- Natal Chart for Carl Jung, 26th July 1875, 19:24, Kesswil, Switzerland, Placidus Houses, Mean Node.
- Natal Chart for Bill Gates, 28th October 1955, 22:00, Seattle, USA, Placidus Houses, Mean Node.
- Natal Chart for Garry Kasparov, 13th April 1963, 23:45, Baku, Azerbaijan, Placidus Houses, Mean Node.
- Natal Chart for David Bowie, 8th January 1947, 09:00, London, UK, Placidus Houses, Mean Node.
- Natal Chart for Bob Marley, 6th February 1945, 02:30, St. Ann's Bay, Jamaica, Placidus Houses, Mean Node.
- Natal Chart for John Cleese, 27th October 1939, 03:15, Weston-super-Mare, UK, Placidus Houses, Mean Node.
- Natal Chart for Arnold Schwarzenegger, 30th July 1947, 04:10, Graz, Austria, Placidus Houses, Mean Node.

References

1. Statistics at www.britannica.com.
2. Information courtesy of the Akashic Records.
3. Information source, Wikipedia.
4. www.now.tuffs.edu.
5. The Planetary Suite by Gustav Holst.
6. www.classicfm.com.
7. Information source, Wikipedia.
8. A reference by the German astrologer, Thomas Ring.
9. www.cam.ac.uk.
10. Information source, Wikipedia.
11. www.metoffice.gov.uk.
12. www.brittanica.com.
13. Information source, Wikipedia.
14. www.goodtherapy.org.
15. Information source, Wikipedia.
16. www.choosingtherapy.com.
17. Information source, Wikipedia.
18. www.pandorafms.com.
19. Information source, Wikipedia.
20. Bill Gates and Dr. Fauci were the targets for Covid conspiracies.
21. Information source, Wikipedia.
22. www.premierchess.com.
23. www.ichess.net.
24. Information source, Wikipedia.
25. www.youtube.com.
26. Information source, Wikipedia.
27. www.storyofsong.com.
28. According to the Akashic Records, there are many forms of halls of learning in spirit — including those that encompass music from every realm of possibility.
29. Information source, Wikipedia.
30. www.imdb.com.
31. Information source, Wikipedia.
32. Information source, Wikipedia.

Epilogue

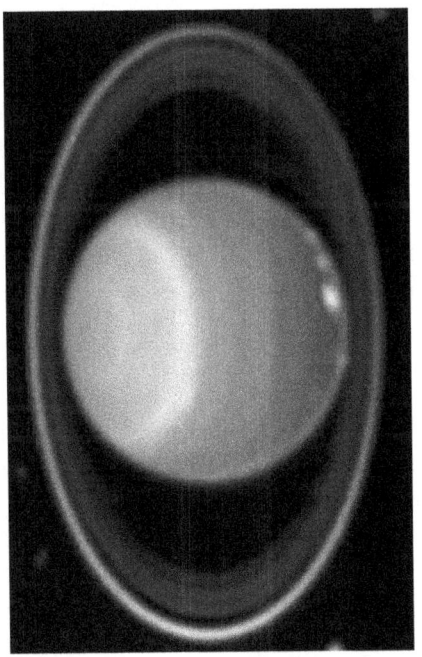

> *"When you change the way you look at things, the things you look at change."*
> Wayne Dyer [1]

Conclusion: The Future is Uranus

Wayne Dyer was an innovative visionary. Hence, he was a man whose ground-breaking principals were set firmly in the future — quintessentially Uranian. Some would say however, that he was a man who oozed intellectual genius. Thus, Dyer's work focused mainly on the principles of motivation, self-actualization, and assertiveness. For the most part, these are all innovative Uranian characteristics.

So, in his natal chart, Uranus is combustible; meaning it is closely conjunct to the Sun. Therefore, Uranus is 'hot stuff,' so to speak. The Sun and Uranus also connect to Neptune, via trines. Aquarius rules its natural eleventh house domain, with the esoteric ruler of Aquarius, Jupiter in the first house, which is intercepted, and exactly trines the MC. These planetary principalities would most likely account for Dyer's motivational and futuristic style of teaching.

Ahead of schedule, Dyer shifted his focus to more spiritual and higher-minded matters. This was most likely the result of Jupiter's conjunction to Saturn, which mostly centers on the acquirement of wisdom and knowledge throughout maturity, hence adulthood. Moreover, the extreme Uranian influence in his chart would also account for the sudden and frequent spells of criticism, which Dyer received about his life work, and which occurred throughout the entire course of his life. [2] Most likely, the result of the Sun-Uranus conjunction.

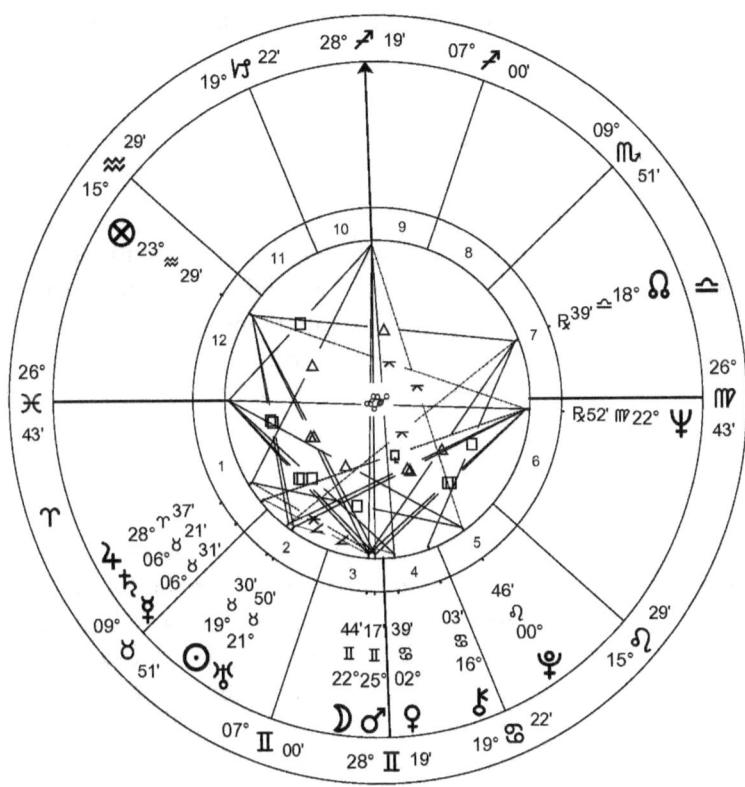

Natal Chart for Wayne Dyer, 5/10/1943, 03:13, Detroit, Michigan

Neptune's degree is pitted, according to Lilly; to which the effects would impact Uranus through the trine. Thus, trines are not always favourable aspects; especially when they are impacted by deficient degrees. Neptune is also in detriment in Virgo, and tenants the sixth house of health matters.

Consequently, Dyer was diagnosed with Leukaemia. This was around the time transit Uranus crossed his Ascendant, and opposed Neptune. Soon after his death however, the coroner recorded a verdict, which indicated that there was no trace of leukaemia in his body. Perhaps, the initial diagnosis was in fact a misdiagnosis — considering Neptune was involved. Or perhaps, he had eliminated the disease from his body?

Interestingly, compelling Uranian souls, like Dyer, do possess the capability of performing such a 'master stroke' of Uranian ingenuity.

Uranian Ingenuity

Uranus helps us to understand exactly where to surrender old habits. It also teaches us how to take chances, in order to shift obstacles, which are otherwise 'surplus to requirements.' Thus, Uranus orchestrates powerful and necessary changes. Uranian shifts also include the 'complete elimination' of illness and disease from the body. Uranus represents the essential place to where, and how we acquire inspiration. Uranus's energy is representative to the 'fulfilment of truth.'

All of these principles were the fundamental essence of Dyer's teachings.

A Uranian Style Death

When Wayne Dyer died in 2015, transit Uranus conjoined his South Node, and opposed his North Node. It also linked to his Sun and Uranus conjunction via a semi-sextile. Thus, his death was the result of a sudden heart attack (Sun-Uranus conjunction). Hence, this is an impending health characteristic of the Sun/Uranus conjunction in his natal chart. Once activated via transits, it can lead to sudden heart attacks, epilepsy and tumors, depending on the condition of the transit. Before, and around the time of his death, transit Saturn was opposing the Sun-Uranus conjunction, with transit Neptune squaring it.

Ironically, Pluto (death) occupies the fifth house. The fifth house is naturally ruled by the Sun; and which rules over the heart. Pluto tenants the Sun's rulership sign of Leo. Furthermore, Pluto trines the Ascendant. Uranus lies at the midpoint of the Ascendant-Pluto trine. At his death, Dyer didn't incur any underlying and unnecessary suffering, which was reported in the media. Moreover, Dyer's chart implied that he did live a typical Uranian life — coalescing the reactionary elements of both composure, and disruption.

Unbeknown to him however, Wayne Dyer's teachings were focused on the ingenious vibrations, which are associated with the much talked about Age of Aquarius. Overall, this meant that his solar combustible Uranian instincts were enhanced by this elevated force in his chart; hence mostly via his domicile eleventh house.

In addition, Dyer's Uranian intuition would have been further enhanced via the position of his part of fortune; hence in Aquarius. Thus, Wayne Dyer was a human representation of the Age of Aquarius.

Uranian Reforms – Hence the Age of Aquarius

For the most part, Uranus has always been considered to be a disruptive influence — both individually and collectively. In some respects, this formidable impression is true. But, Uranus is only disruptive when we resist, mostly through fear, the 'lightning changes,' which are necessary for our evolutionary and intellectual development. Curiously, Uranus is the only planet that is encompassed by a unique exocarp, which is both homogenous, and vibrant.

The unpredictable energy of Uranus parallels Earth. This is because in Greek mythology, the Earth helped to create Uranus — emerging from primeval chaos. When Uranus appears suddenly in our field of vision via transit, for the most part, we panic. This is because, from a psychological perspective, we only see chaos emerging in our lives. Therefore, if Uranus creates nothing but chaos, particularly via difficult transits, there is something intellectually wrong in our lives, which needs urgently addressing.

Alternatively, if the embers of chaos are still glowing at the beginning of a Uranus transit cycle, its vibrant and interchangeable energy field will have the potential to transform the embers into something more fulsome, and exhilarating — despite the overall condition of the transit. Thus, the purpose of Uranus is to liberate the mind from the ashes of despair.

Uranus symbolizes the ability to realize the importance of ecstacy and euphoria — reformative innovations that nutrify the brain. Developed through ingenuity, ecstacy and euphoria are the intended and reformative themes of the Uranian (Aquarian) Age. Hence, ecstacy and euphoria are Uranian awakening reforms, which reverberate from invention, and from extensive intellectual creativity.

Meanwhile, let us briefly cite a few more examples of why Uranus continues to be troublesome. Uranus is however, all about the liberation of new ideas, and the freedom of expression (awakenings). Moreover, Uranus is concerned with the emancipation from oppression, and sudden sweeping changes, which bring about necessary reforms, especially within an intellectual capacity. Thus, once the intellect has been 'progressively reformed,' new technologies are invented.

Whereas the Sun, (Uranus's sphere of polarity), presides over self-importance, and the self-image of the individual, Uranus rules over the collective influence of humankind — specifically in an intellectual capacity. Characteristically, this means that Uranus stimulates the collective influenced brain, in order to impart shared ideas, and intentions. It does this via the brain's neuro impulses, in order to enhance and unite these shared ideals for the purpose of liberating humankind.

One such example was the abolishment of slavery. Thus, this was a prime example of 'liberating the collective' from patterns of energy, which have run the course of time. Alternatively, when lightning strikes, it invariably inflicts damage; particularly upon infrastructure. Damaged structure however, can be rebuilt into something more superior, and much more efficient. Lightning discharges are intended to orchestrate necessary changes, which may have been previously overlooked in some way, or even ignored. Thus, lightning discharges are similar to the 'light bulb moment.' Ordinarily, sudden changes occur, because they should have happened previously.

Uranian reforms are for the most part, deemed as sudden and unprepared for occurrences. Furthermore, Uranian reforms are 'progressively essential,' especially for the ultimate survival of humankind. Without the influence of Uranus in our lives, humankind would be shackled in the psychological chains of despair.

Speaking in a positive capacity, Uranus represents the seed of anticipation, exhilaration, and the arousal of the cerebrally-enhanced senses. Equally, this planet represents the seeds of delirium, indifference, and disintegration. All of these positive/negative qualities are the intellectual conditions — synchronized within the cosmic brain, which symbolizes the essential purpose of the Aquarian Age.

Positive/Negative Uranian Programming

Whether we accept it or not, robotics is an essential part of modern Uranian programming; and the Aquarian Age. Androids, for example, which are essentially 'humanoid robots,' and are not to be mistaken for the popular operating systems for mobile phones. Originally, androids were only glimpsed upon in science fiction, and were designed mostly for the purpose of the liberation of the collective — supporting humankind mostly within a technological capacity.

Alternatively, androids, especially when programmed correctly, can greatly assist us with our intellectual progression. Thus, human beings can work alongside these robotic devices, in order to augment new ideas. For instance, androids can help us to design, and thus develop entirely new generational computers, which will liberate the collective influence from the psychological concept of drudgery, hence non-progression. These are the essential characterizations, which are associated with the Age of Aquarius.

Unfortunately, the technological devices of today are unwittingly orchestrating health problems; particularly those of a psychological nature. For example, the overuse of technology is partly responsible for the escalation of anxiety and depression, which are essentially fear-based conditions. There are also many people, who believe, that robots will eventually take over the world; and human beings will become their slaves. Once again, this is purely a science fiction perspective. Robots are essentially an enhanced form of computers, and they are not sentient. Therefore, they cannot possible impersonate our deeper, fundamental, and most cherished human qualities.

Perhaps, the main concern today however, is the distinct shortage of intellectual/creative brain potential. Thus, this distinct absence has been condensed across a large percentage of the populace, which have become somewhat robotic, as a result. Large swathes of the population have become completely void of new ideas, and new ways of thinking. In essence, many human brains are considered to be 'intellectually void.'

Most concerningly, is that when a new form of technology is invented, the very essence of its programming becomes immersed in the illiterate and uninformed conditionings, which mostly surround the current mindless, and automated generation. This notion also applies to the techno geeks, who have extremely high IQs, but very low soul values, or even common sense. In some cases, they have even implied that they are in fact soulless. Personally, I don't believe this to be the case. It is far more likely that this generation have simply 'lost their way,' particularly in a spiritual/intellectual capacity.

Meanwhile, the subverted manipulation of the smartphone is a classic example, which enhances this non-progressive thinking. It has already been proven by some of the top scientific minds, that the overuse of these devices can also be responsible for brain tumors; and other diseases. But unfortunately, very few see the significance, or the dangers posed by this 'negligent cerebral insurgence'— scrutinizing the misuse of these technological devices.

Nevertheless, the smartphone's programming could be further enhanced by the reforming ideas, and the radical input of the collective. This is the case, especially at this point in our collective evolution, hence the twenty-first century, which symbolizes finding meaning and purpose in the age of reason. By and large, a 'collective intellectual amplification of ideas,' would mean that rather than becoming overwhelmed and obsessed by the functions of a particular type of technology, we, as a collective influence, could help to safely enhance and harness the overall purpose of these devices. Just a thought!

Ultimately, these far-reaching measures would help to benefit humankind in its collective and scientific development; especially if we could eliminate, for example, the harmful of non-ionizing radiation, which is dangerously emitted by the smartphone. Mental imagery, hence ideation is one such measure, that will eliminate radiation, especially when it's purposely applied via a collective influence.

To be more precise, we could build up a mental picture in our collective minds, which would help to 'winnow out' the smartphone's radiation.

Ultimate Uranian Collectiveness

These are all prototypical examples of Uranus functioning at the collective (eleventh house) level of consciousness. At the individual level of consciousness however, wherever Uranus is positioned in the natal chart, it can assist the individual to liberate the house, and everything associated with it. Wayne Dyer was an advocate for these Uranian functions.

If Uranus tenants the seventh house for example; either natal, or in a solar return chart, and its condition is positive, it can help to liberate those souls who are being targeted with the restraints of social violence; particularly those who are the victims of difficult and oppressive marriages. When I say positive, I mean when Uranus isn't unsettled by the oblique negativity, which is posed by the existence of quincunxes and oppositions. Ideally, when a planet's expression is considered to be wholly positive, it will necessitate a delicate and balanced blend of conjunctions, sextiles, squares and trines, yes even squares. If Uranus, is afflicted in the chart, by too many negative aspects, then the term difficult oppressive partnerships and marriages often becomes the subject matter of this planet in the seventh house.

Moreover, from a seventh house position, Uranus offers its own form of humanitarian justice, by providing insight that will help to reawaken the brain, despite the planet's condition. Therefore, those who endure psychological abuse have technically been transformed into 'slave robots' by their abusers. However, this concept bears little difference to those who have become modern-day slaves to the smartphone, and other forms of technology.

Meanwhile, from the twelfth house, Uranus acts in much a similar fashion. However, rather than becoming slaves to a physical abuser, these individuals become a robotic slave to their own intellectual thoughts, or consciousness. From the twelfth house, Uranus's influence is often untenable — unleashing terrifying thoughts. As a result, these individuals can become hysterical over the simplest of things. In effect, their thoughts can easily become their ultimate enemy.

In addition, dreams can often involve the presence of frightening aliens, that also become subsequent enemies. Alternatively, dreams can involve unfathomable machines that take over everything; similar to the film, *The War of the Worlds*. The important thing to remember here is that they are only abstract illusions, which have become ingrained on our inner most thought patterns. Remember, the purpose of Uranus is the liberate us from all forms of oppression — no matter where this planet resides in the natal chart.

Notwithstanding, those who have Uranus placed in either Leo, Scorpio, Sagittarius, Aquarius, or Pisces, or if Uranus tenants the fifth, eighth, ninth, eleventh, or twelfth houses, are best provided intellectually to assist the rest of humankind adapt to the radical changes, which are associated with the Aquarian Age.

Conceivably, this revolutionary epoch symbolizes the future of humankind.

Personally speaking, I envisage an advanced intellectual world; and one where ground-breaking new technologies play an important role in the liberation of humankind. Thus, liberation from corruption and subversion. It is the inevitable conclusion to the current leaning, which gravitates towards momentary intellectual chaos, and potential destruction.

References

1. Wayne Dyer was an American self-help author, and a motivational speaker. He died in 2015.
2. The psychologist Albert Ellis was a repeated criticizer of Dyer's work.

About the Author

For over thirty years I have worked as a psychotherapist, and a spiritual healer. And, I am the honored author of six medical and evolutionary astrology books, which are published via the American Federation of Astrologers. In addition, I have been a successful composition writer of over five hundred articles that have appeared in The International Survey for Astrological Research, The Mountain Astrologer, The Astrological Association of Great Britain, The New Zealand Journal of Astrology, Elfin, and Kindred Spirit. Furthermore, I am also a regular contributor to Wanda Sellar's Astrology and Medicine Newsletter.

As a spiritual teacher I emphasize the importance of having spiritual faith, and psychic perception — touching upon why we should not lose sight of these important birth rights — while here on Earth. Presently, so many individuals have renounced their spiritual heritage for the acquisition of power, greed, mass consumerism and hatred. And, so many individuals have lost sight of who they are — omitting the possibility that we are all part of a collective influence, which upholds us all as spiritual beings on a human journey.

Alan Richards-Wheatcroft

Afterword

I was very honored to be asked to write this Afterword, as Alan's work is directly from his heart, and his many years of experience as an astrological guide. He's also a wonderful and kind person whom I'm grateful to know.

Uranus The Awakener shines a bright light on the multiple understandings of the ways people experience Uranus in their unique life journeys.

In my early astrology education I learned that we don't feel the effects of the outer planets very much, as they represent generational tendencies, and deep-seated psychological compulsions on an individual level. However, unlike the other outer planets, this electrifying powerhouse shows up differently, with more of an abrupt impact when its aspects and transits are so placed to jolt a person from their current paradigm.

Alan gives a clear understanding about the energy of Uranus and its power to shake up our worlds. He carefully demonstrates how people respond to the Uranus energy — how Uranus sizzles into our lives and shakes up current understandings, work, family, relationships and health.

As I read the book I was careful to pay attention to the important themes of what Uranus brings, keeping in mind my own, somewhat troublesome and amazing experiences with it over the years. The reader will easily identify this for themselves as they take in the information. As troublesome as it can at times appear to be, there is always a method to the work of this quirky, blue giant, and if we understand what has come to pass in its work in our minds, our lives, and our karma, we can see that we are better for having had the Uranian experiences.

Interestingly Edgar Cayce stated that the planet closest to the zenith in our natal chart shows where our souls have sojourned in between lives, the energies we experienced before we incarnated. My natal Uranus is at the zenith, which just figures for my strange, quirky life journey, and now my understanding of it is much clearer. So, from one Uranian to another, I hope you find light and understanding in this wonderful book!

Celeste Nash

Index

Other Titles Published by the American Federation of Astrologers (AFA)*
- Aal & Subramanyan/Astrology by Moonlight
- Adams/Understanding Retrogrades
- Addey/Harmonic Anthology
- Adler/Predictive Astrology
- Alexander/Magickal Astrology
- Alexander/Planets in Signs
- Antepara/Aspects: Powerful Keys to Personal Transformation
- Arroyo/Astrology, Karma & Transformation
- Arroyo/Astrology, Psychology and the Four Elements
- Arroyo/Chart Interpretation Handbook
- Arroyo/Experiments & Experiences with Astrology
- Arroyo/Exploring Jupiter
- Arroyo/Person-to-Person Astrology
- Arroyo/Relationships and Life Cycles
- Ashcroft-Nowicki & Norris/The Door Unlocked
- Ashman/How to Survive Mercury Retrograde
- Ashman/Intuition and your Sun Sign
- Ashman/Roadmap to Your Future
- Ashman/Sun Sign Karma
- Ashman/Sun Signs & Past Lives
- Astrolabe/World Ephemeris Midnight 2001-2050
- Astrolabe/World Ephemeris Noon 2001 - 2050
- Avelar & Ribeiro/On the Heavenly Spheres: A Treatise on Traditional Astrology

- Avery/Astrological Aspects
- Avery/The Rising Sign: Your Astrological Mask
- Banzhaf & Theler/Keywords for Astrology
- Barclay/Horary Astrology Rediscovered
- Bell/Midlife is not a Crisis
- Bell/Planetary Threads
- Benjamine/Astrological Lore of all Ages
- Bennett/Astrology: Secrets of the Moon
- Beversdorf/Vedic Secrets to Happiness
- Bills/The Rulership Book
- Bishr (Tr. Holden)/The Introduction to the Science of the Judgments of the Stars
- Blackledge/William Lilly: The Man Who Saw the Future
- Blackwood/12 Faces of the Goddess
- Blackwood/A Lantern in the Dark
- Blake/Vocational Astrology
- Blaschke/Astrology: Language of Life Vol 1, Progressions
- Blaschke/Astrology: Language of Life, Vol 3, Handbook for the Astrologer
- Blaschke/Astrology: Language of Life Vol 2, Sabian Aspect Orbs
- Blaschke/Astrology: Language of Life Vol 4, Relationships
- Blaschke/Astrology: Language of Life Vol 5, Holographic Transits
- Bloch & George/Astrology for Yourself
- Boehrer/Declination: The Other Dimension
- Bogart/Astrology and Meditation
- Bogart/Astrology and Spiritual Awakening
- Bogart/Astrology's Higher Octaves
- Bogart/Planets in Therapy
- Bohannon/North and South Nodes: Guideposts of the Spirit
- Bohannon/Your Solar Return
- Bonatti (Dykes Tr)/Bonatti on Basic Astrology
- Bonatti (Dykes Tr)/Bonatti on Elections
- Bonatti (Dykes Tr)/Bonatti on Horary
- Bonatti (Dykes Tr)/Bonatti on Lots
- Bonatti (Dykes Tr)/Bonatti on Mundane Astrology
- Bonatti (Dykes Tr)/Bonatti on Nativities
- Bonatti (Dykes Tr)/Bonatti's 146 Considerations
- Borstein/The Moon's Nodes
- Bowser/An Introduction to Western Sidereal Astrology 3rd Edi-

tion
- Brady/Astrology a place in chaos
- Brady/Brady's Book of Fixed Stars
- Brady/Predictive Astrology
- Brady/Predictive Astrology: The Eagle and the Lark
- Brahy/Confidential Recollections Revealed
- Brittain/Planetary Powers: The Morin Method
- Brown/Cosmic Trends
- Bryan/Houses: A Contemporary Guide
- Bunker/Astrology's Hidden Aspects
- Bunker/Beginner's Guide to Astrology
- Bunker/Quintiles and Tredeciles
- Burk/Astrology: Understanding the Birth Chart
- Burk/Complete Node Book
- Busteed & Wergin/Phases of the Moon - (OOP – Limited copies available)
- Cameron/Predictive Planetary Periods: Hindu Dasas
- Campbell/Asteroids Interpreted
- Campbell/Amazing Asteroid Stories
- Campbell/Forensic Astrology: Solving Crimes with Astrology
- Campion/A History of Western Astrology, Vol. I
- Campion/Astrology and Cosmology in the World's Religions
- Campion/Astrology, History and Apocalypse
- Campion/Book of World Horoscopes (2004 updated)
- Campion/The Dawn of Astrology
- Canfield/Brother Pluto Sister Eris
- Canfield/Eris in Signs, Houses, Aspects
- Canfield/Uranus
- Canfield/Yankee Doodle Discord
- Carelli/The 360 Degrees of the Zodiac
- Carter/The Astrological Aspects
- Charubel-Sepharial/The Degrees of Zodiac Symbolized
- Christino/Foreseeing the Future
- Christino/The Best of Al H Morrison
- Christino/What Evangeline Adams Knew
- Circle Books Aspect Finder
- Clark/From the Moment We Met
- Clark/The Family Legacy
- Clark/Vocation

- Clement/Aspect Patterns – (OOP Limited copies available)
- Clement/Mapping Your Birthchart– (OOP Limited copies available)
- Clement/Mapping Your Family Relationships– (OOP Limited copies available)
- Clement/Mapping Your Sex Life– (OOP Limited copies available)
- Clement/Planet-Centered Astrology– (OOP Limited copies available)
- Clement/The Astrology of Development– (OOP Limited copies available)
- Clifford/Astrologer's Book of Charts
- Clifford/British Entertainers: The Astrological Profiles
- Clifford/Getting to the Heart of Your Chart
- Clifford/Horoscope Snapshots
- Clifford/Solar Arc Directions
- Close/Self-Evident Astrology Book I: Decoding the Solar System
- Clow/Awakening the Planetary Mind
- Clow/Chiron: Rainbow Bridge Between..
- Cochrane, David/Astrology for the 21st Century
- Cochrane, David/The Astrology of Bipolar Disorder: A Scientific Breakthrough
- Cochrane, David/Vibrational Astrology - The Essentials
- Coley/Clavis Astrologiae Eliminata: Key to Whole Art of Astrology
- Coley/Clavis Astrologiae Eliminata: Key to Whole Art of Astrology
- Cornelius/The Moment of Astrology
- Costello/The Astrological Elements: Earth and Air
- Costello/The Astrological Elements: Water & Fire
- Costello/The Astrological Moon
- Costello/The Weiser Guide to Practical Astrology
- Cragin/Astrology on the Cusp
- Cragin/The Astrological Elements
- Cramer/Dictionary of Medical Astrology
- Cramer/How to Give an Astrological Health Reading
- Crane/A Practical Guide to Traditional Astrology
- Crane/Astrological Roots: The Hellenistic Legacy
- Crane/Between Fortune and Providence

- Cruthirds-Schmiedlin/Astrology Using Asteroids Simplified
- Crowl/The Degrees
- Cunningham/Divination for Beginners
- Cunningham/Healing Pluto Problems
- Cunningham/How to Read Your Astrological Chart
- Curry/Understanding Human Design
- Daath/Medical Astrology
- Darling/Essentials of Medical Astrology
- Darling/Essentials of Medical Astrology
- Darr/Transits
- Davis/Astrolocality Astrology
- Davis/From Here to There: An Astrologer's Guide to Astromapping
- Davis/Horary Astrology
- DeFouw & Svoboda/Light on Relationships
- DeJersey & Taves/Destiny Times Six
- Devlin/Astrology and Past Lives
- Devlin/Astrology and Relationships
- DeVore/Encyclopedia of Astrology
- Dimino & Sherwin/East Joins West
- Discepolo/Transits and Solar Returns
- Discepolo/Transits and Solar Returns
- Doane/30 Years Research
- Doane/Astrology's Wide Influence
- Doane/Blending Astrology, Numerology and Tarot
- Doane/Contest Charts
- Doane/Contest Charts
- Doane/How to Read Cosmodynes
- Doane/How to Read Cosmodynes
- Doane/Modern Horary Astrology
- Doane/Profit by Electional Astrology
- Doane/Secret Symbolism of Tarot
- Doane/Secret Symbolism of Tarot
- Dobyns/Finding the Person in the Horoscope
- Dobyns/Progressions, Directions and Rectification
- Dobyns/The Node Book
- Dominguez/Practical Astrology for Witches and Pagans
- Donath/Approximate Positions of Asteroids 1851 - 2050
- Donath/Asteroids in Midpoints

- Donath/Asteroids in Synastry
- Donath/Asteroids in Synastry
- Donath/Asteroids in the Birth Chart
- Donath/Have We Met Before?
- Donath/Houses: Which and When
- Donath/Minor Aspects Between Natal Planets
- Donath/Patterns of Professions
- Donleavy/The Whirling Winds
- Doser (Dykes(ed))/Financial Significators in Traditional Astrology
- Doser (Dykes(ed))/Professional Significators in Traditional Astrology
- Doser/Astrological Prediction: A Handbook of Techniques
- Dreyer/Healing Signs
- Dreyer/Vedic Astrology
- Dukelow/Coalescent Horoscopes
- Dukelow/Transpluto
- Duncan/Astrology: Transformation & Empowerment
- Duz/A Practical Treatise of Astral Medicine and Therapeutics
- Dykes (ed.)/The Book of the Nine Judges: Traditional Horary Astrology
- Dykes (tr)/Astrology of the World I: The Ptolemaic Inheritance
- Dykes (tr)/Introductions to Astrology: Abu Ma'shar & al-Qabisi
- Dykes (tr)/The Forty Chapters of al-Kindi
- Dykes (tr)/Works of Sahl & Masha'allah
- Dykes (Tr/Ed)/Astrology of the World II: Revolutions and History
- Dykes/Apotelesmatics Book III: On Inceptions
- Dykes/George/Brennan/Traditional Astrology in the 21st Century CD - In Honor of James Holden
- Dykes/Traditional Astrology for Today
- Ebertin/Applied Cosmobiology
- Ebertin/Auxiliary Tables: Calculating Stellar Positions
- Ebertin/Combination of Stellar Influences
- Ebertin/Cosmic Marriage
- Ebertin/Directions: Co-Determinants of Fate
- Ebertin/Fixed Stars and Their Interpretation
- Ebertin/Rapid and Reliable Analysis
- Ebertin/The Annual Diagram:Forecasting Using 45-degree

Graphic Ephemeris
- Ebertin/The Contact Cosmogram
- Ebertin/Transits
- Edwards/Astropsychology: A Journey to Yourself
- Edwards/Medical Astrology for Healing
- Einhorn/The Little Book of Saturn
- Eleftheriadis/Horary Astrology: The Practical Way to Learn Your Fate
- Escobar/144 Doors of the Zodiac
- Eshelman/Horoscope Calculation
- Fagan & Firebrace/Primer of Sidereal Astrology
- Falconer/Astrology and Aptitude
- Farley/Astro Mind Maps
- Faugno/Your Fertile Hours
- Finey/The Sacred Dance of Venus and Mars
- Fleuret/Astrological Keywords: A Reference Manual
- Fleuret/Astrological Keywords: A Reference Manual
- Flynn/Astrology and Weight Control: Jupiter/Pluto
- Forrest/Skymates II
- Forrest/Skymates, Revised Edition
- Forrest/The Ascendant
- Forrest/The Book of Air
- Forrest/The Book of Earth
- Forrest/The Book of Fire
- Forrest/The Book of Neptune
- Forrest/The Book of Pluto
- Forrest/The Book of the Moon
- Forrest/The Book of Water
- Forrest/The Changing Sky
- Forrest/The Inner Sky
- Forrest/The Night Speaks
- Forrest/Yesterday's Sky: Astrology and Reincarnation
- Gansten/Primary Directions: Astrology's Old Master Techniques
- Garner/A Cosmic Dialogue
- Garrett/Health in the Horoscope
- Garrett/Karma in the Horoscope
- Garrett/More About Retrogrades
- Garrett/Relationships
- Garrett/Unlocking Interceptions

- Garrison/The Lunar Gospel
- Gauquelin/Cosmic Influences on Human Behavior
- Geary (Ed) Astrology the New Generation
- Geffner/Astrological Markers of ADD and ADHD
- Geffner/Astrology for Career Success
- Geffner/Creative Step-Parenting
- Gehrz/Anthology Book One - Vettius Valens of Antioch - Not Available
- Gehrz/Astrological Remediation: A Guide for the Modern Practioner
- Geisler, Pat/Chocolate Sauce
- Geisler, Pat/The Plain Vanilla Astrologer
- Gemming/Mystical Secrets of the Stars
- George/Ancient Astrology Volume Two
- George/Asteroid Goddesses
- George/Astrology and the Authentic Self
- George/Finding Our Way Through the Dark
- Gilbert/Potential Fulfilled: Accident Pattens
- Gillen/The Key to Speculation on the New York Stock Exchange
- Glenn/How To Prove Astrology
- Goldsmith/Moon Phases: A Symbolic Key
- Goldsmith/Zodiac by Degrees
- Grail/Astrology of Dwarf Planets: The Galactic Dimension of Creation Mythology
- Grant/Vol I: Elementary Astrology
- Grant/Vol II: Analysis of the Horoscope
- Grant/Vol III: Synthesis of the Horoscope
- Grant/Vol IV: Predictive Astrology
- Grasse/Signs of the Times
- Grasse/Under a Sacred Sky
- Grebner/Decanates
- Grebner/Everything Has a Phase
- Grebner/Lunar Nodes
- Green/EA Glossary: Guiding Principles of Jeffrey Wolf Green Evolutionary Astrology
- Green/Essays on Evolutionary Astrology
- Green/Evolutionary Astrology: Pluto & Your Karmic Mission
- Green/Medical Astrology: Astrological Correlations to the Anatomy/Physiology and the Chakra System

- Green/Neptune: Whispers from Eternity
- Green/Pluto Vol 1: Evolutionary Journey into the Soul
- Green/Relationships: Our Essential Needs
- Green/Uranus: Freedom from the Known
- Green/Your Horoscope in Your Hands
- Greenbaum/Temperament: Astrology's Forgotten Key
- Greene/Horoscope in Manifestation: Psychology and Prediction
- Greene/Outer Planets and Their Cycles, The Astrology of the Collective
- Grell/Keywords
- Grell/Keywords
- Gullfoss/The Complete Book of Spiritual Astrology
- Gunzburg/AstroGraphology
- Hall/Good Vibrations
- Hall/Karmic Connections
- Hall/Patterns of the Past
- Hall/The Book of Why
- Hamaker-Zondag/Aspects and Personality
- Hamaker-Zondag/Physchological Astrology
- Hamaker-Zondag/The House Connection
- Hamaker-Zondag/The Twelfth House: The Hidden Power in the Horoscope
- Hamaker-Zondag/The Yod Book
- Hannan/Predictive Techniques: Annual Harmonic Chart
- Hansen/An Astrological Journey of the United States
- Harvey/Anima Mundi: The Astrology of the Individual and the Collective
- Hayes/Astrology of Identity
- Heimsoth/Homosexuality in the Horoscope
- Henson/Degrees of the Zodiac
- Henson/The Vertex: The Third Angle
- Hill/Vocational Astrology
- Holden(Tr)/Paul of Alexandria: Introduction to Astrology
- Holden(Tr)/Rhetorius the Eqyptian
- Holden/A History of Horoscopic Astrology, 2nd Edition
- Holden/A History of Horoscopic Astrology, 2nd Edition HB
- Holden/Biographical Dictionary of Western Astrologers
- Holden/Five Medieval Astrologers
- Holden/The Judgments of Nativities

- Hopewell & Llewellyn/The Cosmic Egg Timer - 2011 Edition
- Hopewell & Llewellyn/The Cosmic Egg Timer
- Hopewell & Llewellyn/The Cosmic Egg Timer
- Hopewell/Aspect Patterns in Colour
- Hopewell/Aspect Patterns in Colour
- Hopewell/The Living Birth Chart
- Howell/Jungian Symbolism in Astrology
- Howland/American Histrology
- Huber/AstroLog I: Life and Meaning
- Huber/Astrological Psychosynthesis
- Huber/Astrology and the Seven Rays
- Huber/Reflections and Meditations in the Signs
- Huber/Transformation: Astrology as a Spiritual Path
- Hughes/Book of Marriage Charts
- Hughes/Planetary Hour Dial
- Hunter/Black Moon Lilith
- Idemon/Through the Looking Glass
- Ishikawa/Pocket Sized Ephemeris 1900-2050 (English)
- Jakobowsky, Frank/Astrological Discoveries
- Jay/Interpreting Lilith
- Jay/Lilith Ephemeris 2000 - 2050
- Jayne/A Preface to Prenatal Charts
- Jayne/Aspects to Horoscope Angles
- Jayne/Progressions and Directions
- Jayne/The Best of Charles Jayne
- Jones/The Soul Speaks
- Kellogg/The Yod: It's Esoteric Meaning
- Keyes/Parallels to Midheaven and Ascendant
- Kimmel/Altered and Unfinished Lives
- Kimmel/Cosmobiology for the 21st Century
- Kozminsky/Zodiacal Symbology
- Lavoie/Alphee's Horary Astrology - The Master's work
- Lavoie/Four Paths to God
- Lavoie/Horary at Its Best
- Lavoie/Horary Lectures
- Lavoie/Lose this Book and Find it With Horary
- Lehman/Astrology of Sustainability
- Lehman/Classical Astrology for Modern Living
- Lehman/Magic of Electional Astrology

- Lehman/Martial Arts of Horary Astrology
- Lehman/The Book of Rulerships
- Lehman/The Ultimate Asteroid Book
- Lehman/Traditional Medical Astrology
- Levin/The Manual of Harmonics
- Levine/Breakthrough Astrology
- Lilly/The Astrologer's Guide
- Lindanger/Your Sun's Return
- Lineman & Popelka/Compendium of Astrology
- Lineman/Eclipse Interpretation Manual
- Lineman/Eclipses: Astrological Guideposts
- Lineman/Your Prenatal Eclipse
- Llewellyn's 2022 Daily Planetary Guide
- Llewellyn's 2022 Sun Sign Book
- Llewellyn's 2023 Daily Planetary Guide
- Llewellyn's 2023 Moon Sign Book
- Lustrup/Pluto: Transforming the New You
- Lyons/Astrology Beyond Ego
- Lyons/The Machine Stops: The Mayan Long Count
- Lyons/Your Hidden Face: Projection in the Horoscope
- Mann/Astrology for the Absolute Beginner
- Marr/Prediction I
- Marshall/Understanding Children Through Astrology
- Martin/Your Destiny Discovered Astrology for Believers
- Masha'allah (Holden Tr)/Six Astrological Treatises
- Mason/Art of Forecasting Using Diurnal Charts
- Mason/Aspects Between Signs
- Mason/Delineation of Progressions
- Mason/Forecasting with New, Full, and Quarter Moons
- Mason/From One House to Another
- Mason/Lunations and Predictions
- Mason/Understanding Planetary Placements
- Mason/You and Your Ascendant
- Maternus (holden Tr)/Mathesis
- Maternus (holden Tr)/Mathesis
- Maternus (holden Tr)/Mathesis HB
- Mayeda/Lucky Stars-Lucky Life: The Powerful Influence of Conjunctions in Astrology
- Mayeda/Ten Key Features of Fame and Fortune: Astrologers Look

into the Celestial DNA of Celebrities
- McClung/The Hyperion Symbols
- McCormick/Deductive Interpret. of Natal Horoscope
- McDevitt/Why History Repeats
- McDow & Graziano/ACD/LD Method of Progressions
- McRae/Understanding Interceptions
- McWhirter/McWhirter Theory of Stock Market Forecasting
- Mercury Retrograde Cards - (3 cards)
- Michelsen/Uranian Transneptunian 1900-2050
- Milburn/Progressed Horoscope Simplified
- Miller/Astrology's Twelve-Planet Tree of Life
- Miller/Designs for a New Age
- Miller/Intercepted Planets: Possibilities for a New Age
- Miller/Interceptions: Heralds of a New Age
- Miller/Pagan Astrology for the Spirit and the Soul
- Miller/Saturn: Redrawing the Outlines of Our Lives
- Miller/The Lunar Nodes to Pars Fortuna: Journey and Goal
- Morin (Tr J Holden)/Book 23 Astrologia Gallica - Revolutions
- Morin (Tr J Holden)/Book 24 Astrologia Gallica - Progressions and Transits
- Morin (Tr J Holden)/Book 26 Astrologia Gallica
- Morin (Tr J Holden)/Books 13,14,15,19 Astrologia Gallica
- Morin (Tr LaBruzza)/Book 18 Astrologia Gallica - Strengths of the Planets
- Morin (Tr. Holden)/Astrologia Gallica Book 16: The Rays and Aspects of the Planets
- Morin (Tr. Holden)/Astrologia Gallica Book 17
- Morin (Tr. Holden)/Astrologia Gallica Book 25
- Morin(Tr. J Holden/Book 22 Astrologia Gallica Direction...
- Morinus/Astrologia Gallica Book 21 (Horoscope Interpretation)
- Munkasey/Astrological Keywords Signs of the Zodiac
- Munkasey/House Keywords and More...
- Murphy & Rosato/The Math of Astrology
- Nagle/Winning with Astrology
- Negus/Interpreting Composite & Relationship Charts
- Newman/Declination in Astrology
- Noel/Reinventing Astrology
- Nolle/Chiron: New Planet in Your Horoscope
- Noonan/Classical Scientific Astrology

- Noonan/Fixed Stars and Judicial Astrology
- Palmer/ABC Basic Chart Reading
- Palmer/Astro-Guide to Nutrition and Vitamins
- Palmer/Astrological Compatibility
- Palmer/Gambling to Win
- Palomaki/Pluto: Key to the Expansion of Consciousness
- Paul-Wolf/Personal Lunation Charts
- Pearce/The Textbook of Astrology
- Penfield/Bon Voyage
- Penfield/Horoscopes of Africa
- Penfield/Horoscopes of Europe
- Penfield/Horoscopes of Latin America
- Penfield/Horoscopes of the Asia, Australia and the Pacific
- Penfield/Horoscopes of the USA and Canada, 2nd edition
- Penfield/Stars Over England
- Phillipson/Astrology In The Year Zero
- Porphyry (Holden Tr)/Porphyry the Philosopher
- Randall & Campbell/Sacred Symbols of the Ancients
- Richards-Wheatcroft/Astrology for Self-Healing: The Essential Guide
- Richards-Wheatcroft/Discovering Faith in Neptune's Ocean
- Richards-Wheatcroft/One Body Many Illnesses
- Richards-Wheatcroft/Pluto's Season for Ashes
- Riske/Astrometeorology
- Roberts & Borkowski/Signs and Parts in Plain English
- Robertson/Cosmopsychology: Engine of Destiny
- Robertson/Eighth House
- Robertson/The Moon in Your Life
- Robertson/Transit of Saturn: Critical Ages
- Rodden/Mercury Method of Chart Comparison
- Rodden/Modern Transits
- Rodden/Money: How to Find it With Astrology
- Rowland/True Crime Astrology
- Rudhyar/Astrology of Transformation
- Ruiz/Interpreting Empty Houses
- Ruiz/Prediction Techniques Regarding Romance
- Sakoian & Acker/Astrological Anthology
- Sakoian & Acker/The Inconjunct
- Sakoian & Acker/The Transiting Planets

- Sakoian and Acker/Decanates and Duads
- Sakoian and Acker/Transits Simplified
- Sargent/How to Handle Your Human Relations
- Sasportas/Twelve Houses
- Sehested/Vol 2: Chart Interpretation
- Sehested/Vol 3: Tables and Reference
- Sharman-Burke and Greene/The Astrologer, the Counsellor and the Priest
- Silva/Astrology and Psychology
- Silveira de Mello/Declinations
- Silveira de Mello/Decumbitures and Diurnals
- Simmonite/Horary Astrology
- Simms/Astrology and the Power of Eight
- Simms/Twelve Wings of the Eagle
- Simms/Your Magical Child
- Sky, Sylvia/Tetrabiblos for the 21st Century - "The Bible of Astrology"
- Smith/Transits of the Planets
- Solibakke/The Mahabote Families
- Stacey/Uranus Square Pluto
- Stiopei/Pluto the Power of Transformation
- Stone/Delineation with Astrodynes
- Swatton/From Symbol to Substance
- Terry/The Progressed Moon Around the Zodiac
- Tebbs, Complete Book of Chart Retification
- Tompkins/The Contemporary Astrologer's Handbook
- Van Toen/The Mars Book
- Von Klockler/Astrology and Vocational Aptitude
- Wakefield/Cosmic Astrology
- Watters/Horary Astrology and the Judgment of Events
- Watters/Sex and the Outer Planets
- Weber/Arabian Parts Decoded
- Weber/Astro-Geology of Earthquakes and Volcanoes
- White/The Moon's Nodes and Their Importance
- Wickenburg/In Search of a Fulfilling Career
- Wickenburg/Journey Through the Birthchart
- Wickenburg/Your Hidden Powers
- Williams/Financial Astrology
- Williams/Simplified Astronomy for Astrologers

- Willner/The Rising Sign Problem
- Wilson-Ludham/Power Trio: Mars, Jupiter and Saturn
- Wilson-Ludlam/Dear Mae R
- Wilson-Ludlam/Healing Thru the Centers
- Wilson-Ludlam/Horary, The Gemini Science
- Wilson-Ludlam/Interpret Your Rays thru the Planets
- Wilson-Ludlam/Letters to 22 Astrologers
- Wilson-Ludlam/Living the Good Life
- Wilson-Ludlam/Ten Lessons in 7 Universal Rays
- Wilson-Ludlam/Yielding to Spirit
- Wilson/Astrology of Theosophy
- Wise/Houses of the Zodiac
- Wynn/Key Cycle
- Yacoubian/Psychid Self-Defense and the Zociac
- Ybarra/Emotional Dimensions of Astrology

This list reflects the current catalog and is subject to additions or deletions.
www.astrologers.com

www.ingramcontent.com/pod-product-compliance
Lightning Source LLC
Chambersburg PA
CBHW070842160426
43192CB00012B/2277